Winter's Children

Winter's Children

A Celebration of Nordic Skiing

RYAN RODGERS

University of Minnesota Press
Minneapolis
London

Frontispiece: Cross-country skiers traverse the frozen St. Croix River in Interstate State Park on the border between Minnesota and Wisconsin, circa 1945.

Published by the University of Minnesota Press
111 Third Avenue South, Suite 290
Minneapolis, MN 55401-2520
http://www.upress.umn.edu

ISBN 978-1-5179-0934-5 (hc/j)

A Cataloging-in-Publication record for this book is available from the Library of Congress.

Printed in Canada on acid-free paper

The University of Minnesota is an equal-opportunity educator and employer.

28 27 26 25 24 23 22 21   10 9 8 7 6 5 4 3 2 1

Contents

Skis line the walls of a Norwegian State Railways warehouse in 1948.

Prologue

I wanted to outski the champion. I figured I could. Born 160 years ago, Torjus Hemmestveit had won the world's first ski marathon in Norway using a single pole, before immigrating to Minnesota. I'd signed up for the American Birkebeiner with old Torjus in my sights. His time was mediocre by today's standards but was a good goal for me: I hadn't skied much in years and was no longer young.

I was running on the country roads between fields of corn and soy in the town where I lived in Wisconsin just across the border from Minnesota. Torjus's brother Mikkel had given skiing exhibitions here in the 1880s, schussing down the slopes of the St. Croix River Valley in what would have been a taste of home to settlers of Norwegian descent and a titillating display of a strange and wild sport to others. Those Hemmestveit boys were the best in the world for a time, coached by the great Sondre Norheim, a Norwegian peasant who became a skiing star for a decade in middle age before immigrating to America and giving up his bones to the North Dakota prairie.

When I'd started running a couple of months before, I'd had to stop every mile, but now I was able to finish a five-mile loop without walking. Jogging against dusk, I passed the end of a long driveway and stopped. A pair of skis leaned against a split rail fence, with a handwritten message on a sheet of notebook paper taped to the fence stating that the skis were giveaways. They were Norwegian Normarks, wooden skis from the 1970s, the same kind that had introduced a generation of Americans to cross-country skiing in the long-awaited boom for the sport. I'd been obsessing over old wooden skis for months, and this felt like fate. I ran home as quickly as I could, grabbed my car, drove back, and snatched those beauties up.

They had barely been used. Their bottoms bore a little wax residue and a couple of tiny nicks, but the original three-pin bindings showed no wear. I didn't have three-pin boots, but I did have a pair of clunky touring boots and bindings collecting dust in my garage. When I took the boots off the shelf and turned one of them over, a chipmunk's stash of shelled sunflower seeds poured out.

I unscrewed the old three-pins and, to my relief, didn't have to drill into the old skis because the replacement bindings screwed right into the same holes. Again, I thought the stars were aligning. I sought waxing instructions from a wooden ski enthusiast I'd befriended and followed his instructions for preparing the skis. I scoured the bases with mineral spirits and ordered pine tar. Some of these old skiers I'd been talking with spoke fondly of pine tar—it was always the smell. The daughter of a champion Duluth skier who had been dead for nearly sixty years tenderly recalled her father applying the sticky stuff in their family's kitchen and the odors wafting off the skis. An aging man who had for twenty years maintained a ski trail system as a pledge of loyalty to his dead best friend wrote a poem describing the passion that motivated him to clear windfall in the summer and groom trails in the winter. "For the love of the smell of pine tar on the base of a wood ski," it started. He'd written the poem on a napkin for an honor he had received, read it aloud at a ceremony, and thrown the poem away. He said he didn't remember the rest.

The season was looking good. Snow fell for two days. The Twin Cities of Minneapolis and St. Paul had several inches on the ground by December 1. Duluth and northern Wisconsin were buried in two feet. Yoopers in the Upper Peninsula of Michigan had been skiing since before Thanksgiving. I popped open the tin of pine tar. It was black and thick like molasses. The Normarks were made of hickory, amber colored with flecks of dark grain. I layered a film of tar onto their bases with a paint brush and then used a butane backpacking stove to torch the tar. You're supposed to hold the torch to the skis until the tar bubbles, but not so long as to char the skis. The blue flame licked the skis until tiny bubbles rippled across the tar. The hot pine tar did smell good, of conifers and solvents. The scent would linger in my garage for weeks.

I wiped the base of the skis until the towel came away clean. The bases were darker now, and the wood was sealed for a time from moisture. I put on the touring boots, grabbed the woodies, and left the garage for the early winter's eve, stepping into the bindings and skiing into the woods next to my house. After the snow, the sky was hyper-clear, with Orion back home for winter and Sirius huge and bright like a sticky gob on a lens. The skis were light and soft, lively on my feet. I'd learned about another champion skier who had come to Minnesota from Norway, Peter Fosseide, who had inspired two generations of Minnesotans to ski cross-country when next to nobody was doing it. This old Norwegian skied into his nineties. Holding ski poles, he used to lift up his hands and say, in the Norwegian accent he never lost, "Life is good with two of these." On a cold clear night in a promising start to winter, I agreed.

The snow was untracked, but I was following something unseen. The motions felt as old as time, and, as far as our species is concerned, they pretty much are. I had been surprised to learn, though, how new to the North American continent skis are. For me, the ski had always been there, with my dad waxing his synthetic Fischers atop the washing machine in the basement of my childhood home, even with his mother, one-half Norwegian, whose old wooden pair was stashed in her closet in the farmhouse sewing room, where my brother and I slept when we visited. When she was younger, she cruised her cow pastures on them. In this country, skis went back only a few generations beyond her, but for her Norwegian forbearers, and for the legions of Scandinavian immigrants who settled in the Midwest, a reliance on and affinity for the ski extended back through millennia.

This book is not a comprehensive look at the almost unfathomably long history of Nordic skiing but rather a celebration of an often-intertwined array of people and places that illuminate the sport's role in the cultural fabric of the Upper Midwest. I tried to illustrate as many notable ski characters—both historic and contemporary—as possible, but, sadly, I was unable to acknowledge many due to a lack of time and space. The following pages skew Minnesota-centric, in part because of where I live but more notably because no other state in the nation possesses the combination of a cold northern latitude, a high concentration of Norwegian Americans, and a relatively large population base. As a result, Minnesota has more Nordic skiers than anywhere else in the United States and offers a nonpareil network of groomed trails and youth ski leagues. Wisconsin and Michigan, particularly in the Upper Peninsula, have their own wealth of Nordic ski history and culture, which I attempt to illuminate here. The Dakotas, which were once home to a thriving Nordic scene, and Chicago make cameos as well. In a place defined by winter's tight and lasting grasp, Midwesterners long ago learned that the best way to cope with the objective hardships of a northern climate is by embracing the recreational possibilities that come with snow. For skiing's earliest practitioners, though, the name of the game was survival.

♠

In northern places outside North America, the ski's history runs incredibly deep. Invented three and a half thousand years before the wheel, its place of origin is unclear. No one can say for sure whether the first humans who donned long boards lived in northern Europe or Asia, though both sides of the debate have their adherents. What we do know is that the ski evolved from the snowshoe. In the grips of an ice age that froze massive stores of seawater, the Bering Land Bridge emerged between today's Siberia and Alaska. Ancient people migrated across the land bridge sometime between 35,000 BCE and 15,000 BCE, bringing snowshoes but not skis. The ski would not reach North America in any lasting way until the nineteenth century, when it was introduced by Norwegian immigrants, most notably in the Midwest.

The world's oldest ski fragment, from 6000 BCE, was recovered in 1960 from a midden pile in northwestern Russia. The fragment was likely left by the people who would become Scandinavia's earliest settlers, as they made their way to their new homeland. They would eventually be known as Sami. The ancient chunk of ski was a wooden tip with a carved figure of an elk's head protruding from its underside. The elk's head faced backward and probably worked as a climbing aid, like kick wax or fish scales. The elk head tip was found in a peat bog. Stone Age skiers stored their skis in the plentiful northern bogs during the summer to keep the skis from drying and cracking and to maintain the curved tip that had been bent into shape by heating the wood over a fire. Thanks to ancient skis cast away or lost, some two hundred have emerged from the bogs of Scandinavia. The elk head ski is by far the oldest.

A dhuc de ſitu , & qualitatibus eius .

One of the many woodcut illustrations from *A Description of the Northern Peoples*, written in 1555 by Swedish archbishop Olaus Magnus. According to historian Roland Huntford, Magnus's book, the "first to expound on the charms of the northern winter," was also "the first to offer an authentic disquisition on snow and skiing in print."

The oldest intact ski dates from 3200 BCE. Ditch diggers found it in 1924 in Kalvträsk, Sweden. At a remarkable fifty-two hundred years old, the Kalvträsk ski is six and a half feet long and six inches wide. The width would have been excessive for the groomed classic tracks of a modern-day local ski trail, but its ample breadth would have excelled at staying on top of the snow. Bindings were attached through four holes drilled vertically through the midsection of the ski, which had been planed flat for the user's foot to rest on. The Kalvträsk has two contemporaries: the Salla ski from Finland and the Drevja ski of Norway. As opposed to the binding mounts of the Kalvträsk, which would have adversely affected glide by leaving the binding strap exposed beneath the ski, causing friction on the snow, both the Salla and the Drevja skis used mortise slots cut horizontally through the width of the skis. Fifty-one hundred years later, the Strand Ski Company of Wisconsin, the world's largest ski producer at the time, used

The hand-colored woodcut *Jompa with Wolf* by Sami artist John Savio (1902–1938) was produced circa 1928–34.

similar mortise slots to mount its bindings. The basic design of the ski is ancient indeed.

The Sami lived a nomadic life tied to reindeer, which required skis for daily use. The Norsemen, who migrated to Scandinavia after the Sami, likely learned how to ski from them. Between the eighth and eleventh centuries, these Norse Vikings lived in permanent villages. They farmed and hence were not as reliant on their skis as the Sami. As a result, they were not as skilled on skis either; yet, what set the Norsemen apart was, according to ski historian Roland Huntford, that they were the first culture to embrace skiing in their literature as part of their identity. One old Norse saga told the fable of an eleventh-century king who, when threatened by a commoner who was a better skier, ordered the commoner to ski a treacherous slope in hopes of killing the man.

The Norse even had a ski goddess named Skade. Written of in the thirteenth century, Skade loved nothing more than skiing and bow hunting. She married another god named Njord, but their divergent tastes in home prevented marital bliss. As a sea god, Njord lived on the coast, while Skade was at home in the mountains. The couple agreed to split their time between coast and crag. After a spell in the mountains, Njord bemoaned:

> Mountains are my curse
> It was dreary to hear
> The howl of wolves
> Instead of the song of the swans.

Skade was similarly disenchanted by her time by the sea:

> I could not sleep,
> Next to the sea,
> Because of the screech of birds.

The couple separated, and Skade returned to her beloved mountains to ski. She later married the more suitable Odin, and they had many children. Centuries later, in 1889, a women's ski club in Norway elected to name their club Skade despite the objection of one of its members. Skade, this member grumbled, should be disqualified for having had two lovers. Skade's story was, the woman said, "indelicate," and her reputation was "by no means unblemished." The club ignored this complaint, and the name remained.

The old ski tale best known today occurred in same century as when the Skade story was written. For decades in the late twelfth and early thirteenth centuries, Norway was engulfed in civil war. It was a class war, with the wealthy, landed Baglers battling the landless, roguish Birkebeiners. The term *birkebeiner*, meaning "birch legger," had been first used as a slight, mocking the poor people for wearing leggings of birch bark, but in true rebel fashion the term was co-opted.

The Birkebeiners regarded a man named Haakon Sverresson as their king. He died after a bloodletting treatment early in 1204. Sverresson was not known to have any heirs, but some months after he died one of his former concubines arrived at the Birkebeiner court with an infant son she said was Sverresson's.

Living in Bagler territory, the mother and child were vulnerable. Around the end of 1205, a Birkebeiner party set off with the toddler to bring him to safety in Nidaros (present-day Trondheim), which was a Birkebeiner stronghold. A blizzard stalled the skiers near Lillehammer. The two best skiers set off with the young king and carried him over the mountain to Østerdalen and later to Nidaros. The toddler king matured in safety. As an adult, King Haakon IV enjoyed a long reign, ended the country's centuries-long spate of civil war, and brought Norway into a cultural golden age. Centuries later, Haakon's escape route would be memorialized in the Birkebeinerrennet ski race, first in Norway and then in Wisconsin.

Three hundred years later, in 1520, an eerily similar event occurred in Sweden that would likewise be memorialized in a ski race. Gustav Ericson Vasa, a young aristocrat, fled across the countryside from Christian II, the Danish king who controlled much of Scandinavia. Christian II had raised Vasa's ire a short time before by inviting Vasa's parents, along with other Swedish royals, to Stockholm for what was supposed to be a reconciliation party. Later dubbed the Stockholm Bloodbath, the party was a ploy to gather the king's adversaries within killing range. Vasa's parents were executed along with one hundred others.

In Mora, Sweden, Vasa tried to stir local men into rebellion against the king, though they were not enthused by the idea. Vasa continued west, trying to build a rebel army. The men in Mora soon learned that Christian II was going to raise their taxes. A murder in their aristocratic class had not sufficiently provoked them, but higher taxes did. The Mora men decided they would join Vasa in revolution and sent their two best skiers to catch him and give him

Ullr, the Norse god of sport, is depicted on skis in an eighteenth-century Icelandic manuscript.

The Norwegian legend of the Birkebeiners is depicted in Knud Bergslien's famous painting from 1869, *Skiing Birchlegs Crossing the Mountain with the Royal Child.*

the news, reaching him in the town of Sälen. Vasa gathered his troops and battled the king, eventually winning and becoming king of the newly independent Sweden in 1523. Norway, though, remained under Christian II's control. Centuries later, this event would inspire the Vasaloppet in Sweden, which in turn inspired Minnesota's Mora Vasaloppet.

Members of Norway's Skiforeningen (Association for the Promotion of Skiing) pose with their long boards, circa 1883.

1

Just Add Norwegians

1840s–1900

The first known skier in the United States was a Norwegian immigrant named Gullik Laugen. In 1841, in southern Wisconsin, Laugen and a friend strapped on wooden skis in Rock Prairie and set off across the snow-covered grass toward Beloit to buy flour. When Laugen's American neighbors saw the strange ski tracks, the seasoned prairie folk let their imaginations run wild. What kind of creature could have left those unceasing parallel tracks in the snow? The local consensus, voiced by an individual regarded as the best naturalist in town, concluded that an unknown monster roamed the prairie, transporting itself by mysterious and terrible means. Even the naturalist, Laugen reminisced in 1869, couldn't answer the settlers' most pressing concern: "whether this freak of nature attacked and devoured human beings."

Ski wasn't yet an English word in the mid-nineteenth century. The term was Norwegian and came from an Old Norse word referring to a split piece of wood. Early chroniclers struggled to describe skis. In 1853, the *Minnesota Pioneer* reported that a Norwegian had arrived in St. Paul on "Lapland snow skates." The skates of this unknown Norwegian were "strips of smooth wood, about six feet long and three inches wide. . . . The wearer partly shuffles along by moving alternately his feet, and shoves himself behind at the same time, with a long staff." With his single pole, the unnamed

SNOW SHOE
RACES.

THIRD ANNUAL MEETING

OF THE

ALTURAS

SNOW SHOE CLUB

AT

LA PORTE,

Plumas   County.

FOUR DAYS' RACING

COMMENCING ON MONDAY,

February 22d, 1869.

$600 IN PURSES

"DOPE IS KING."

PROGRAMME.

FIRST DAY.—Club Purse of $100 00, free
for all.

2d Race. Club Purse of $50 00, free for all
but the winner of the first race.

SECOND DAY.—Club Purse of $75, free for all.

2d Race. Club Purse of $50, free for all
but the winner of first race of this day.

THIRD DAY.—Club Purse of $50, free for all.

2d Race. Club Purse of $25, free for all but
the winner of the first race of this day.

FOURTH DAY.—Club Purse of $150, free for
all. $125 to the winner and $25 to second man.

2d Race. Club Purse of $100, free for all
but the winners of the first race of this day.
$75 to the winner and $25 to the second man.

Purses for Boys, will be made up during the
week.

Racing to commence at precisely one o'clock
each day. All entries for each days' racing must
be made before 11 o'clock, A. M., with the Secretary. Entrance $1.

If on Monday, February 22d, 1869, the weather
should be unfavorable, the races will be postponed
from day to day until favorable.

By order of the Club,
JOHN CONLY, Pres't.

ALEX. H. CREW, Sec'y.

Norwegian had skied from Lake Superior to St. Paul in a day and a half.

Pastor Olaus Frederik Duus arrived in Wisconsin from Norway in 1854 to serve seven congregations scattered across the frontier between Stevens Point and Lake Winnebago. Duus traveled extensively between the churches, primarily by a horse-pulled sled. He corresponded with his father in Norway, in one missive detailing how an ice storm coated the landscape's ample snowpack with a thin crust that made conditions unsuitable for his horse. Duus was, as he put it, "too fleshy" to walk on top of the ice crust, so he borrowed a pair of skis and went "crashing and creaking" to his church.

Usually ambivalent about America, he showed rare introspection when describing the vast change that he and so many other immigrants were experiencing. When his father asked whether he should encourage more folks back home to immigrate, Duus hesitated. "I neither want nor dare to," he said. "However, I do not know of anyone who does not live far better than in Norway." The American culture, though, was lacking. Duus complained about a man with three wives; two were suing the man. "The most shameful, villainous actions are here taken as a matter of course," he said.

Yet Duus was swayed by material opportunities. He bought a property and sold it a short time later for a profit of twenty-three hundred dollars. He excitedly told his father that in 1856 he would earn a salary of thirteen hundred dollars, collect fees for ministerial services, receive free board, get sixty dollars to buy firewood, and

"Dope" on this advertisement from the 1860s referred not to a nineteenth-century narcotic but to homemade ski wax made from pine pitch, turpentine, and whale spermaceti. Good dope, which had names like Skedaddle and Breakneck, was essential in the early ski races in California gold mining camps. The Norwegian miners called their twelve-foot-long skis *snowshoes*; they put them on and would schuss straight down the mountainsides. One racer's speed was calculated at eighty-seven miles per hour.

Norwegian grouse hunters return on skis to a mountain cabin near Filefjell, 1907.

have access to forty acres for farming. As an added bonus, Duus said, "I shall be rid of the troublesome Neenah congregation, and then my work shall be much more pleasant."

"The poor deer have suffered a good deal because they cannot escape the hunters on skis," Duus wrote. "The men tire a deer, and several times they have been able to walk right up to one and plunge a hunting knife into it. More than a hundred deer have been killed by the Norwegians here." After Duus finished condemning the heavy hunting, he mentioned that two of the ski-slain deer were currently in his larder. He closed his letter sarcastically: "We are in the highly praised America and *everything is all right, you know.*" Two years later his wife died. At the age of thirty-five, Duus returned to Norway permanently with his two young boys.

Scandinavian immigrants often hunted on skis. One Norwegian, Halvor

An illustration from 1856 depicts bear hunters departing a cabin in Sweden.

Hjelstad, who in 1868 settled near Glenwood, Minnesota, went hunting on skis one day with his dog. The canine ran up to a hole in the snow and started yapping, so Hjelstad approached. A black bear crawled from its den, clumsy and groggy in midwinter. Hjelstad staved in the bear's head with the ax he was carrying.

Hjelstad skied for other reasons as well. Surrounded by Swedes, on Sundays he would seek out preferable company by skiing some miles to visit with four Norwegian families from his native region of Telemark. "When he approached the slope leading to the little Chippewa River," a friend recalled, "Halvor would sashay gracefully down the slope of the river until he found a narrow place, then he would retrace his ski marks and get a good start down the slope and jump across the narrowest place in the stream." In Hjelstad's native province of Telemark, skiing had been of great importance for generations. Telemark was an especially rugged region of narrow valleys beneath mountain peaks where farmers eked out a living on the slopes that were less steep than others. It was no wonder the region for a time produced Norway's (and perhaps the world's) greatest skiers.

♠

That same year, from the Telemark village of Morgedal, a forty-three-year-old peasant named Sondre Norheim rose from obscurity to become the world's first star skier. Norheim has been dubbed the "father of modern skiing," and his humble mountain cottage is a shrine to skiing history buffs. Three times the torch ceremonies for the Winter Olympics have begun from fire lit in the Norheim cottage's fireplace hearth.

When Christiania (later Oslo) hosted its third annual national ski competition in 1868, on a slope called Iversløkken near its city center, skiing as an organized sport was still in its infancy, even in Norway. The competition would eventually move to the legendary Holmenkollen hill, where it continues today. The prize money of about ten dollars would have attracted Norheim. He and his wife, Rannei, had five living children and struggled to get by. Rannei was steady and industrious, selling needlepoint to support the family, while Norheim's fondness

Sondre Norheim's rural Norwegian cottage in the idyllic mountain surroundings of Morgedal in Telemark.

An excited crowd awaits the next ski jumper at Holmenkollen, near Norway's capital city, Christiania, circa 1900.

for fiddling, dancing, and skiing kept him from excelling at his trades of farming and carpentry.

Norheim set out on skis for the Christiania competition, 110 miles distant. The story goes that Norheim, dressed in simple garb, was jeered at as he made his way to the big race. Once in action, however, any mocking of Norheim turned to adulation. The race was a two-and-a-half-kilometer loop that combined downhill, cross-country, and jumping. Norheim finished with a time of eighteen minutes and fifty-five seconds, half a minute ahead of second place. One newspaper gushed of his run down the final slope: "With his ski stick carried like a fashionable cane in one hand, and his cap in the other, he set off at a whirlwind speed, and as if it was the most natural thing in the world."

Hungry for a national identity after centuries of foreign rule, the

Sondre Norheim's jumps from the roof of his Morgedal cottage barn made him a legend in Norway. More than a century later, the Norwegian tourism industry would celebrate his legacy with images like this one, with the caption "Ski jumping before breakfast improves the appetite!"

educated classes of Christiania would turn Norheim into a folk hero. Through no fault of his own, Norheim's legend would become so inflated that the false claims threatened to detract from his status as the boldest, fastest, and most stylish skier of his time. His mastery and panache were key in transforming skiing from a utilitarian practice of rural Norwegians into an activity that transcended sport and would define a nation.

A host of reputable sources still credit Norheim with a laundry list of outrageous accomplishments, such as single-handedly inventing the Telemark turn, the Christiania turn, slalom skiing, the waisted ski (resembling the modern downhill ski, with the end wider than the middle), and the binding heel strap made from birch root. Thanks to the sober scholarship of ski historians like John Weinstock and Roland Huntford, we know that

Norheim personally developed none of these things. Norheim may have been the first to execute a deft Telemark turn in front of the capital city ski fans, but he was simply skiing in the superior style of his home province.

When the Christiania skiers watched Norheim, they couldn't help but notice that their own skills paled in comparison. A capital city newspaper admonished the downhill technique of a typical local skier: "He runs down the slope, legs widely straddled, with a stiff, crouching stance, and trunk leaning forward, a ridiculous figure." Nor did the Christianians know how to ski in proper cross-country fashion. "[They] ran off as they normally do when marching quickly, that is, they lifted the skis from the snow and stamped them down to the accompaniment of the sound of squelching on the ground. Very few had the gliding movement that makes the ski an easy, useful means of transport."

For the tournament in 1870, the Central Association, Norway's new ski racing organization, invited Norheim to demonstrate proper technique. The economic opportunity was sorely needed for Norheim and his Telemarking protégés. In the coming years, they would sell their skis in

Christiania skiers and spectators make a winter trek to Holmenkollen, circa 1900. The hill and its celebrated ski jump would define Norwegian competitive skiing for decades.

Sondre Norheim inspired generations of young Norwegian skiers, especially the children of Morgedal, where this photograph was taken in the 1890s.

Christiania, put on exhibitions, and teach skills. Witnessing Norheim's exhibitions was a formative experience for the coming generation of skiers.

At the competition five years later, Norheim was slow in the cross-country portion of the race. He took sixteenth place. He was fifty years old, and his racing career was finished. The Central Association presented him with a silver trinket and a gold coin for his contributions to the sport before releasing him to Morgedal and his peasant life of subsistence farming. With his glory days behind him, Norheim moved to North Dakota and eventually died in a sod hut. He was buried in an unmarked grave and forgotten for sixty years until, with seemingly celestial timing that heralded the long-awaited rise of cross-country skiing in America, Sondre Norheim's memory would dawn again.

🌲

Norwegian artist Christian Krohg depicted the first ski competition at Huseby Hill in this drawing, circa 1883.

The Hemmestveit family also lived in Morgedal, in a small farmhouse perched on the side of a mountain. The Hemmestveit kids—Mikkel, Torjus, Aasne, and Halvor—watched Sondre Norheim's skiing exploits through their cottage window, as he ripped through the meadows and launched off improvised jumps, which included the snow-covered roofs of hillside houses. "It was like Sondre never quite grew up," Mikkel reportedly said later in life. "He was more boy than most of us." When the Hemmestveits were old enough, they joined Norheim on Sundays. Sister Aasne won a village race, though her gender would preclude her from having the skiing opportunities of her brothers.

The first time a Hemmestveit placed in a major competition was 1879, at the annual Christiania competition, now held at Huseby Hill. With Swedish king Oscar II, Norway's ruler, in attendance, eighteen-year-old Torjus took second place. A local paper noted: "The ski is the poor man's horse . . . and a good horse at that," mentioning that Torjus and eight other Telemarkings had come to town by skiing 110 miles through the wilds. The writer continued: "Skiing is democratic in the best meaning of the word, since nobody is so poor that he cannot acquire a pair of skis. . . . At the same time skiing is a pleasure for the better-off: it expands the chest that has shrunk at the desk. It fills the senses with joy in God's glorious free natural world."

Those lines are a great distillation of a key point of evolution in skiing's history, pinpointing the tension between skiing as the practice of poor mountain folk who skied frequently and well out of necessity meeting the modern recreation for personal and community growth, laced with a spiritual aspect. The Norwegians had a word for this rather profound definition of skiing: *idraet,* literally translating to "ski sport" but with greater meaning. In the coming decades, they would proselytize this view of skiing to a world audience.

Right after the 1881 Huseby competition, Torjus Hemmestveit Sr. and his two sons Torjus and Mikkel conducted a multi-week ski school, teaching their Telemark gospel to the heathen urban skiers. The school was open to both men and women. A local paper pointed out that the substantial stock of skis for sale in the city had sold out: "There was hardly a decent pair of skis obtainable in the whole town."

Ski manufacturing was a cottage industry during this time. Wood for skis was harvested and dried in the fall, and then the skis were crafted on winter evenings. Even the poorest tenant farmer could fashion skis

A skier leaps from the precipice during one of the first jumping competitions at Huseby Hill, 1880s.

for his family. Norheim and Torjus Sr., like many Telemarking men, were noted ski makers. Near Lillehammer in 1882, young ski maker Simen Rustad opened the world's first ski factory. He used a waterwheel to power a saw that produced more skis than could be achieved by hand. A neighbor chided him, saying that with all the time he had wasted setting up the ski factory he could have instead made many boats. The Rustad family would go on making wooden skis until 1980. Following Rustad, Norway's ski industry was for many years an amalgam of small-scale producers. Immigrants in Minnesota would create their own standard for ski production in the American tradition of mass production. Mikkel Hemmestveit would eventually found perhaps the first ski company in the United States, though in the early 1880s he was still a teenager and his brother Torjus a young man in his early twenties. The brothers were on the cusp of a decade that would bring them great change and a little fame.

The Hemmestveits had dark hair; they were quick, compact, wiry, and good at dancing. One account described Mikkel as weighing not more than 135 pounds, while another claimed 175. In 1883, the annual Christiania race had become too big for a club to run, so, for the first time anywhere for any sport, Norway formed a national sporting entity to execute the tournament. In another first, instead of an all-in-one race with elements of downhill, cross-country, and jumping, a separate cross-country race was held, and a racer's time would be combined with his jumping score to determine overall place: *Nordic combined* was born.

The celebrated Hemmestveit brothers, Mikkel and Torjus *(center)*, were early stars of the Aurora Ski Club in Red Wing, Minnesota. After winning medals at tournaments throughout the Midwest, they were photographed with fellow club members Paul Honningstad *(far left)* and B. L. Hjermstad *(far right)* around 1891.

Torjus, Mikkel, and more than a dozen other Telemarkings traveled by train to Christiania to compete in what was now dubbed the King's Cup. Taking the train allowed them to bring more skis to sell. Torjus won the cup, with his younger brother Mikkel runner-up. Telemarkings took nine of the top ten places. That night they hit the town, scandalizing the city dwellers by drinking heavily and criticizing the king—at least that's what the papers reported the next day. One paper snobbishly derided the Telemarkings as "monkeys" and "farmers." King Oscar II, a Swede, didn't wield as much control as the Danish kings had, yet Norway was still under foreign dominion. In this era of embryonic Norwegian nationalism, the Telemarkings fit right into the mold that Sondre Norheim had cast of the rural Norwegian—rough, independent, disconnected from the foreign power structure, and unmatched in spirit and on snow. In the newspaper's toadyism to a foreign king and hostility toward its rural citizens, another reason why commoners took their chances on America was clear.

♠

The legendary Sondre Norheim in America, 1890s.

At age fifty-nine, Sondre Norheim followed his oldest son and daughter and immigrated to America with Rannei and their three youngest children. The Norheims arrived after a ten-day journey in a small berth on a ship with twenty other immigrants. They stayed in Kasson, Minnesota, with their oldest son, who had adopted the name Ole Saunderson (son of Sondre). In 1888, Sondre and company headed west to McHenry County, North Dakota, a short way east of Minot. In May, Norheim signed documents declaring his intent to become an American citizen. He received 160 acres to homestead near the Mouse River, where he and Rannei built a sod hut. They enjoyed visiting their neighbors across the river, who dubbed Rannei "Lena Claypipe" for her smoking habit. Norheim taught the neighbor's son, Olaf Nelson, to ski. Loaning the boy his skis, Norheim made a jump for Olaf on a knoll above the Mouse River.

As an elderly gentleman in the 1960s, Olaf Nelson described Norheim as a reticent man who never talked about his life in Norway. Alas, it sounded as though Norheim had indeed finally grown up. Still, his skiing inspired legends on both sides of the Atlantic. When snow rendered the negligible prairie roads impassable, Norheim carried the mail on skis. One story had Norheim skiing a batch of important mail all the way to Montana. Another tale told of Native Americans watching Norheim and marveling at how he danced across the snow. Norheim died at age seventy-two in March 1897, at the end of a brutal prairie winter. He may have initially been buried on his farm but was ultimately moved to the cemetery of the Norway Lutheran Church, perched above the Mouse River. Upon Norheim's death, the village of Morgedal held a ski festival and gave speeches in his honor. In America, the father of modern skiing lay forgotten in an unmarked grave.

♠

In Norway, the Skiforeningen, or Association for the Promotion of Skiing, which had been founded in 1883 (and is still thriving today with fifty thousand members), declared the future of skiing was in cross-country and not in jumping or running downhill. By this time, ski jumpers were soaring longer distances, so no longer could any Ole walk off the street and hurl himself over a small jump without risking life and limb. A gulf was forming between the casual dabbler and the committed jumper. Skiforeningen's focus on cross-country made the sport accessible to regular folks who did not want to break their necks. City dwellers who worked in offices could get fresh air and stay fit. As a result, numerous ski shops started popping up in Christiania.

Showcasing the cultural distance between the capital and surrounding rural regions, in 1886 Norwegian physicians debated whether cross-country skiers' bodies could survive the physical strain of long races. Doctors nervously monitored that year's eleven-kilometer cross-country King's Cup race at Huseby Hill, which Mikkel Hemmestveit won. An attending physician noted: "Not one of the skiers showed any signs of overexertion, exhaustion, or having suffered organic injury as a result of the considerable exertion." The following year, organizers lengthened the race to twenty kilometers. Outside the capital, in places like Telemark, farmers constantly skied lengthy, grueling cross-country courses while hunting,

Prompted by the Skiforeningen, cross-country skiing boomed in popularity during the late nine-teenth century as city-dwelling Norwegians, long boards in hand, embraced the outdoors at skiing destinations like Frognersæteren, a fashionable café north of Christiania.

gathering firewood, and even fetching and schlepping hay from higher fields for livestock.

A chronicle of the stupendous endurance of frontier Scandinavians came from the exploits of a pair of Sami skiers on a scientific expedition to Greenland in 1883. The team had failed in its attempt to be the first to cross Greenland and was about to turn back. The trip leader, a Finno-Swede nobleman and artic explorer named Adolf Erik Nordenskiöld, asked the only two skiers in his party to scout the route ahead. In the context of formal arctic exploration (as opposed to the daily life of Scandinavians living

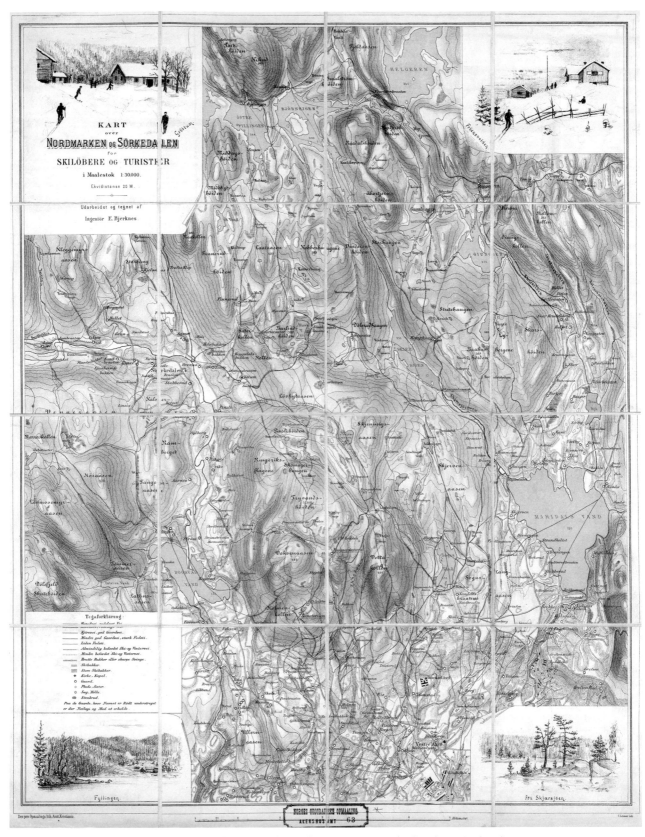

This touring map from 1890 shows the massive network of trails at Nordmarka, north of Oslo, that has been used by Norwegian skiers for generations.

above the Arctic Circle), skiing was not an established means of travel, so Nordenskiöld's use of it was revelatory. The two Sami skiers, Anders Rassa and Pavva Lássa Tuorda, were from northern Sweden. They set out on this last-ditch reconnaissance carrying minimal gear and skied, by their estimation, 230 kilometers before they ran out of drinking water and turned back. They arrived back at camp after being gone for fifty-seven hours and skiing a 460-kilometer round trip. The Sami were not overly exhausted on their return and raved about how good the skiing had been.

When the expedition reported its adventures to the outside world, many people didn't believe the pair had skied so far. Fridtjof Nansen was one of the doubters. A few years later, inspired, Nansen would use skis on the first successful crossing of Greenland; his journey would attract international news and play a role in popularizing skiing as sport. But in 1883 Nansen was a skeptic.

In 1884, Nordenskiöld, to test whether the Sami could have actually skied that far, organized a race of 220 kilometers in northern Sweden called the Nordenskiöldsloppet. Sixteen skiers, mostly Sami, competed (eight of the top ten finishers would be Sami), though Anders Rassa did

Sami skiers Anders Rassa and Pavva Lássa Tuorda prepare to depart camp during Adolf Erik Nordenskiöld's scientific expedition to Greenland in 1883.

not. He said he didn't care whether people believed him; he didn't think 460 kilometers was all that far anyway. He had skied farther on wolf-hunting trips. Pavva Lássa Tuorda entered the race and won with a time of a little over twenty-one hours. In third place was a poor Sami farmer named Apmut Arrhman. He was a small, sinewy guy and had been mocked for his humble appearance as he skied 90 kilometers to reach the start of the race. Nearing the finish line, he struggled with a damaged ski and thought a pull from the bottle of aquavit he carried in his pack would help. Instead, the booze made him fall asleep. Despite the nap, Arrhman took third place and won £250. He skied home to find his wife furious at him for being gone so long. While he had been out skiing, a bear had attacked their cattle. Arrhman put his skis back on, tracked the bear for 50 kilometers, killed it, and skied back home. Meanwhile, the educated classes in Christiania continued to debate whether a human body could withstand an 11-kilometer race. In 2016, Red Bull, the caffeine- and sugar-rich soda that sponsors many extreme sports, revived the Nordenskiöldsloppet. Still 220 kilometers and using the original course from 1884, the race attracted more than four hundred entrants in 2019.

♠

Though the cautious approach of ski officials in Norway was amusing, their organization was essential in developing the sport and further influenced Norwegian immigrants in the American Northwest (as the Upper Midwest was then known) to start a ski circuit. Ski clubs began popping up in the region in the mid-1880s, forming the basis of organized skiing in America.

The real spark was a good old dose of indignation. In 1885, eastern newspapers editorialized that Minnesota was unfit for human habitation in winter, even likening St. Paul to Siberia. Local bigwigs in the capital city of the state retaliated by planning a winter carnival to showcase the virtues of February in the northland. The St. Paul Winter Carnival was to promote delightful cold weather sports through clubs. In November, the Scandinavian Ski Club, arguably the first ski club in the country, formed in St. Paul. An organizer later recalled that in the early 1880s skiing had been so unknown in the Twin Cities that he'd had to intervene on behalf of a group of Norwegian boys who had set up a ski jump in a city park.

THE FIRST COUPLE OF SKIING

In a key development for the ski sport, the Nordenskiöldloppet transformed one ski skeptic into a believer. Prior to the race, Fridtjof Nansen had scoffed at Baron Nordenskiöld's skiing claims, but when Nansen successfully led the first expedition to cross Greenland, in 1888, he used skis. Nansen's expedition was huge news, and he wrote a popular book stating that skiing had been instrumental in his crossing. Nansen and his wife, Eva, became boosters for the growing new sport.

The couple had actually met while skiing. Like Nansen, Eva was an upper-class urbanite. Social norms dictated that girls of her class could ski for fun as children, but they needed to quit the sport and concentrate on becoming proper ladies as they matured. Eva kept skiing and as an adult scandalously skied alone in Nordmarka, the wooded region north of Christiania that was, and still is, laced with ski trails.

On Easter 1892, Eva and Fridtjof skied over Hardangervidda (a massive mountain plateau), likely making her the first woman to traverse the prominence on skis. Their trip also established the Easter ski journey, a tradition that continues today, when throngs of Norwegians flock to the mountains on skis. Eva had sewn herself a special outfit for the journey, which, aside from being more comfortable than a long, cumbersome ladies' dress, served to purposefully shock people. Eva's woolen ensemble included a pair of loose pants covered with a dress that hung past her knees—that the shape of her legs could be discerned was highly offensive to many.

After being skewered in the newspapers, Eva admonished her detractors: "Can anyone seriously maintain that women become more immoral by skiing, even if together with men?" Women skiing in trousers wouldn't become common until the 1920s. Thinking back on previous ski trips, she celebrated the *idraet*: "The many health-giving tours in winter form the brightest and happiest memories that life has given me. They hold the unadulterated beauty of all life and Nature in a lovely indelible image, which has exercised a purifying influence on my spirit." ▲

Fridtjof and Eva Nansen, 1890

A police officer had threatened to arrest the boys for "attempted suicide" until the organizer convinced the officer otherwise.

To drum up enthusiasm for the winter carnival, trainloads of carnival boosters brought the party to Minnesota's larger towns. At 5:00 p.m. on January 19, 250 people, the vast majority of them men, set out from St. Paul to Red Wing. Earlier that day, Red Wing had formed its own club, named the Aurora Ski Club. Members of the Aurora club met the St. Paulites at the train station and marched in a rowdy procession down Main Street, setting off fireworks on their way to the music hall. The crowd hoped the governor, Red Wing's own Lucius Hubbard, would make an appearance so that they could bounce him. Bouncing was a new tradition with the Winter Carnival: an individual would be placed on a large blanket held by a ring of people who would toss the person high into the air. The governor prudently stayed away, but Red Wing's mayor was bounced. The crowd chanted "Up, up" as another man was bounced in the music hall to test "the hardness of the ceiling with his toes," a newspaper reported.

Ornate illustrated posters advertised special train routes between Chicago and the Twin Cities that shuttled visitors to the 1888 St. Paul Winter Carnival.

In the days of the Winter Carnival ski competitions, skiers would promenade through the streets, as these members of the Aurora Ski Club did through downtown St. Paul.

The carnival promoters were remarkably effective at generating interest in a previously arcane winter pursuit. "All men and boys in the city seem to be more or less touched by the ski frenzy," the *Red Wing Daily Republican* reported. Women and girls were left out of the fun. During the train visit, while the men bounced each other, the ladies, "decorated with St. George's crosses," served drinks.

On another day, uniformed St. Paul skiers and winter carnival promoters boarded the party train and chugged twenty miles east to Stillwater. Perhaps some in Stillwater were still sore that St. Paul had been chosen over the St. Croix River town as the site of the state capital thirty years earlier because the resulting newspaper write-up about the visit was wonderfully sententious. The *Stillwater Messenger* ridiculed the uniforms worn by the visiting ski club: "The mackinaw blanket *uniforms* worn were no novelty in this lumbering center and were no more attractive or picturesque than are those of our own boys of the woods when they slick up in the dandy attire of new clothes preparatory to a winter's hard and honest work in the pineries." The *Messenger* huffed on about the terrible new habit of bouncing, which was "not very funny" and contained "some elements of danger and brutality."

The following week, the *Messenger* and the *St. Paul Pioneer Press* debated correct pronunciation of the word *ski*. "It isn't pronounced sky, not yet skee," the *Pioneer Press* proclaimed. The correct way to say this strange new word was in fact *she*. The *Messenger* argued back: "He who would avoid scandalizing the Scandinavians will pronounce it 'skee' and avoid 'sky.'" The local papers weren't alone: an 1893 article in *Outing Magazine* said the correct way to say the word was *she*.

When sixty members of the Scandinavian Ski Club, clad in blue jackets and pants, marched while carrying their skis on their shoulders during the Winter Carnival parade, the newspaper described the skis as "long and curious shoes." Club members exhibited downhill runs on Robert Street. Recapping the carnival, the *Pioneer Press* praised the Aurora Ski Club and another from Minneapolis, claiming, "St. Paul is the first city in the country to boast organization of a club to use skis as implements of sport." Other ski clubs soon formed in Eau Claire, Wisconsin, and Stillwater. The Eau Claire and St. Paul clubs have lasted to this day.

By the 1890s, the jumping exploits of the Hemmestveit brothers had made them famous on both sides of the Atlantic, and they were featured prominently in an article in *Outing Magazine* in 1893.

🌲

In Christiania, Mikkel Hemmestveit won the King's Cup in 1885 and then again in 1886, when he was twenty-three-years-old. But his status as Norway's best skier was not enough to keep him from emigrating. That summer Mikkel hopped a ship bound for America and settled in Minnesota with his cousin, who had a farm in Lake Ida Township, forty-five miles northeast of Fargo, North Dakota. During Hemmestveit's first American winter, the Norman County Ski Club coalesced around him, just in time for Mikkel to compete in the second annual St. Paul Winter Carnival, held on January 25, 1887. The first Winter Carnival had featured a ski exhibition, but the competition portion had been canceled because of warm weather. The ski contest at the second Winter Carnival was the first in the Midwest.

Members of St. Paul's Scandinavian Ski Club built a jump and a mile-long cross-country course on Halsted Avenue (on the Mississippi River floodplain where the Holman Field airport is today). The twenty-foot-high jump would, the newspaper claimed, "send the runner at least forty feet

Members of Norwegian ski clubs pose in front of the ice palace at the 1886 St. Paul Winter Carnival.

out in mid-air." The skiers were grouped into divisions based on ability. Twenty-three competed in the first-class division. Each skier jumped three times and then sprinted the one-mile cross-country run, which was timed. The fresh-off-the-boat, reigning King's Cup champion did not disappoint. Mikkel jumped more than sixty feet and skied the course in four and a half minutes, more than a minute ahead of the runner-up. Later in the carnival, Mikkel was enlisted to perform a skiing exhibition near the site of the future capitol building in St. Paul. Skiers from St. Paul and St. Croix Falls, Wisconsin, tried recruiting him to move to their respective towns.

Two weeks later, Mikkel traveled to Red Wing for the Aurora club's first tournament. The Aurora club was exclusively male, and only Scandinavians were permitted to serve as officers. Female involvement was limited to preparing food and decorating the hall for the post-competition banquet. The Red Wing contest did not have a cross-country portion, but Mikkel won thirty-five dollars in gold by jumping thirty-seven feet off a six-foot-high jump. He earned a little extra for putting on another exhibition, in which he went fifty feet farther up the bluff and skied down "with an ease and grace unsurpassed." What innocent times these were for skiing, when the length of a Midwestern slope was too long and too high. Equipment was, of course, part of the equation—the long wooden skis had no hardened edging, and the bindings at worst were merely leather straps to slip one's toes under and at best the same backed up by a leather strap and buckle that went behind the skier's heel. The gear and newness of the sport, as well as the objective hazards of ski jumping, resulted in frequent injuries. The *Zumbrota News* reported that three members of the town's new Viking Ski Club had suffered severe sprains. "While trying to use her husband's skis," the paper printed, Stella Barteau broke her leg. "If Zumbrota ski fever holds out very long, it will be necessary to build a hospital to take care of its many victims."

♠

Mikkel Hemmestveit spent the 1887–88 ski season in St. Croix Falls, Wisconsin, drawn to the town by an offer from businessman H. U. Hetting to partner on a ski manufacturing company—and the Excelsior Ski Company was born. Mikkel founded the St. Croix Falls Ski Club, which welcomed women. The club practiced on what was called Mount Pisgah, a glacially

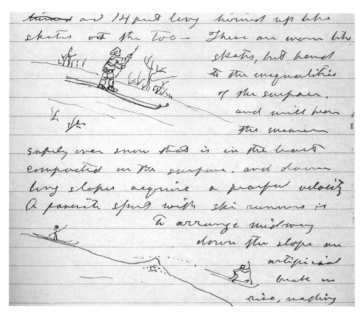

Pastor Elijah Edwards, who lived in Taylors Falls, Minnesota, in the 1880s, gazed across the St. Croix River at Mikkel Hemmestveit and the St. Croix Falls Ski Club while they practiced, as he described in his journal, a "peculiarly Scandinavian sport." The skier's descent was like a swoop of a bird, "only swifter and more terrible," wrote the reverend. "A favorite sport with the ski runners is to arrange midway down the slope an artificial break or rise, reaching which the ski-runner with all his accelerated velocity springs into the air."

The town of Albert Lea in southern Minnesota formed an active ski club in the mid-1880s. The club's president was Gilbert Gulbrandson, a prominent banker. In 1888, a squad of eight skiers from the club was photographed in Minneapolis during a tournament at Kenwood Hill.

formed esker that butts up to the edge of downtown.

St. Croix Falls was a logging town situated on the border with Minnesota and the banks of the river it had been named after. Ski fever swept through the town and the neighboring community across the river where the local newspaper was published. "Skis are all the 'Go' now," the *Taylors Falls Journal* reported. The Excelsior Ski Company was an exciting new enterprise. Other businesses paid for their own advertisements—the grist mill in nearby Franconia, the watch and jewelry shop, the dry goods store, even Peter Trump's saloon (when Trump died of a stomach ailment, the *Journal* eulogized that he had been very liberal, industrious, and generous, having given away half of his earnings to charity). But Excelsior never had to advertise. Everything it did was front-page news, whether it was Mr. Hetting traveling to St. Paul to sell skis or the factory adding steam boxes to increase production. Mikkel, whom the paper called Mr. Hammondsworth, traveled downriver to Franconia and Osceola to give Sunday skiing exhibitions. Membership in the St. Croix Falls Ski Club quickly grew to sixty-five, including most of the businessmen and society leaders in town. Everyone wanted a piece of the hot new sport. What the *Journal* failed to acknowledge, because Mikkel was a newcomer and an immigrant, was that the town's enticing ski buzz was entirely thanks to his presence. Mikkel was merely "second lieutenant" of the ski club, after H. U. Hetting and Hetting's son. When the ski season started and Mikkel dominated the tournaments, the honor, the *Journal* claimed, "all belongs to the Saint Croix Falls Ski club."

For a smattering of towns in western Wisconsin and eastern Minnesota, a proper tournament schedule took place that winter, with jumping contests in La Crosse, Eau Claire, Red Wing, and St. Paul. La Crosse had a new club, the Norske Ski Club, which recruited a number of non-Scandinavians they called the American Faction.

Women formed ski clubs as early as the late nineteenth century but wouldn't be welcomed as full members of the sport for many years. Members of a ladies' ski club in Christiania pose here in the 1890s.

The club admitted women, who were exempt from membership fees. Both men and women were required to wear uniforms, and they skied together, at least during practice. At the time of the tournament, fifteen of the fifty-eight Norske club members were women. The *La Crosse Republican* mentioned Mary Davidson, calling her the "champion lady ski runner of the world." Davidson, a recent immigrant from Norway, didn't ski in the competition but put on an exhibition that won "the delight of the crowded and jubilant multitude." In the coming decades, the very few women ski

"Norwegian sport at Ishpeming, Michigan" embellished for the pages of *Harper's Weekly* in 1892.

jumpers who practiced the sport were almost always relegated to jumping in exhibitions and not allowed to compete. The same was true in Norway. Women were generally encouraged to ski casually but not competitively, as competition supposedly threatened their "femininity." This view would hold for nearly a century.

In Ishpeming, Michigan, the Norden Ski Club organized its own jumping contests on Lake Angeline Mine. Norden was the first ski club to form so far north. In terms of American settlement, heading north was akin to traveling back in time. In 1860, Ishpeming had only a thousand residents. By 1890, two years after the Norden club's first contest, however, the population had boomed to eleven thousand, fueled in large part by the iron ore mines. Norden was the first of the many legendary Iron Range ski clubs.

The American ski tournaments were purely jumping competitions. Cross-country did not fascinate onlookers like jumping did. In February 1888, at the King's Cup in Norway, Torjus Hemmestveit won the cross-country race, which had been drastically lengthened to fifty kilometers and came to be regarded as the world's first ski marathon. Academic concerns over the human body's ability to withstand such exertion had faded. Torjus's time was four and a half hours—pretty average for a mediocre racer by today's standards. The winner of the fifty-five-kilometer classic-style American Birkebeiner race in 2020, for example, finished with a time of less than two and a half hours. Torjus, though, was using a single pole. Using two poles, which the Finns had been doing for years, had been banned at the King's Cup until the year before. Behind Torjus and finishing in fourth place was a man using two poles. Despite the man's failure to crack the top three, when the other racers and the fans watching saw two poles in action, the kinesiology of the technique just made more sense as the faster and more enjoyable way to ski. "Two sticks will . . . soon be . . . usual," a journalist covering the race correctly predicted. The journalist noted another advancement: some of the racers were "thinly clad in knit-wear jerseys and ditto trousers." Previously the outfit of the skier had been

In the days of Sondre Norheim and the Hemmestveit brothers, skiing was accomplished primarily with a long single pole, often illustrated with dramatic effect in the European press.

heavy work clothes, but now skiers were beginning to dress for speed, following the lead of competitive ice skaters, another popular Norwegian sport of the time.

The Hemmestveits were kicking butt on both sides of the Atlantic. Mikkel and his St. Croix Falls teammates wore new uniforms of "light brown Mackinaw goods with blue and white trimmings; knee pants with leggings; blue sash and blue and brown caps." Mikkel placed first at all four tournaments that season. In Eau Claire, on what was dubbed the steepest and longest ski run in the world, he jumped seventy feet, soaring "like an eagle . . . so powerful and elegant." In La Crosse, he won a gold watch and chain. He did not disappoint at the Winter Carnival, where the steep pitch of the jump caused many ski runners to fall.

The season's last contest was at Kenwood Hill in Minneapolis, near Cedar Lake. In a ceremonial start, skiers from Eau Claire, Albert Lea, Red Wing, St. Paul, St. Croix Falls, and Stillwater, led by a drum corps and

Ski runners at the Kenwood Hill tournament in Minneapolis, 1888. An estimated three thousand people, some climbing trees for a better view, watched as members of the Norwegian Turn and Ski Club, Vikings Club, and Der Norske Twin Forening soared from a jump facing the yards of the Minneapolis and St. Louis Railway.

police brigade, began marching from the Cedar Riverside neighborhood of Minneapolis. The colorfully costumed skiers paraded with their skis on their backs down Washington Avenue in Minneapolis toward Union Station near the Hennepin Avenue bridge. Flag bearers waved flags from the United States and Norway. Skiers hooted, "Tuch-hey-son-son-son," a supposed Viking war cry. At the depot, the skiers piled onto an eleven-car train and rode to Kenwood Hills for the contest. Onlookers climbed trees and freight cars to get a better view. In the words of historian Helen White, who in the 1980s did exhaustive research on the Hemmestveits:

> The bugler took his place to sound the beginning of the contest. The starter called "Number One!" and the call was taken up all down the hill. Number One arranged his skis, grasped a small balancing stick in his hand, bent slightly forward, and in a moment he was dashing down the course like a rocket. On nearing the *hop* he would crouch slightly, like a lion about to spring, and then he was sailing through the air over the hop, landing from 60 to 80 feet from where he took the leap. . . . When some less skilled runners fell after jumping and rolled down the hill "hurly burly" fashion, everyone laughed. The successful jumpers were greeted with an admiring call which the *Tribune* interpreted as "ak heverapper" (beautiful)!

Mikkel finished his perfect season with a jump of seventy-two feet, for which he received a parlor clock worth forty dollars, a silver cake dish, and five dollars cash.

♠

Signs of decay within the St. Croix Falls Ski Club were evident by the end of the 1887–88 season. Behind Mikkel in first place, Red Wing's Aurora club took six of the top eight places at the Winter Carnival tournament. The St. Croix Falls club hosted raucous parties with the St. Paul club, for which the capital city skiers arrived on a special train and in one case didn't leave until 3:00 a.m. The night's program consisted of marching, eating, and drinking, but not skiing. Once Mikkel left for his farm in western Minnesota after the season ended, the club became a strictly social enterprise. Laden with local bigwigs and hangers-on, the St. Croix Falls club hosted dances and a euchre party. The Excelsior Ski Company continued operations for the time being. The paper proudly announced that skis had

The "Sky Crashers" of the Aurora Ski Club, photographed in Red Wing, Minnesota, circa 1890. *Top row, left to right:* B. L. Hjermstad, Paul Honningstad, unknown, Mikkel Hemmestveit, and Torjus Hemmestveit; *(bottom)* Christian Boxrud, Erik Giswold, unknown, Lars Jamtars, and Nels Klifton (from Ishpeming).

shipped to St. Paul and fifty pairs were available for sale to local residents.

In the fall of 1888, residents of St. Croix Falls strutted about in their fashionable ski club uniforms. Mikkel and his wife, Bergit, moved to the town in what was expected to be a permanent relocation. The *Taylors Falls Journal* eagerly awaited the twin towns' return to skiing glory and wrote in early December that "the Ski business in this place is booming." A competitor to the Excelsior company popped up and boasted skis made of local bitternut hickory and rock elm lumber. Meanwhile, Minneapolis was planning a major tournament, and a fantastic cross-country race was slated for December. Skiers would race 141 miles from Minneapolis to La Crosse over two days. Sadly, the race never happened.

The weather refused to cooperate. By late January, the *Taylors Falls Journal* conceded: "The outlook for sports on skis this winter is rather dubious." In St. Paul, the Winter Carnival ice palace melted. The only tournament that season was in Stillwater, at the Mulberry Street Hill, where Mikkel won the first prize of fifteen dollars. While the St. Croix Falls Ski Club planned a gala for George Washington's birthday, the Aurora Ski Club trained in the tradition of the *idraet,* going on weekly forty-mile cross-country jaunts when the conditions allowed. With a strong team already in hand, Aurora club boosters offered Mikkel a job at the Red Wing Furniture Factory, where he would be free to make skis to sell on the side. Mikkel and Bergit left St. Croix Falls for Red Wing in 1889.

🌲

Torjus Hemmestveit, the reigning King's Cup champion, immigrated to Minnesota in 1888 with his wife, Tone, and young son, also named Torjus. They settled with relatives near Ada, in the northwest of the state. Like in Norman County a few scant years before with Mikkel, an Ada ski club formed around Torjus in time for the winter tournaments of the coming season.

Red Wing's Aurora club continued to press the ski sport. In advance of a January 1890 tournament it hosted, the club updated its red, white, and blue uniforms. The old ensemble consisted of a white mackinaw coat, blue knee breeches and belt, and a red hat. Maybe skiers wanted something more subtle—or perhaps their feelings had been hurt the season before when a St. Paul skier teased the Aurora club that they looked more like a choir than a ski team. The new uniforms were less gaudy: dark blue (or black) with bands of yellow trim.

Skiers from La Crosse, Eau Claire, and Ishpeming traveled to the tournament. Also present was the Ada club, pitting the Hemmestveit brothers against each other. In front of a crowd of a few thousand, Mikkel and Torjus took first and second place, the younger brother besting the older on the home course of his new town. At the gala following the tournament,

Despite a visible lack of snow, a ski exhibition at Glenwood, Minnesota, featuring Torjus and Mikkel Hemmestveit was held in 1890. Glenwood would be known in later years as a popular hub for ski competition.

The Norden Ski Club of Ishpeming, Michigan (pictured here in 1889), was known for wearing distinctive checkered wool in competition.

Mikkel was awarded forty dollars in gold and Torjus twenty-five dollars in silver. The county attorney, Frank Wilson, gave a speech in which he praised the *noble sport* of Norway. "The languid debauchery of the south," the lawyer prattled in the midst of a night of drinking, eating, and dancing, "is happily not the pleasure of the Norseman."

By the end of the year, with a job offer at the furniture company alongside his brother, Torjus had moved to Red Wing, assuring the Aurora club's dominance. This must have been a fine time for Torjus and Mikkel. The brothers were together again, in more comfortable living conditions than they'd had in Norway. They both had young families in a community that had made such efforts to welcome them. The skiing couldn't compare to the mountains of Morgedal, but a person could only expect so much.

Organization of the American ski sport advanced in late 1890, when Midwestern clubs founded the Central Ski Association of the Northwest, the country's first ski league. The member teams included Eau Claire, Red

Wing, Ishpeming, Minneapolis, Stillwater, St. Croix Falls, and St. Paul. The first league tournament was in Ishpeming on January 23, 1891.

The Ishpeming tournament kicked off with a boisterous two-mile-long parade. A cadre of uniformed police and an eighteen-piece Scandinavian band led two hundred marchers from downtown to Lake Superior Hill. Five thousand people came out for the tournament and watched with breathless interest as Torjus won first place and Mikkel second. A reporter with the *Ishpeming Daily Press* was quite impressed by Mikkel and went on to describe the Telemark style of jumping, which in America would be dubbed "Red Wing" style:

> Hemmestveit is a small man, but the amount of nerve and muscle in his firmly built body would suffice to make two average men. . . . Standing with one foot slightly advanced, his skis close together, and leaning forward he sped down the steep hill. At the jump he gathered himself for the leap, and with a mighty bound sailed into the air. Twice he gathered himself together and leaped while in mid-air, raising himself as a bird would raise. . . . The cheers that arose when he came safely to the ground . . . seemed to rend the firmament.

🌲

The high times for the Hemmestveits and the young ski league did not last. Mikkel and Bergit, who was pregnant, planned on traveling to Telemark after the ski season to sell some property and give birth to the baby in Norway. But in March 1891, Bergit died giving birth to a son in Red Wing. The baby died soon after; mother and son were buried in the same coffin. The Hemmestveits' woes only worsened. Tone, Torjus's wife and mother of two young children, died a few months later from tuberculosis. The brothers' siblings, Aasne and Halvor, emigrated from Morgedal to help their widower brothers and surviving nephew and niece. Halvor, of course, joined the Aurora team.

The three brothers jumped together for two seasons. Torjus and Mikkel still won their share of tournaments, but they were no longer a sure thing. In their final season of 1892–93, Torjus jumped 103 feet, beating by a single foot the American record Mikkel had set two years earlier. Red Wing hosted a big tournament in February that Mikkel won, with Torjus and Halvor

SEE ARTICLE ON "WASHINGTON'S MATRIMONIAL MONUMENTS" ON PAGE 71. SEE ALSO
ARTICLE ON NEW YORK CITY POOL-ROOMS ON PAGE 70.

FRANK LESLIE'S
ILLUSTRATED
WEEKLY

VOL. LXXVI.—No. 1951.
Copyright, 1893, by ARKELL WEEKLY Co.
All Rights Reserved.

NEW YORK, FEBRUARY 2, 1893.

[PRICE, 10 CENTS. $4.00 YEARLY.
13 WEEKS, $1.00.

WINTER SPORTS IN THE WEST—FLYING ON SKIS—THORGER HEMMESTVEDT'S GREAT JUMP OF ONE HUNDRED AND THREE FEET AT RED WING, MINNESOTA.—Drawn by Miss G. A. Davis.—[See Page 70.]

Torjus Hemmestveit's record-setting jump at Red Wing, featured on the cover of *Frank Leslie's Illustrated Weekly* in 1893.

placing fourth and fifth. In an exhibition run, Torjus and Mikkel jumped together, holding hands as they launched, soared, and landed.

That same year, Halvor moved to western Minnesota and Mikkel returned to Morgedal. Mikkel would never again see his brothers. Torjus remained in Red Wing a while longer, married Tone's younger sister, and continued jumping with the Aurora club and making skis. The Red Wing *Advance Sun* noted in late 1893 of his production: "The orders thus far have been far in excess of the output." The economic bubble created in the boom decades following the Civil War burst with the Panic of 1893, and the American economy tanked. When the Central Ski Association met late that year, no club offered to host a tournament. Unemployment was skyrocketing. None of the club communities wanted to assume the financial risk associated with hosting a tournament.

Organized skiing faded, though local interest remained. *The North,* a Midwestern newspaper for Scandinavian Americans, opined that "if the ski sport in this country is to be developed to what it ought to be viz. one of the grandest and most healthy sports on earth, the 'ski boys' must go to work and show what they can do in the way of a distance run." This was a rallying cry for the *idraet*—skiing *profundi,* that ideal of skiing as not just sport but a means of experiencing God's nature while improving one's own health and the well-being of the community. It was a call that would be sounded for the better part of a century with limited success.

The U.S. economy continued to lag. In 1896, Torjus and his family moved back to Norman County, Minnesota. He began farming again, near his brother Halvor and sister, Aasne. Torjus supplemented farming with carpentry work, rarely talking about his ski career. A house fire in 1898 destroyed whatever artifacts he had from his glory days. A granddaughter recalled that after a good snow Torjus would demonstrate proper Telemark technique by jumping off his barn roof. As a boy he'd watched Sondre Norheim jump barn roofs in Morgedal until he had been old enough to do it himself, and when his own kids skied well enough they joined him, while the younger ones jumped off snow-covered straw piles. "As soon as the children were old enough," the granddaughter wrote in a county history, "they were out skiing cross-country without the aid of poles."

Torjus died in 1930 and was buried in the Telemark Church cemetery in Pennington County, Minnesota. His descendants are scattered around the state.

A jumper soars over the crowd at Union Park in Negaunee, Michigan, 1907.

2

Yump, Ole, Yump!

1890s–1910s

Although the Panic of 1893 derailed the young Central Ski Association, the economic depression that followed paradoxically spurred the rise of the world's first mass producer of skis. For a half century, the Twin Cities area would be home to a flourishing ski industry, prompted when, in 1896, a Norwegian named Martin Strand left Superior, Wisconsin, and moved back to Minneapolis after his land surveying business went under. He was thirty-three years old and hustling for work. One winter's day, Strand watched a dozen boys skiing down a hill on crude skis fashioned from barrel staves. Later Strand recalled, "It made me realize the United States really didn't know the sport of skiing. There were skis, but they had been made by Norwegians living here for their own use. No one ever had tried to make them popular with Americans and no one, of course, had a ski factory." The first ski boom years and the Excelsior Ski Company had already been forgotten, making space for a new crop of boosters to step up.

Strand had left his family farm in central Norway in 1883, where he hunted rabbits on skis, cut grass with a scythe, and harvested grain with a cradle. Like many Norwegian immigrants, he left a life of the land with thin margins. Later described as "a slight man and rather under medium height," Strand arrived in New York City as a twenty-year-old who knew no English and carried in his pockets a dollar and a half and a train ticket to

When Martin Strand first sojourned into the wilds of northern Wisconsin and Minnesota, forest survey crews relied on snowshoes for transportation. By 1903, when this photograph was taken, skis were more common.

Minneapolis. Decades later, in an unfinished autobiography, Strand would write with characteristic grandiosity: "I began life in this country with empty hands."

Yet, his first years as an American went smoothly. He moved in with his brother and two uncles in Minneapolis, joining an immigrant community of twenty other Norwegian families. He quipped in a newspaper interview, "I had no feeling of being in a strange country except that I couldn't speak English." Strand enrolled at the University of Minnesota and studied civil engineering. His uncle ran a surveying crew and gave Strand a job as a rodman. One of his first summers in America he worked on a crew laying tracks for the new Soo Line through the virgin woodlands of northern

Wisconsin. "That country was so wild then that the partridges did not know enough to be afraid of a man," he wrote.

In 1888, Strand moved north to take a post as a draftsman in the city engineer's office in Superior. Located next to Duluth at the western end of Lake Superior, the city had tripled its population in just a few years, creating much need for surveying. Giddy speculators claimed the city would surpass Chicago as the Great Lakes' metropolis. Strand started his own surveying business. He traveled again into the surrounding old growth forests, marking section lines for the loggers. The loss of these forests would haunt him in his old age. In 1892, though, the future was luminous, and Strand's success enabled him to travel for pleasure to Norway, England, and Scotland.

Then the bottom fell out. The shaky nature of Superior's speculative-based economy became evident with the Panic of 1893. "Things got tough," Strand remembered. "All I could find was some work running out section lines for lumberjacks, but even that gave out in 1896 and I went back to Minneapolis to work for a railroad at the magnificent sum of fifty dollars a month." The new job lasted only a few months before Strand was laid off in the fall. This was especially troublesome considering he had just married a woman named Rinda Titterud in June. Titterud was born in Minneapolis though, based on her name, was obviously not far removed from Norway. She and Strand had likely known each other for years in the city's tight-knit Norwegian community.

"There was no such thing as county relief in those days," Strand said. "Either you worked or you didn't eat. When the first

At the turn of the century, a pair of staves from an old barrel was all one needed to fashion a pair of skis. In this photograph circa 1903, the Ellestad children of Lanesboro, Minnesota, use barrel stave skis in their backyard.

Martin Strand could afford the luxury of traveling back to Norway as a tourist in the 1890s. Capitalizing on the fresh mountain air, early posters advertised the country as "The Sanatorium of Europe."

snow fell I was desperate, but the snow gave me an idea." That idea came from the boys skiing on barrel staves, a notion he may have developed from the cumulative effect of seeing boys on shoddy skis over the course of years.

He bought two and a half dollars' worth of tools and hired a carpenter for fifteen cents an hour to plane and carve boards in his basement. Strand used Rinda's tea kettle to steam and bend skis in their kitchen. He made seventy-two pairs of skis with this method and carried samples about Minneapolis while looking for buyers, finding his first client in a downtown department store with a rather lackluster pitch.

"What have you there?" the store buyer asked Strand.

"Skis," Strand said.

"What do you do with them?"

"Slide on them," Strand said, and that deft answer was apparently enough to close his first ski sale.

At some point in the late 1880s or 1890s, Strand became acquainted with another of the century's most important ski boosters, Aksel Holter. Holter would be best known for his later years in Ashland, Wisconsin, where he became the nation's most vocal proselytizer of the *idraet*. Called Ak (rhymes with hack) by friends and family, Holter was ten years younger than Strand. During his first years in America, he worked in a livery stable and as a hack driver, private coachman, and house painter.

Aksel Holter, 1920s.

As a boy in Christiania, Holter had attended the capital's annual ski competitions, watching in awe as Sondre Norheim and his fellow Telemarkings demonstrated their skill. He begged his father for a pair of genuine Telemark skis made of pine, but he had to settle for a cheap regular pair made from spruce. Eventually, his father gave him Telemark skis, and Holter won a youth ski race on his sweet new boards. Like Strand, though, Holter's contributions to skiing came not from his competitive ability but in his earnest promotion of the sport. Upon arrival in the United States, Holter lived for several years in St. Paul, and this is likely when he and Strand formed a relationship that would influence the style of millions of skis that poured out of the Twin Cities.

A vintage Strand touring binding affixed to a pair of antique skis.

Strand's fortunes improved for a while, though after a few good years he would hit a rough decade. He continued making skis on the side after landing a stable job in 1897 with the Great Northern Railway. During the last full winter of the century, in which sixty-three inches of snow fell, doubtlessly a good season for selling skis, Strand was the only ski maker listed in the Minneapolis city directory. In 1904, the Strands lost a baby. The next year, the Minneapolis directory indicated that Strand was selling insurance for New York Life, as well as running the Strand-Youngquist Manufacturing Company, which he had started with a friend. He and Frederick Youngquist were still the only ski makers in Minneapolis. Their business was at 2646 Twelfth Avenue South, which is today a playground in the Phillips neighborhood. In 1905, Strand was the first to display skis at the Minnesota State Fair. His skis were made from Norway pine, Georgia pine, and southern white ash. Opposing what most people believed throughout the era of wooden skis—being a contrarian fit right into Strand's character profile—he favored southern white ash over hickory. He told fairgoers that hickory was good but too heavy for most skiers. By 1907, Strand and Youngquist had parted ways. Two years later, Youngquist and his wife died from tuberculosis, leaving four orphans. Martin and Rinda lost another baby.

Fridtjof Nansen and other famed explorers relied on skis produced by the L. H. Hagen Company of Christiania. In this photograph from 1894, members of Nansen's Antarctic expedition pose in front of the ship *Fram*.

Strand glossed over this era in his memoir, neatly compartmentalizing the grief he had endured and blithely boasting that by quitting the railroad he "gave up a good position at a good salary that I could have had for life. My friends thought I was crazy, or as one said, 'Not crazy exactly, but next to it.'" Strand went on: "There is a certain game or sport in running your own business." He told an anecdote about a lawyer he knew who traded professional stability for independence and set up his own practice. The lawyer answered an inquiring friend as to how he was doing: "'Just fine. I made two hundred and forty dollars the first month. Of course,' the lawyer said. 'It was only forty dollars in cash, but it is worth two hundred dollars more to be your own boss!'" Strand's view was an intriguing mix of American entrepreneurial spirit coupled with the stubbornly independent nature of the Norwegian peasant.

Meanwhile, Aksel Holter had started his own ski company in Ashland, basing his skis on the design of an esteemed Norwegian manufacturer. Holter imported seven pairs of hickory skis in 1900 from the L. H. Hagen Company in Christiania. Legendary arctic explorers over the years, such as Fridtjof Nansen, Roald Amundson, and Admiral Richard Byrd, used Hagen skis. The Hagens would serve as the template for the millions of skis churned out of the Midwest in the coming decades, made not only by Holter but also by Strand and the companies that sprang up in Strand's wake.

In 1905, the Tajco Company of Portland, Maine, set the paradigm of how skis would be sold in the United States when it both published a book on skiing that doubled as a catalog and opened the country's first ski shop. Tajco's catalog was the first book published about skiing in the United States and only the second book published on skiing in the English language. The prior year the first ski book in English, *The Ski-Runner*, by E. C. Richardson, was published in London. Tajco's catalog, *The Winter Sport of Skeeing*, not only marketed its wares but featured articles on how to ski and showcased studio-shot photographs of live models on skis in front of painted backdrops, some of which were lifted directly from Richardson's book. The pictures featured both men and women, including one whose caption stated "Women Find Skeeing Is the Ideal Sport."

Tajco skis were top-notch and expensive: prices ranged from $3.50 to $18 a pair. In 1905, the average American worker made ten dollars a week. Tajco's less expensive skis sold well, but high-end models didn't, and the company went out of business within a couple of years. Martin Strand

"It Is Indeed an Ideal Outdoor Winter Pastime."

One of several staged photographs in Tajco's 1905 catalog, *The Winter Sport of Skeeing,* the first book about skiing published in the United States.

＊

professed respect for the quality of Tajcos but remarked that he himself made only "skis that people will buy—cheap skis." Strand would emulate Tajco by including articles and photographs in his catalogs, in addition to showcasing his latest ski models.

🌲

Ole Mangseth left his family home in Elverum, Norway, for America in the first years of the new century. In his early twenties, Ole was a respected ski jumper in Norway and wasted no time getting on skis in America. After partnering to farm with his brother John, who had been in the country for a couple of years, the Mangseth boys settled in Spooner, Wisconsin, about halfway between Superior and Eau Claire. "When winter came," Ole later wrote, "we began to look around for a hill." They didn't find one to their liking and "were forced to give up the search."

By the next winter, the Mangseths had moved thirty-five miles south-west to Frederic and the neighboring rural area of Seven Pines, where they found several splendid ski hills. "John got busy and made skis," Ole recalled. "After a little work on a hill, we were ready for action." Neighboring farmers came out to see what on earth the Norwegians were up to. The farmers had never seen skis before and queried the Mangseths until the brothers tired of trying to explain themselves, telling the farmers to wait and see. The Mangseths itched to jump again, not having felt the rush of flying through the air for years.

John jumped first and landed smoothly. Ole recalled that his brother flew ninety feet, though this was probably an exaggeration brought on by a space of four decades. The jumpers in the Midwest ski league that was about to spring up wouldn't soar much farther aided by tall jumps constructed of wooden scaffolding. Ole didn't elaborate on what "work" he and his brother had done to prepare the hill, whether that included tree removal or the construction of a snow or wooden ramp. Considering

Ole Mangseth with his three boys: (from left) Ronald, who would win the national Class D championship; Otto, who in the words of his son "wasn't much of a jumper"; and Rolf, future three-time national junior class champion. The photograph was likely taken in 1923 at the national ski jumping tournament held that year in Minneapolis.

OLE MANGSETH, COLERAINE

CHESTER CREEK SKI HILL.
DULUTH, MINN.
PHOTO BY LARSON.

Ole Mangseth high above the Chester Bowl ski hill in Duluth, 1910.

they were on a neighbor's property, it is doubtful they built any sort of scaffolding. More likely, they augmented a steep natural slope by building a snow ramp.

Ole's first jump didn't go well. He took "an awful spill, and nothing could be seen at the bottom but a flurry of snow and a jumble of legs, arms, and ski tips." The farmer who owned the hill was displeased by the reckless behavior occurring on his property. He threatened to put a stop to the foolishness but was placated when he saw Ole "crawl out of the snow with skis and bones in good condition," as Ole explained in his own words, "and he decided to let us try again. The next Sunday, we had a large crowd of spectators, who had come to see the 'two crazy Norwegians from Seven Pines.'" Mangseths would be soaring from American ski jumps for the next fifty years.

The erstwhile Northwest hadn't seen a major ski tournament since 1893, though this would change with the dawning twentieth century. The economy was slowly recovering, and a wave of inventions began to tilt everyday life toward the modern. Indoor plumbing, the internal combustion engine, electrification, and telephone service became increasingly available. Optimism and a sense of empowerment were high.

Aksel Holter moved to Ishpeming in 1900 (later relocating to Ashland in 1905). He became close friends with another great adherent of the skiing

In 1906, the National Ski Association promoted its second tournament in a boisterous advertisement, calling it the "Greatest Exhibition of Skiing Ever Witnessed in America."

A jumper leaps from the ramp at one of the early tournaments in Ishpeming, Michigan, circa 1904.

idraet, Carl Tellefsen. Tellefsen had founded the Trondheim Ski Club years before in his native Norway, and he had been in Ishpeming since 1888, working as a banker. Holter's and Tellefsen's individual passions for skiing were remarkable and overbearing. Paired up, the effect was a tempest of *idraet* fever—to them, skiing was more religion than hobby. The duo revived the Norden Ski Club, which they rebranded as the Ishpeming Ski Club, removing the foreign word to appeal to a broader base.

In February 1901, the Ishpeming club hosted the first American ski tournament of the century. The club hosted regular tournaments and races for a mostly local group of competitors over the next few years. In 1904, Holter invited the Mangseth brothers to compete. The Mangseths were eager to reconnect with other skiers and, lugging their skis, caught the train from Wisconsin to Ishpeming. How exactly Holter and the Mangseths knew each other is unclear. The brothers were too young to have known Holter in Norway. Perhaps they'd met in the United States, or maybe Holter knew of them only by reputation.

"We had quite a time boarding our train in Frederick," Ole Mangseth wrote. "Everybody looked at us, wondering what our purpose was in carrying boards with us. The brakeman told us that this was not a lumber train." As they had done with the suspicious farmers, the Mangseths assuaged the wary brakeman and then spent much of the long train ride to Ishpeming fielding questions from fellow passengers about their curious boards.

The Ishpeming tournament featured a cross-country ski race. In Norway, cross-country races, or "distance runs," were fifteen to twenty miles. Organizers shortened the Ishpeming race to eleven miles because it was "not thought best to follow the old custom here." Race organizers were well aware of the disinterest in cross-country racing. Fostering enthusiasm would be better served by starting with a short race and hoping to attract adherents. Only five of the eight skiers who started the race even finished. A recent Norwegian immigrant named Matt Johnson won easily, with his shirt collar "not even damp" at the finish line. His competition didn't fare as well: the "other riders were almost done up." The *Mining Journal* noted that "the boys would rather jump than participate in distance contests." As followers of the *idraet*, which demanded skiers be skilled in all facets of the sport, Holter and Tellefsen were obligated to convince the region's skiers to embrace cross-country as much as they did jumping. Cross-country racing continued in Ishpeming through the coming years, including divisions for women and children, but remained limited in appeal. Tellefsen's ambition was to shift from hosting frequent home region tournaments to executing a big northwestern contest reminiscent of the prior decade.

♠

In Red Wing, the ski culture remained strong, if unfocused. A boy named Buddy Borgen was born in 1896. When he was five or six years old, his father, an engineer at the Red Wing Sewer Pipe company, used the company boilers to steam and bend a pair of boards to make skis for the boy, fashioning the bindings from rubber straps. Borgen and his buddies skied from their neighborhood south across Birchwood Park to jumps they had built on nearby hills called Coon Hill, Devil's Dropoff, and Barrone's. For the rest of the century, Buddy Borgen and his sons would form the heart of Red Wing ski jumping, through boom times and eventual bust. Buddy's son Jerry would struggle to keep the prospect of jumping in Red Wing

A lone skier from the Aurora club looks out over the flats in the South Bush Street area of Red Wing, Minnesota.

alive, all the way until his death in 2018. Jerry would eventually found the American Ski Jumping Hall of Fame and Museum in Red Wing's St. James Hotel, a staggering testament to ultimate fandom.

On New Year's Day 1903, the Aurora Ski Club, which had trundled on informally since losing the Hemmestveits, held a local meet with nine men and nine boys. Later that winter, acting on an invitation from Tellefsen to put on a jumping exhibition, a dozen members of the Aurora took the train to Ishpeming. The Aurora's reputation was evidently still the gold standard for American jumping. The Ishpeming paper dubbed the Aurora crew the "skiing dudes" for the skiers' flamboyant dress. Aurora jumper Eric Iverson stepped off the train in the frontier of Ishpeming wearing a chinchilla overcoat, derby hat, red scarf and necktie, and particularly pointy-toed patent leather shoes. The Red Wing jumpers showed off their skills to the Ishpeming club with sufficient panache that what had previously been known as Telemark style now became "Red Wing" style.

♠

Interest in organized competition continued to grow. The following winter, Ishpeming hosted a jumping tournament with thirty men and nine boys from around the region (this was the same tournament the Mangseths competed in after schlepping their skis on the train from Frederic). Ishpeming native Conrad Thompson won the overall, and fellow local Leonard Olson made the longest standing jump with a leap of seventy-seven feet. This contest would come to be regarded as the first American national jumping championship. At a meeting in the afterglow of the successful tournament, the Ishpeming club decided to make the contest an annual affair, to be held on Washington's birthday and called the National Ski Tournament of America.

Some of the nation's top jumpers gather for a tournament in Mount Horeb, Wisconsin, 1914.

Carl Tellefsen gave a rousing speech, praising the "splendid comradeship" of the club and the "great aggregation of ambitious ski veterans" before expressing his adherence to the *idraet*. Tellefsen expounded on "the purity of this gallant sport" and, in a tack similar to one that Aksel Holter would pick up after Tellefsen's early death, railed against the morally inferior sports—"football, baseball, or a 100-yard dash"—which were tawdry by comparison and marred by conflict. Skiing was not merely a sport; skiing was a course that one could follow through life, on which the skier would make like-minded friends, revel humbly in God's creation, and keep one's community strong through individual health and the positive influence of tournaments.

Duluth jumper John Ruud, surrounded by adoring fans at the National Ski Tournament in 1909. During competition, Rudd landed four successful somersaults on skis that measured just five feet, four inches.

"Remember that we are all Americans and not Englishmen, Swedes, or Norwegians, and that there is no discrimination shown and no favors. The best man gets there," Tellefsen said in a valiant attempt at building an egalitarian meritocracy, at least for able-bodied men of northern European extraction. That Tellefsen bothered to mention "Englishmen" in the Scandinavian crowd was likely a reference to one of the club's members, John Greenway, a young mining bigshot from a venerable eastern family. Greenway would soon start an important ski club in Minnesota.

Tellefsen's dream was that skiing would sweep across the northern United States and become a national obsession in America, as it was becoming in Norway. "We may not see the effect of our effort on the growing

The dream of boosters like Carl Tellefsen and Aksel Holter was to make skiing the new national pastime. In following decades, organizations like the Minneapolis YMCA (seen here in the 1920s) would begin to promote skiing among its regular activities.

generation at once," he predicted, "but we will before long when every kid will demand a pair of skis as a household necessity. That is the way to develop a healthy mind in a healthy body."

Tellefsen had been trying for years to revive a governing ski body to fill the void left by the dereliction of the Central Ski Association. By 1905, enough interest had coalesced for him to shepherd the few existing ski clubs into an umbrella organization called the National Ski Association (NSA), and on February 21 five clubs voted to approve the organization's bylaws. The NSA established specific rules for jumping to determine style points during competition. To Holter and Tellefsen, mastery of form exhibited through style was as important as distance. This was a tenet of the *idraet,* with its emphasis on craft over the individual. Decades later, the NSA would become the United States Ski and Snowboard Association, which is today the governing body for skiing in the country. Of the original five clubs of the NSA—the St. Paul Ski Club; the Stoughton Ski Club near Madison, Wisconsin; the Grand Rapids Ski Club in Michigan; and, of course, the Ishpeming Ski Club and Aurora Ski Club—the St. Paul and Ishpeming clubs have survived the ensuing 116 years.

The official communication of the National Ski Association, the *Ski Sport,* overseen by Aksel Holter, covered the annual activities of the growing organization. This copy was owned by three-time national junior class jumping champion Rolf Mangseth.

The Englishman whom Tellefsen mentioned, John Greenway, was an employee of the Oliver Iron Mining Company, a subsidiary of U.S. Steel. Greenway had been a captain for Teddy Roosevelt's Rough Riders. Roosevelt described Greenway as "a strapping fellow, entirely fearless, modest and quiet . . . ready to respond with eagerness to the slightest suggestion of doing something." In the NSA's first year, Oliver Iron transferred Greenway from Ishpeming to northern Minnesota, where he was to run a new mining operation called the Canisteo District and commence massive iron ore removal from the small boomtown of Bovey, a short distance northeast of Grand Rapids.

Greenway's go-getter attitude that impressed Roosevelt became evident. Instead of basing his mining operation from Bovey, Greenway carved a new town from the neighboring forest less than a mile away. Only a year old, Bovey was already known "for its rowdy bars and many gamblers and prostitutes . . . its unfinished look, grubby streets and a high incidence of typhoid fever." Unlike Bovey, the new town was carefully planned by

EVEN O. FLADVAD'S OPEN-AIR LIFE

In 1905, sixty-three-year-old Even O. Fladvad resorted to a campaign of badgering and bribery to convince his fellow Red Wing skiers to join him for a cross-country excursion. Fladvad was a Norwegian immigrant and longtime club member. He no longer jumped but volunteered as a judge during tournaments. Unlike the rest of the club, Fladvad remained a cross-country enthusiast. A friend named B. Eide said of Fladvad, "Being of nature an outdoors man, the skis were quite convenient adjuncts to his open-air life." Eide was referring to the Norwegian concept of *friluftsliv,* which translates to "free-air life." *Friluftsliv* was similar to the *idraet* in its synthesis of nature and personal well-being. That the Norwegian language has specific words for such concepts helps explain why Americans continue to be fascinated by Scandinavian culture.

Fladvad couldn't convince his fellow club members to join him on the cross-country outing so he offered a free meal as a reward. On Sunday, February 5, Fladvad led forty-eight reluctant skiers across the countryside. "The other members did not seem to fancy much this," said Eide. Fladvad had previously laid out a three-mile course that crossed a number of fences, declaring that no skier was "permitted to take off his skis before crawling through a fence." (Fences were considered a desirable feature of a ski course.)

They made their way to the farm of Hans Johnson for dinner. Fladvad had told Johnson to expect twenty skiers. Poor Johnson nearly fainted when four dozen hungry skiers arrived outside his door. Unable to resist a free meal, fourteen others arrived on horse-drawn rigs. Fladvad's run didn't improve cross-country's standing in Red Wing. Yet, the next day, Fladvad and Eide ventured onto a backwater of the Mississippi River for a ski, enjoying the free-air life. ▲

The outdoor philosophy of *friluftsliv* was promoted by the Norwegian Trekking Association. Here a group of skiers gather at the association's ski cabin at Ulriken near Bergen in 1908.

A jumper in 1938 drops toward the landing slope beneath the Itasca Ski and Outing Club's slide. The jump had been perched on the hill above Trout Lake, in Coleraine, since 1908 until the club relocated the jump in 1941.

Greenway, and he named it Coleraine after the president of the Oliver Iron Mining Company, Thomas Cole.

Although not a skier himself, Greenway quickly started a ski club to entertain his miners. Called the Itasca Ski and Outing Club, it would produce some of the nation's top jumpers and remains today one of the few ski jumping clubs left in Minnesota. With typical gusto, Greenway had a ski jump built of old railroad ties by the end of 1905. The jump was located on the shores of Trout Lake, and the first local skier to run it, Sigurd Peterson, crashed and broke his shoulder. This inauspicious start notwithstanding, Greenway invited NSA club skiers for a meet in February 1906. His friend G. G. Hartley (a Duluth businessman whose myriad interests ranged from mining to celery farming), who had platted the rough town of Bovey, provided a silver trophy made by Tiffany's of New York.

By this time, the Aurora club had recruited Ole Mangseth to Red Wing.

Barney Riley, the "Wild Irish Rose," in flight on his home slide at Coleraine, Minnesota.

Mangseth won the Itasca club's inaugural tournament and then defended his title the following two years. In what would remain a standard practice at tournament venues, if a jumper won a tournament three years in a row he could keep the trophy permanently rather than temporarily for one year, so the Tiffany's cup became Mangseth's. In 1907, at Ishpeming, Mangseth set a new American distance record by jumping 114 feet. Greenway lured Mangseth away from Red Wing with a job as a painter for the Oliver company, and Mangseth moved to Coleraine with his wife, Constance, and son, Rolf.

By the end of the decade, ski jumping was becoming a mainstream sport throughout the snowy reaches of the country. NSA membership quickly grew to twenty-two clubs and more than one thousand jumpers. The era's favorite jumper came from Coleraine and first made waves in 1908. At the national tournament in Eau Claire, an eighteen-year-old named Barney Riley won the Class C, or Boy's Class, division. At five foot five, Riley was the only notable Irish jumper in the tournament, and his success enthused Eau Claire's sizable Irish population. The city's chief of police, named O'Brien, claimed he was going to hang a picture of Riley in the police station; the Reverend Father Connolly said Riley's victory made him feel ten years younger. Onlookers hoisted Riley on their shoulders and carried him about while singing songs in his honor. The Norwegians tried to claim him as one of their own by dubbing him Rileyson, and later Scandinavians gave him the nickname Irish Swenska, or Irish Swede. Riley's most descriptive and lasting nickname was the Wild Irish Rose. He won the national Class B championship both of the next two years. His toothy grin and increasingly bowlegged stance frequently showed up in newspapers in the coming years.

🌲

Despite cross-country skiing's lack of popular appeal and organization compared to jumping, many Midwesterners skied in the early twentieth century, particularly those in communities where Scandinavians had settled. Most Americans still lived in rural areas, and in the snowy northland skis were a tool of casual sport and practical locomotion. The best-selling novelist Walter O'Meara was born in the northern Minnesota town of Cloquet in 1897. He wrote in a memoir in 1974 that as a boy "skiing was not only a sport but a

A beautiful example of the careful craftsmanship in early ski design, this antique ski from the collection of Duluth skier Adrian Watt may have been made by a Finnish family on Minnesota's North Shore in the late 1800s or early 1900s.

natural way of getting around in winter. We skied everywhere, up and down the snow-paved roads, across the open fields around town, into the woods and swamps in search of Christmas trees or rabbits." O'Meara and his classmates skied to school and leaned their skis against the schoolhouse exterior while they were in class. People in Cloquet made their own skis, bending their boards with the help of a steam pipe at the local sawmill. O'Meara "longed for a pair of Finnish skis. They were lovely—long and narrow, with a high crown of polished wood on which was often burned an intricate design."

Ishpeming held regular cross-country races into the 1920s. Cross-country "races were a customary part of the ski season," an NSA publication reported. However, "interest waned in the 1920s," which was an indulgent

Contestants gather for a cross-country ski race in Ishpeming, Michigan, 1910s.

way of saying that interest in organized cross-country racing went from little to near none. Ishpeming's Finnish community tried to keep things going by sponsoring cross-country races and offering gold and silver medals as prizes. One of these races in 1906 attracted only nine entrants. As ski historian John B. Allen wrote: "[The NSA] tried to promote cross-country races, but that was work and sweat, as unheroic to perform as it was unspectacular to watch."

Purists kept pushing, however, and added a cross-country race to the roster of national championship events. The fourth annual national championship in 1907 left Ishpeming and began its peripatetic tour around the country, landing for the first and only time in Ashland, Wisconsin. Aksel Holter had moved to Ashland in 1905 and brought home the tournament.

Holter ensured the *idraet* was being followed by organizing and adding to the roster of

The "Iron Man," Asario Autio, a Finnish immigrant from Ely, Minnesota, won the first U.S. national cross-country championship.

jumping events the first national cross-country championship, an event that continues to this day. During its first running, the cross-country course covered nine miles of "somewhat broken territory, up, down, through ravines covered with heavy underbrush, over level fields with fences to be climbed," and concluded with five miles across a frozen lake. Red, white, and blue streamers marked the racecourse, which was officiated by members of Chicago's Norge Ski Club. A Finn from Ely named Asario Autio won easily, finishing more than two minutes ahead of his nearest competitor. Dubbed the Iron Man, Autio declared himself the "Champion of the World" and put out a standing bet of one hundred dollars that no one could beat him. Whether anyone took him up on the offer is doubtful. Autio's colorful persona flashed brightly and then disappeared from America's young world of skiing.

🌲

Two weeks before the Ashland nationals, Ole Mangseth, jumping with the Aurora, broke the American distance record when he jumped 114 feet in Red Wing on January 23, 1907. The previous record had been set only three days earlier by Ole Feiring of the new Duluth Ski Club when he had jumped 112 feet. Feiring was the defending national champion going into the Ashland tournament, though Olaf Jonnum from Coleraine outjumped him to become the new champion. The name Olaf is a form of Ole, both meaning "ancestor's descendant." The top three skiers of the time were named Ole in one form or another.

Things got stickier on February 12 when Red Wing hosted a tournament. Ole Feiring won, Ole Mangseth took second, and Olaf Jonnum finished third, followed by Ole Larson of Duluth and Ole Westgaard of Ishpeming in fourth and fifth places. Cries of "Yump, Ole, yump!" cut through the cold air of tournaments. Ole wasn't necessarily the most popular chap

The Duluth Ski Club was organized in 1905 and quickly became a top contender in jumping competitions. In this 1909 photograph from the sixth national tournament, a skier in the clubhouse prepares for a leap.

A humorous postcard lampoons Norwegian ski jumping at Fergus Falls, Minnesota.

out there, but there were a lot of Oles running the slide. *Yump*, of course, meant "jump," shouted by Norwegians who pronounced *j* as *y*, as was done in the home country. Norway's influence in the American jumping scene was clear.

The NSA always held its annual meeting during the festivities surrounding the national tournament. At the 1907 meeting in Ashland, a contentious issue arose that would divide the ski jumping community for many years. Ever since ski jumping competitions started in America twenty years earlier, top jumpers had collected lucrative cash prizes. Purists like Aksel Holter felt that money sullied the motives of the skiers, who should be focused on perfecting technique and not on breaking records. Money also gave an unfair advantage to ski clubs in larger cities with more cash to throw around. Holter suggested that top finishers receive patches and medals instead of cash. His suggestion was not well received. Three-quarters of the competitive skiers at the meeting opposed this attempt to "bar out professionals." They did not want to maintain amateur status for the purity of the sport; they wanted to get paid. Unlike Holter, who by this time owned his own business, and the banker Carl Tellefsen (who would die suddenly the next year), the vast majority of the competitive skiers were

A poster for a jumping tournament in Red Wing, Minnesota, in 1911 boasted prize money awarded to the nation's top jumpers.

of the working class, many with families to support. Ski jumping took time and money, and the jumpers took umbrage with the prospect of losing the carrot of cash prizes. Under such opposition, Holter and the NSA caved, but the skiers likely didn't grasp Holter's conviction: he was not about to give up his mission of purifying the sport.

♠

Aksel Holter's ski factory, located at West Fourteenth Street between the Omaha and Northern Pacific train lines, was up and running in Ashland by the time of the 1907 national championships. The year of the big tournament, Holter sold ten thousand pairs of skis. Some of these he contracted for Alfred Andresen and Company, a Minneapolis business that slapped its name on skis and other household goods like waffle irons and frying pans and sold them to the region's Scandinavian population.

A few years later, Holter sold his company to the Minneapolis ski maker Martin Strand. The reasons that prompted Holter to unload his (by all appearances) successful ski company are murky. Holter's granddaughter, Patra, who grew up in the house next door (and was yelled at by Holter for climbing in his apple tree), understood that there had been friction between Holter and the town of Ashland: he wanted to expand his business, but the town was not supportive. Perhaps turning his beloved *idraet* into a business had sullied the purity of the sport for Holter. In 1911, Strand presented Holter with a handsome silver teapot, now on display in the U.S. Ski Hall of Fame in Ishpeming, with the engraving: "Presented to Aksel H. Holter by Martin A. Strand, SKI MFR." Patra Holter, who donated the cup to the museum, suspected the teapot commemorated Strand's acquisition of Holter Skis.

Strand had just come off a beater of a year. In a shop he occupied at 2427 University Avenue Southeast in Minneapolis, near the University of Minnesota, Strand and his foreman, Ole Ellevold, made toboggans and oars in addition to skis. Business was good, and in the spring of 1910 Strand ordered more machinery in advance of what he hoped would be a good snow year. On May 28, a dry and windy day, Strand asked a neighboring business owner to stop burning refuse. The neighbor declined, and soon the fire spread, engulfing Strand's shop. Athletes from the nearby university ran over to help, but wind fueled the fire's spread, and they were unable to stop it from devouring the business. All of Strand's lumber, skis, and machinery were destroyed.

Strand hurriedly leased a building less than two miles away at 2306 Hampden Avenue in St. Paul. This industrial niche

Some of Aksel Holter's skis featured the name of Alfred Andresen and Company, a Minneapolis firm known for its manufacture of rosette and krumkake irons. This rare surviving example is in the collection of Rick Scott, a distant cousin of Holter who would ski in the original American Birkebeiner in 1973.

of the St. Anthony Park neighborhood would become the heart of the Twin Cities ski industry. Strand's time here, though, would be extremely limited. Just after he and Ellevold had the business back up and running, in December another fire destroyed Strand's new factory. For the second time in a year, all of Strand's materials and equipment were lost. Unbeknownst to Strand, the lease of the Hampden Avenue property stipulated that a fire would void his rental agreement. As Strand recalled, Ellevold "knew the second fire almost broke me and he knew it automatically cancelled my lease on the building. I didn't know that, but he did and he bid up on the lease so I was forced out." Ellevold met with the property owner of the burned-out factory behind Strand's back and took over his former boss's lease, leaving Strand's ski company homeless.

Martin Strand again found a new factory home, this time forty miles to the east. In April 1911, Strand entered into an agreement with the city of New Richmond, Wisconsin, which was sorely in need of an economic boost. The Willow River Lumber Company, a major employer in town, was slowly going out of business. New Richmond ponied up six thousand dollars to build Strand a factory and would charge him no rent for five years. Strand took out a bond with the city for fifteen hundred dollars and pledged to keep at least twenty employees on his payroll. Construction began immediately.

An advertisement for Aksel Holter's ski factory in Ashland, Wisconsin, in the 1911–12 issue of the *Ski Sport*, published by the National Ski Association.

A group of competitors representing Red Wing's Aurora club and the Norse Ski Club of Lanesboro pose for a photograph before departing for the Benson Ski Hill Tournament in 1917. The man holding the megaphone is Lanesboro resident Olaf Thompson, whose deep bass voice announced tournaments nationally.

The factory boasted city water, steam heat, electric lights, and a location alongside the Omaha line railroad tracks. By the time Strand moved into the finished facility on June 15, he had orders for fifteen thousand pairs of skis. The first skis rolled off the line in mid-July, and the factory hummed to fill orders for the coming winter. It seems likely Strand would have purchased Holter's business during the second half of 1911 or after he'd secured his new factory and increased his means of production.

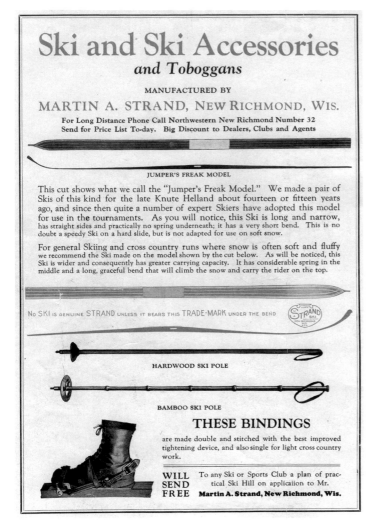

Catering to the ski-jumping craze of the 1910s and 1920s, Martin Strand began advertising the "Jumper's Freak Model" alongside his other skis, poles, and bindings.

Strand's wife and two surviving sons moved from Minneapolis to join him in New Richmond. They rented a house nearby and then built their own the following year at 325 East Second Street. With the aid of an architect, Strand designed the house himself in a style called the "construction effect," a grasp at early modernism in which some of the framing timber was left exposed. The house resembled a European chalet and featured a second-story summer sleeping porch for Strand. The house was less than a mile from the ski factory, and it's easy to imagine trim Strand walking briskly to work early each morning in his trademark winged-collared shirts, crisply starched. At the age of forty-seven, Strand had finally found his permanent home.

Strand skis cost as little as one dollar and as much as eight dollars, which was still less than half of what high-end Tajcos cost a decade earlier. In 1916, each Strand ski was handled twenty-two times during production. Every board was planed, steamed, put in a bending rack, and cured for forty-eight hours. The now recognizable ski was sanded to "satin-smoothness." A "sharp little steel chain" neatly bored in the mortise slot for mounting the bindings. All that was left in the production process was varnishing and mounting the binding, for which Strand used "an effective fastening of his own patenting." In 1922, Strand received a patent for an automated ski-shaping machine.

Aug. 25, 1925.

M. A. STRAND

1,551,178

AUTOMATIC WOOD SHAPER

Filed May 27, 1922

3 Sheets—Sheet 1

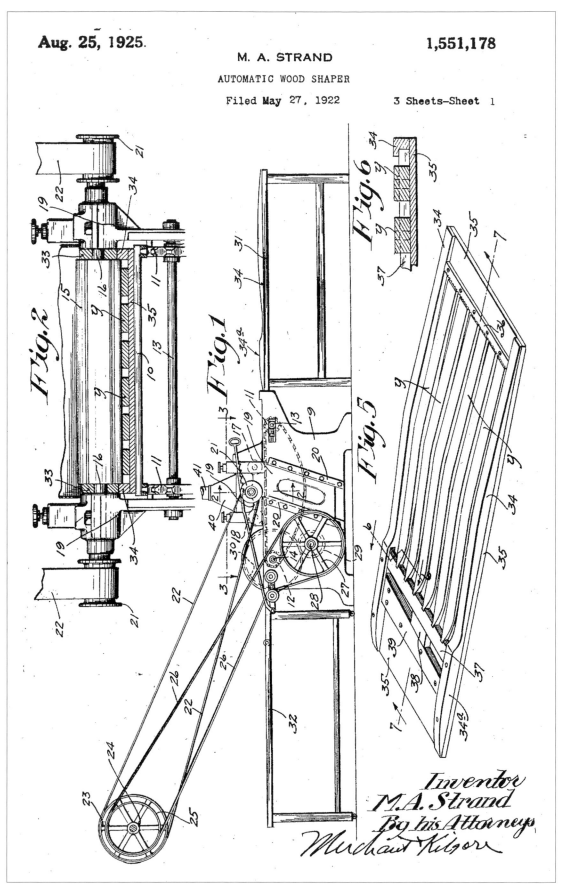

The 1922 design for Martin Strand's patented automatic wood shaper.

Craftsman Anton Jonson at work in the Strand ski factory in New Richmond, Wisconsin, circa 1914.

His automatic wood shaper used a mess of belts, cogs, and blades to cut up to six skis at a time from roughly shaped boards.

Strand sold a number of other products made of steam-bent wood. In addition to skis, he produced oars, paddles, and toboggans and even tried his hand at children's potty chairs (which bore the moniker Restwood Nursery Seat and featured a Fire King glass pot insert). He produced paddles and sleds for years, but by all appearances the potty chairs never caught on with consumers. With thirty employees in 1916, he was the biggest employer in New Richmond, and the ranks of his employees would more than double in the next fifteen years. Over two months that winter, Strand shipped five hundred orders of skis to places like Boston, New York, Arizona, and California. He identified himself as the biggest producer of skis in the world. This was likely true. He had no comparable competitor in the United States, while the ski industry in Norway consisted of dozens of small producers.

Strand nursed his ties to the *idraet* and believed his product bettered people. "The best part of the sport," Strand said in 1916, "comes in these cross country hikes, and in this the whole family can participate, young and old, men and women, boys and girls, and it will take folks out into the open when they most need it—when most of them are too closely housed up in overheated and illy ventilated houses, stores, and offices." His eventual successor as the world's biggest ski maker, however, would suffer no similar moral obligations.

Meanwhile, in St. Paul, Strand's erstwhile foreman, Ole Ellevold, incorporated the Northland Ski Manufacturing Company in 1912. Ellevold was a carpenter by trade, and this was likely his first foray into business ownership. His naivete would make him a mark to a new associate. Ellevold founded

Catering to a largely Scandinavian clientele, the Strand and Northland companies advertised in the local Norwegian press. This advertisement for Northland skis was in the *Minneapolis Tidende* in 1914.

The Edge-Grained
Northland Ski
Is a Winner

Ragnar Omtvedt, Verdensmester paa Ski siger:

„Northland Ski

er de bedste jeg har brugt baade her og i Europa". Send strax efter fri illustreret Katalog.

NORTHLAND SKI MFG. CO.,
Midway, St. Paul, Minn.

Northland company president Christian A. Lund dons festive winter attire and poses with skis, 1920s. Lund's coat is similar to one worn by Anders Haugen during opening ceremonies for the first Winter Olympics in 1924.

Northland with two others—a draftsman, Hugo Kjolstad, and an accountant, John Fryer. Just across the street from the new Northland factory, a young Norwegian named Christian A. Lund ran the Gold Coin Chemical Works.

The 1913 *Bulletin of the National Association of Credit Men* listed Lund as selling "Veterinary Remedies and Disinfectants." At least some of Lund's remedies, however, were garbage. Later in the decade, Lund got caught selling cans of inaccurately labeled "Gold Coin Lice Killer." The ingredients listed on these cans boasted formidable-sounding substances such as "Meta-Cresol" and "Para-Cresol," but the content of the cans was actually kerosene. Minnesota's U.S. attorney brought charges against Lund for "adulteration and misbranding of 'Gold Coin Lice Killer.'" Lund pled guilty and paid a ten-dollar fine. It would not be his last run-in with the law.

Minnesotan ski historian Greg Fangel conducted extensive research on the Midwestern ski industry and found that one of the chemicals Lund sold from his Hampden Avenue factory was a wood-preserving oil. Fangel hypothesized that Lund made his in with Northland by selling Ellevold this wood oil for use on Northland skis.

When Northland first offered sale of company stock in July 1913, Christian Lund bought shares. By 1916, Lund was Northland's majority shareholder, and he promptly sent Ole Ellevold packing. Ellevold moved to western North Dakota, where he knew people—people with the surname Strand. But Strand was a common name, so this could be marked as a coincidence: the Strands whom Ellevold ran to when he was betrayed evidently were not related to the former employer he had betrayed. By 1918, C. A. Lund was the president of Northland, a position he would hold for the next forty-nine years.

Lund was publicly reticent. Northland catalogs eventually ran a generic biography on him that was obviously designed to sound exactly as a ski company owner should, emphasizing his youthful skiing in Norway and making the dubious claim that Lund had been a competitive ski jumper. "He has carefully studied the different Norwegian methods of ski manufacture in Norway where the science of ski manufacture has long since reached perfection," claimed a Northland catalog of the early 1920s. Lund hadn't been back to Norway since he emigrated. He lied again and took credit for personally founding the Northland company. Like Strand, Lund would groom his sons to run his company, presumably to avoid the maneuverings of outsider upstarts like himself.

♠

Cross-country ski racing through the 1910s was patchy. The newly founded Park Region Ski Club in Fergus Falls featured a cross-country race as part of its inaugural 1911 tournament. The race went "across rough country to

Though cross-country skiing had yet to capture the public's interest as it would in later years, the ski sport continued to feature prominently in advertising for the St. Paul Winter Carnival.

the broken dam, with 14 fences to cross, and with the return over the same course, a distance of 7 miles." Employing exceptional fence-crossing technique, a recent Swedish immigrant named O. W. Johnson won the race.

The distance of the NSA's 1912 cross-country national championship was shortened to a meager three and a half miles. The defending champ, Julius Blegen, a Christiania native who had immigrated to Minneapolis, held on to his title. The following year, NSA officials tried implementing a professional cross-country class when the event was held in Glenwood, Minnesota, but the lure of prestige didn't attract more skiers. The 1917 cross-country national championship, scheduled for St. Paul, was canceled after receiving not one single entry.

The jumping world had challenges of an opposing sort. At the 1915 national meet in Duluth, the Duluth Ski Club sold fifteen thousand dollars' worth of tickets on the day of the tournament. Fearing robbery, club members worried about transporting the big bag of cash to the bank, so they decided to send two boys with the money, figuring that no one would expect a couple of kids to be carrying a small fortune. The boys loaded the "loot into pack sacks and skied down through Chester Park to the 4th Street Car-line." Adults met the boys at the streetcar and proceeded to the First National Bank to deposit the money. The 1915 Class A jumping title was won by a young yumper named Lars Haugen. Haugen and his brother Anders would be the top American jumpers for the next two decades.

On a Thursday during the spring of 1920, Rinda Titterud Strand underwent what was to be a "slight operation" at Minneapolis's Asbury Hospital. The surgery proved more intensive than expected, but over the next few days she appeared to recuperate. Her husband stayed with her during this time, until Tuesday evening, when Martin Strand returned to New Richmond. The next morning, Strand received urgent word from the hospital that Rinda had taken a turn for the worse. Strand hurried to the city, but when he arrived Rinda had died. She was fifty years old.

The Strands had already lost their three eldest sons. Now Strand was a widower with two surviving young school-age sons, Paul and Martin Jr. Rinda's death headlined Saturday's *New Richmond News and Republican Voice*. In the list of out-of-town relatives present for the funeral were two couples, Mr. and Mrs. H. O. Ellevold and Hjalmer Ellevold with his "Misses." Martin Strand still had a long run ahead of him, but when his time would come, one of his pallbearers was Magnus Ellevold. Despite the business wrangling between Martin Strand and Ole Ellevold, they evidently were indeed related, through marriage or blood, and the families stayed in contact until the end.

Skis are stacked and ready for finishing at the Strand ski factory in New Richmond, Wisconsin, circa 1925.

3

Ski Capital of America

1920s–1930s

Walter Spidahl was born in 1919 in the township of Norwegian Grove, in northwestern Minnesota near Pelican Rapids. His parents had been born in Minnesota to Norwegian immigrants, yet Walter, a third-generation Norwegian American, didn't learn English until he started attending school. Spidahl's formative childhood memory came when he was six and arrived home from school to find his father, Julius, shaving strips with a planer off a ten-foot oaken board clamped to his workbench. The board had fallen off the family's hay manger, its exterior a dull weathered gray, but with planing it took on warm tones of fresh oak. Spidahl asked his father, in Norwegian, what he was doing. "Vi skal se," Julius replied. We shall see.

When Walter came home from school the following day, Julius was again working on the board. Julius gave the boy one guess as to what he was making, and then Walter had to complete his after-school chore. Walter guessed wrong and filled the wood box in the kitchen. He returned to the workshop to find that Julius had cut the board into two pieces. He'd seen his father make sleigh runners, handles for axes and shovels, and sticks for flipping lefse, but this was different.

On the third day, brimming with excitement, Walter ran home from school. Julius was not in his workshop. Walter sprinted to the house, where a grinning Julius met him at the kitchen door with a hug. The boy was

These fifty-nine-inch children's skis from Red Wing are made from birch-wood and date from the late nineteenth or early twentieth century. The ski bindings are simple leather thongs secured to the sides of the skis with a small copper bracket.

taken aback by the humidity in the kitchen. The family's big copper boiler sat on the stove, and in it soaked the two boards. Julius pulled out the boards and showed Walter how he'd carved the tips of the skis into parabolic arcs and attached a leather toe-strap binding in the middle of each. Julius stuck the skis back into the boiler and then, using a crude setup of three chunks of split stove oak and a four-foot length of ironwood, bent the skis into place and left them behind the kitchen range to dry for a few days.

Soon snow fell. After chores, Walter, his older brother, and a neighbor named Leonard Lund set out on skis. The Spidahls each used a single pole, while Lund used two. They spent the day skiing on hilly pastureland. Julius climbed a hill behind the house and proudly watched the boys. When Walter returned, he told his dad, "Tusen takk," or "a thousand thanks," to which Julius replied, "Ni hundre ern ok," or "nine hundred are enough."

In the coming years, Walter skied to school and on jumps built with friends in the cow pasture. One year Julius took him to watch a jumping tournament in Detroit Lakes. Just as it had in Norway, skiing in America brought levity to a hard life. Walter's mother, Inga, had died when he was eleven. Two years later, his younger brother was electrocuted after climbing a power line. When Walter was seventeen, he came home one winter's night to find Julius dead. Walter would live a long life and keep skiing, making a career in the Twin Cities ski industry.

🌲

In 1920, after the Great War, skiers in Fergus Falls hoped to revive interest in "this clean, healthful sport," so that skiing could "again take its place as a leading winter attraction." A ten-mile cross-country race was held on a Sunday afternoon in February. The course headed north out of Fergus Falls and doubled back. The weather was warm and the snow turned to mush, but the skiers raced, and Olaf Aunen won $7.50 for first place with a time of one hour and nineteen minutes.

Like many communities around the Upper Midwest, Fergus Falls had a jump where tournaments were held. The town's club wasn't high profile enough to be a member of the NSA, which by 1925 had grown to include thirty-five clubs. Most were from the Midwest, but some were in such faraway places as Washington, New York, Colorado, and Massachusetts.

Spectators arrived at a jumping tournament hosted by the Park Region Ski Club in Fergus Falls, Minnesota, on horse-drawn wagons and sleighs, circa 1910.

Fergus Falls, however, was somewhat unique for hosting cross-country races. In 1922, Olaf Aunen won another Sunday afternoon cross-country run. Entrants were asked to register with Carl Willer at Willer & Tiesberg's drugstore by 8:00 p.m. the night before the race. The course was six miles long and included a shorter run for boys sixteen and under.

Later in the month, a winter storm dumped a foot of snow across much of the state. Fifty-mile-an-hour winds created massive drifts that shut down highways and railroads. The Fergus Falls *Daily Journal* noted that St. Louis and Roseau Counties requested and received twenty federal agents from Minneapolis equipped with skis, snowshoes, and sled dogs to "battle rum runners and whiskey smugglers carrying contraband into Minnesota from Canada on dog sleds." With the highways closed, the smugglers "resumed operations with Alaskan huskies pulling sledges filled with rum and whiskey." In Duluth, fire chief Ole Norman ordered his crew to work double shifts. The firefighting rigs consisted of horse-pulled sleighs, on which skis were carried for use as needed.

The night before the blizzard, two men from Fergus Falls rode a passenger train eleven miles east to Underwood to attend a funeral. They spent the night there and woke to a snowpocalypse. These two funeral attendants, the *Daily Journal* noted, were "of Scandinavian descent, skiing to them is an instinct, and they were not daunted. They procured skis and pointed them in the direction of Fergus Falls." The men left at 10:00 am and skied along the train tracks, which were occasionally blocked with ten- to twelve-foot drifts. Halfway home, they stopped for lunch at Wall Lake and reached Fergus Falls at 5:00 p.m.

♠

In places less settled than Fergus Falls, skiing remained an indispensable form of winter transportation. Werner Nikander, a Finnish immigrant in Houghton, Michigan, spent several years in the 1920s compiling biographical sketches of Finns, which he published as a book in 1927. Nikander's book, *Amerikan Suomalaisia* (American Finns), mentioned two sisters living near Virginia, Minnesota, in the state's iron-rich northeastern corner, a region known as the Iron Range. An area historian described one of the sisters, Anna Tikkanen Savolainen, as a pioneer social worker. Savolainen skied to the homes of neighbors at any hour to deliver a baby or assist

Young skiers line up at the start of a cross-country race in the Finnish immigrant community of Calumet, Michigan, 1920s.

with the ill. The other sister was Milma Lappila Erikkila, who "utilized skis extensively in her far flung parish work."

Ski jumping was booming as a sport in the northland in a way that certainly would have pleased NSA founder Carl Tellefson. Records of cross-country skiing done for sport (or otherwise) are sparse during this time. In a 1972 recollection in the *Mesabi Daily News*, longtime newspaperman Clarence Ivonen wrote about the Finnish community holding cross-country ski races around Virginia in the early twentieth century. The races happened during the Finnish festival of Laskiainen, an ancient affair that means "sliding time." The festival had pagan origins and later synthesized with Christianity in a way that linked it to Mardi Gras. Laskiainen was in essence a party to add fun to late winter doldrums. Historically, the festival involved a tobogganing contest in which the person who slid farthest

A downhill descent on a bobsled during a Laskiainen festival in Kurkijoki, Finland, 1930s.

would be rewarded with the greatest crop yield the following summer. A sledding contest is still a part of today's festivals. Although present-day Laskiainen festivals don't have ski races, a century ago members of the Finnish community faced off on handmade skis, according to Ivonen. He noted that technique was important but the real trick to winning was to have a friend waiting at a strategic location along the course with a glass of energizing orange juice.

Pat Lanin, who in the 1970s would begin a long ski coaching career in the Twin Cities, grew up north of Virginia near his Finnish grandparents, who had immigrated in the early 1900s. From the time of their arrival in the country and into the 1950s, Lanin's grandparents routinely skied to visit the neighboring farms of Finnish families. A network of tracks maintained by regular travel connected the area farms. The next generation (that of Lanin's parents) shared no interest in this old-fashioned way of travel.

By the 1920s, the Strand and Northland companies were mass-producing skis in New Richmond and St. Paul, but many people, particularly those in rural and immigrant communities, still preferred to make their own. Ski making for homesteading Finns, as it was for Norwegians, was a common skill. But not all ski makers were equal. The best Finn ski makers were called *suksi mestari*, which means "ski smith" or "ski master." The process started in summer. Ski masters would find straight-grained birch or black ash trees and then would cut, cure, and carve the wood. The skis would be soaked, steamed, and bent in the Finn's sauna. As Harold E. Lager, a dentist, Finn, and ski aficionado from the Iron Range, noted in 1979: "The final penetrating and kneading of pine tar with a hot smooth sauna rock to make an eternal running surface was nearly a secret process." The mystery of this process has no doubt only become more arcane, if not been forgotten.

🌲

While the Finns of the Iron Range competed in insular community groups, ski competition at the international level took a step forward with the first Winter Olympic Games, held in Chamonix, France, in 1924. The Olympic skiing events were all varieties of Nordic—cross-country, jumping, and Nordic combined. Military patrol, an early version of biathlon, was also an event, but the United States did not participate. Varieties of alpine or downhill skiing had yet to develop into a widely recognized disparate sport and would not be included in the Olympics for more than a decade.

First cousins Aili Kurkinen and Carl Orjala on skis at John and Maria Orjala's farm, East Lake, Minnesota, 1934.

Northland Skis

Have Stood the Test
That's Why Champions Like Them Best

1924 U. S. OLYMPIC SKI TEAM

Sigurd Overbye	Col. G. E. Leach	Anders Haugen
Harry Lien		LeMoine Batson

Every member ot the team used Northland Skis. Anders Haugen, captain, made the longest standing jump in the International Contest which was held in Chamonix, France, February, 1924.

At the National Ski Tournament held in Brattleboro, Vermont, February 14 and 15, 1924, 8 prize winners out of 10 in Class A used Northland Skis. The following are the names of the winners

*Lars Haugen (Nat'l Champion)	*Henry Hall
Norman Berger	*Harry Lien
*Alf Bakken	Rolf Monsen
*Nels Nelson	*"Bing" Anderson
*Clarence Hall	*LeMoine Batson

*Used Northland Skis

Henry Hall still holds the world's record for the longest standing jump on Skis—229 feet. This record as well as the five preceding world's records were made on Northland Skis.

Send for a Free Northland Booklet on "How to Ski."

Northland Ski Mfg. Co.

Largest Manufacturers of Skis in the World.   17 Merriam Park, St. Paul, Minn.

CARBERY & REED, PRINTERS   176   638 FEDERAL ST., CHICAGO

The 1924 U.S. Olympic Ski Team was sponsored by Christian Lund's Northland company and was featured in special advertising to the ski trade.

Tryouts for the U.S. Olympic Ski Team were held at Glenwood Park in Minneapolis (which in 1938 would be renamed Theodore Wirth Park after the Minneapolis parks superintendent). The team consisted entirely of Midwesterners, with the lone exception of John Carleton from New Hampshire. Carleton was an alternate but was added after a Swedish jumper complained that Minnesotans Barney Riley, Anders Haugen, and Hans Hansen had all competed as professionals and should therefore be disqualified from the Olympics. Confusingly, the

Around 1925, a trio of young ski-jumping contestants shake hands near the slide at Minneapolis's Glenwood Park. Long the heart of the Twin Cities Nordic ski world, the park would be renamed Theodore Wirth Park the following decade.

NSA and the newly formed Fédération Internationale de Ski (the governing international ski body) each had definitions of amateur and professional, and even though the jumpers were later cleared to compete, Riley and Hansen dropped from the squad.

The U.S. Ski Team's coach was none other than the mayor of Minneapolis, George Leach. The National Ski Association dubbed Leach "The Ski-Mayor of the Ski Capital of America." While Leach wasn't a nationally ranked skier, he was an effective promoter. He'd recently survived a dramatic public scandal to win reelection as mayor after being targeted in a nasty political play orchestrated by the Ku Klux Klan. The KKK was on the rise in 1920s Minneapolis, and Leach had drawn its ire by appointing a Catholic as his secretary and by prohibiting police officers from joining the organization. Leach's opponent in the 1923 mayoral election had been Roy Miner, the "exalted wizard" of the local KKK. Miner and his cronies had convinced a woman to say she had had an affair with Leach. Floyd Olson, the Hennepin County attorney, a future governor, and Leach's political rival, successfully prosecuted Miner and four of his minions for libel; they went to prison. Leach won in a landslide.

Leach's Olympic Ski Team included Norwegian-born Ragnar Omtvedt, from Grand Beach, Michigan. Omtvedt had been the national jumping champion four times and had twice set the American distance record, most recently in 1916 with a 192-foot jump at Steamboat Springs. The journal of the National Ski Association described him as a "well built sturdy athlete . . . very proficient in cross-country skiing." La Moine Batson, from Eau Claire, was the youngest member on the team at twenty-five. A "bonny Scotchman," Batson was a student at a normal school. Harry Lien from Chicago skied with the always formidable Norge club and was "rangey in build . . . possessing much confidence and daring"—in short, a "clean cut, splendid sportsman." Lien, a carpenter, was born in Norway and had served the United States in World War I. Another Norwegian immigrant, Sigurd Overby, lived in St. Paul and was a cross-country specialist who would eventually win the national cross-country title three times. A chauffeur by trade, Overby was described as a "small wiry fellow who uses especially constructed skis." The team captain was a bricklayer named Anders Haugen.

Anders Haugen would win the United States' first ever Winter Olympics medal. But, due to a scoring error, fifty years passed before anyone noticed that the medal was rightfully his. Between 1912 and 1928, Anders and his brother Lars won the national Class A jumping championship eleven of seventeen times, with Anders winning four times and Lars seven. They had (no surprise)

George Leach, Minneapolis mayor and coach of the 1924 U.S. Olympic Ski Team, during the Winter Olympic Games in Chamonix, France.

Ragnar Omtvedt fastens his skis at a 1916 competition in Chicago. He was a four-time national jumping champion when he was recruited for the 1924 U.S. Olympic Ski Team.

spent their childhoods in Telemark, where they'd learned to ski as toddlers. Anders was born in 1888 and Lars in 1891. They came to America in their late teens and skied for clubs in Chippewa Falls, Red Wing, Milwaukee, Minneapolis, and Colorado. The Haugens had remarkably long careers for a high-impact sport like jumping. Anders won his final national title at the age of thirty-eight, Lars at thirty-seven. Lars was offered a slot on the 1924 Olympic team, but he declined, choosing to jump professionally for cash prizes. He suggested the team take his brother instead.

The ski events in the 1924 Winter Olympics consisted of eighteen- and fifty-kilometer races; Nordic combined, which tallied jumping scores with the contestants' time from the eighteen-kilometer cross-country race; and the special jumping only competition. Still fueled by a steady flow of Norwegian immigrants, the American team did very well in the games, compared to how they would fare in coming decades. Sigurd Overbye took

By the mid-1930s, star jumpers Anders and Lars Haugen had claimed enough championship loot to fill entire rooms. Here they pose with a fraction of their collection in 1936.

nineteenth in the eighteen-kilometer race and eleventh in the Nordic combined. In the jumping event, Anders Haugen was awarded fourth place, just behind Thorleif Haug of Norway. Haug cleaned up in Chamonix, taking gold in both of the cross-country races, as well as in Nordic combined. In calculating the jumping scores, though, someone made a mistake that cost Haugen his medal. Although Haugen's jump of fifty meters was the longest in the Olympics, on style points he fell behind the two leaders, both from Norway. Calculated properly, Haug's average style score was 17.73, while Haugen's was 17.92. One can thank Norway for the Haug versus Haugen recount.

In 1974, a Norwegian sports historian going over the results from the first Winter Olympics caught the error. Later that year, eighty-six-year-old Anders Haugen traveled to Norway for his rightful due. Thorleif had died in 1934, but his daughter gave Haugen her father's erroneously obtained bronze medal and a kiss on the cheek. Not only was Anders Haugen's bronze medal the first medal won by an American in the Winter Olympics, but to date it remains the only medal won by an American in ski jumping. Another half century would pass before an American medaled again in an Olympic Nordic event.

♠

No doubt skiing in the Olympics was an honor and the trip to Europe exciting, but these were working-class guys who were missing their usual paychecks while they were in France. For them, earning money by skiing well was a practical matter, though purists like Aksel Holter harbored a more abstract view of the relationship between skiing and money. Having lived through the first wave of ski popularity in the Hemmestveit era of the late 1880s, Holter attributed the ski league's failure to the emphasis on prizes and showboating. If people could practice skiing in its pure form, he thought, everyone would be better for it.

In one sense, Holter was decades ahead of his time. The type of skiing he valued would not be similarly appreciated by Americans in any number until the late 1960s. "I love it more than ever," he wrote in the 1925 NSA publication *Ski Sport*. "Whenever possible in most any kind of weather, with snow on the ground, I don my skis and hike off into the woods with all

Virginia Wackerman receives help with her skis from her older sister Peggy in Minneapolis in the mid-1930s. Decades later, Virginia would be better known to a generation of Twin Cities skiers as Jinny McWethy, founder of the North Star Ski Touring Club.

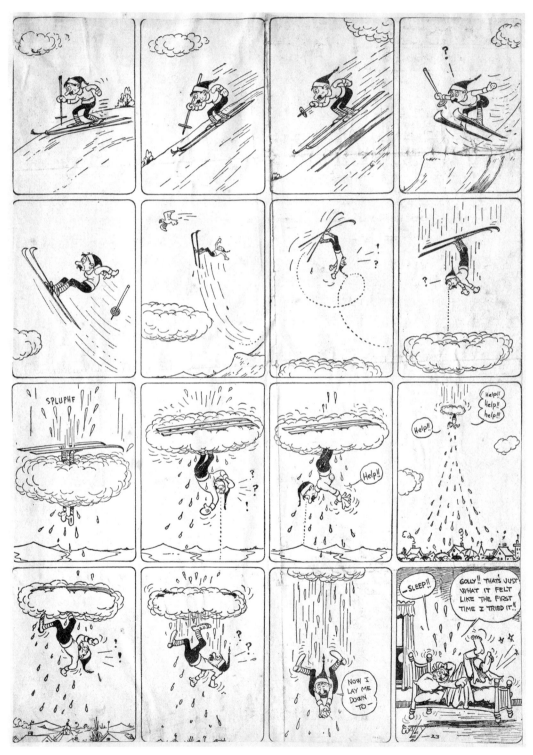

Jumping was popular enough before World War II that it was regularly
featured in newspaper cartoons, such as this one from 1923.

business worries left behind, the fragrance of balsam and spruce filling my soul with harmony, giving me a new lease on life."

From the transcendent exuberance of his prose, Holter revealed himself to be a likely reader of the Wisconsinite-come-Californian John Muir, who was something of a skier and whose greatest works had been published during the preceding decade. The articulation of Muir's spiritually infused nature writing would have appealed

Aksel Holter marching in Superior, Wisconsin, 1920s, with members of the girls' hiking and skiing club he founded with his wife in Ashland, Wisconsin.

immensely to Holter in the way it mirrored the *idraet* and drew attention to the revelation that the once endless commodity of wild places was actually finite, a development witnessed by Holter as the denuded landscape in northern Wisconsin spread ever wider under the logger's ax. "No other sport will get you in such close touch with the beautiful nature of God," Holter wrote. This was heavy stuff for a sport, perhaps more than the average citizen was interested in.

Many good things can be said of Holter. For example, with the ski sport under his ideological leadership in the 1920s, women and girls were more openly welcomed as skiers than they would be for decades. In Ashland, Holter and his wife founded a hiking and skiing club for girls. The girls wore black pants, leather jackets, and tall leather boots, and they practiced outdoor activities in pursuit of spiritual, mental, and physical fitness, giving them license to have the same rugged fun outside as boys did. You could replace the leather with polyester and Gore-Tex, switch out *spiritual health* for the fairly synonymous and currently vogue term *grit,* and you'd have an Outward Bound or YMCA outdoor program of today. Had Holter's view prevailed, the misogyny that curtailed women's skiing in the coming decades may have been avoided.

Duluth jumpers gather near the lodge at Chester Park during a tournament in the 1920s.

At his worst, though, Holter came off like a fire-and-brimstone preacher. In the years since the 1907 national tournament in Ashland, he'd managed to outlaw cash prizes in NSA competition, requiring ski jumpers to maintain amateur status. Following the tone of his hero Carl Tellefsen, he railed against baseball as a cautionary tale on the evils of mixing money and sport—"professionalism is liable to kill this great American pastime"—citing the 1919 scandal in which the Chicago White Sox threw the World Series. The "great American Press," he said acidly, refused to adequately cover the great ski sport, which was, Holter moralized, "beneficial to all mankind, building character and self-reliance in the heart of our youth, creating desires for everything pure and wholesome, teaching that which is of real blessing to individual, family, community, country and nation." Holter presented skiing as a panacea for every conceivable ill and pushed the *idraet* to a degree of ridiculousness. "Skiing," he concluded, "is purely an amateur sport and should never again become professional in any manner or form." Conveniently, Holter did not depend on skiing for his livelihood. He owned a candy and cigar store in Ashland, as well as holding for thirty-two years the cushy-sounding position of "oil inspector" for the state of Wisconsin.

Erling Strom, on the other hand, who emigrated from Norway at the end of the nineteenth century as a young man and would become an important figure in American skiing, supported himself for most of his adult life with a career in the fledgling ski industry. Strom offered a counterpoint to Holter and chronicled the divergence in skiing that began in the 1920s

and snowballed in the 1930s, as mainland European–oriented downhill skiing became more influential than Nordic. Not only were the mainland Euros good skiers, Strom said, "but they were brought up to look upon skiing as a business while in Norway it came closer to being a religion."

Norwegians had introduced skiing to mainland Europe, but the sport soon evolved away from *idraet* ideals. Strom offered an explanation: "Cross-country skiing had never been a necessity in Austria as it had been in Scandinavia, where the farms are spread all over the land much like ranches in Western America. Skis [in Norway] were used for visiting neighbors, for trips to the store or even to church." He explained how the layout of farms and villages was different in the Alps, where people lived clustered together and neighbors, stores, and churches were all in close proximity. As a result, cross-country skiing was unnecessary. The Europeans homed in on the sport's more leisurely and casual qualities, with the

An intrepid outdoorsman, Erling Strom became well known after his participation on countless ski expeditions in the mountain west. During one trip with a group of Minneapolis skiers in 1930, he rescued an injured mountain goat.

emphasis on skiing down the hills for fun as opposed to across the hills for need.

Strom blamed the Norwegians' purist views for the loss of Nordic skiing to mainland Euro skiing in America. This was an oversimplification. Free-heel Nordic skiing was hard work, whereas, done casually, the mainland Europe–based downhill skiing, with a fixed-heel boot, a technology that would develop in the coming years, reflected the grand American ideals of ease and mechanization. Oh, how Holter would have hated the downhill ski culture that enveloped the American ski world after the war; but that would be getting ahead of things. All skiing was still done with a free heel until 1929, when the Kandahar binding offered a fixed-heel option and pushed downhill skiing forward.

♠

In 1924, in response to changing demographics in the United States, President Calvin Coolidge called for a National Conference on Outdoor Recreation. The 1920 census had revealed that for the first time, the country's urban population surpassed its rural population. No longer living on farms, average Americans spent less time outdoors. Coolidge named Theodore Roosevelt Jr., the eldest son of the outdoorsy Rough Rider, as chairman of the conference. For the National Ski Association, this was an opportunity to nudge the *idraet* into the American mainstream.

Gustave Lindboe, who skied with the Chicago Norge club and had recently replaced Aksel Holter as the NSA secretary, was dispatched to Washington, DC, to speak at the conference. "That this great movement in getting the people out-of-doors the year around," Lindboe preached, "will have bearing on every man, woman or child both physically as well as mentally is a certainty." Lindboe pointed out that from the 128 organizations present, the NSA was the only one representing a winter activity. The case he made for getting more Americans skiing was similar to the one used today, namely, skiing is healthy, skiing is fun, and skiing boosts local economies; in addition, and as is also heard today, Lindboe cited the health and robustness of Scandinavians as a model for the benefits of getting outside in the cold.

Then he veered in an unusual turn that his predecessor Holter never would have touched. Lindboe explained that at the national championships

Expanding rail lines throughout the Midwest in the 1920s meant that city-dwelling skiers were only a short train ride away from skiing opportunities. For a few years around 1930, Ogden Dunes, east of Chicago, was home to a massive ski jump, billed as the largest in the nation.

MINNESOTA'S JACK LONDON

Born in 1897, Duluth native Jack O'Brien turned his life of rugged adventure into a successful writing career before dying young. He had an early introduction to death when, paddling a canoe with two friends on the Basswood River (in today's Boundary Waters Canoe Area Wilderness) just shy of his seventeenth birthday, the canoe overturned and both of his friends drowned. O'Brien later served in the Mexican American War and World War I. He started a degree at the University of Minnesota but left college to wander the country, supporting himself with odd jobs.

In 1928, O'Brien joined Admiral Richard E. Byrd's expedition to Antarctica, during which Byrd succeeded in becoming the first person to fly an airplane to the South Pole. O'Brien spent a year on Antarctica supporting Byrd, traveling by sled dog and ski, often in the company of the expedition's second-in-command, the geologist Dr. Laurence Gould, who would later be president of Minnesota's Carleton College. Gould and O'Brien sometimes clashed: Gould was an ambitious academic who would live to be ninety-eight, while O'Brien was a peripatetic free spirit. Byrd chastised O'Brien for drinking too much, while Gould took umbrage with Byrd for authorizing O'Brien's successful book on the expedition, *By Dogsled for Byrd,* which was published shortly before Gould's own book.

By Dogsled for Byrd was O'Brien's start as an author. In 1933, he published *Silver Chief: Dog of the North,* the first in a popular series of novels set in the far north of Canada about a Canadian Mountie and his trusted dog. O'Brien had bonded with the sled dogs on the Byrd expedition, and they doubtlessly cast the model for the canines of his later novels. O'Brien died of cancer in his New York City apartment in 1938 at the age of forty-one. ▲

Jack O'Brien, circa 1928.

Models from Dayton's department store show the latest winter fashions during a photo shoot at the Glenwood Park chalet in Minneapolis, circa 1925.

the year before in Vermont, of all the many ladies present at the gala after the races, only one was wearing makeup (women could only spectate, not race, despite the lip service paid to how skiing benefited women and girls). Confusing the line between health and public expectations of appearance, Lindboe said the ladies were all naturally flushed in their cheeks from standing outside watching the race, and, other than the lone exception, their need for makeup had been obviated by the cheek-tingling air. On another issue hard to relate to today, Lindboe asked the government to help with the problem of police interference with skiing. Apparently, denizens of major cities "feeling the call of the outside" after work were being stopped from skiing in city parks by police.

The goal of the conference was to get the federal government to ensure that outdoor recreation opportunities were available for Americans. Aside from the population's gravitation toward cities, the economy was good, and the labor movement had provided weekends to the working class. More Americans had both the cash to buy automobiles and the time to drive them on the nation's improving highways. A follow-up conference

"As soon as anyone picked up his skis he would jump all over them until they would put his skis on," said Walter Teppen about his dog, Spot, who during the 1920s entertained onlookers by schussing down the landing slopes on modified skis beneath jumps in Duluth and the Iron Range. During a winter parade in 1925, Spot repeatedly ran a model slide mounted on the back of a truck. Two men walked next to the truck, one releasing Spot at the top of the jump and the other catching Spot after he'd launched off its bump.

was held in 1928. The stock market crash the following year, however, interrupted direct progression of the government's views on supporting recreation, but the government was revising its role in the modern age to fit the needs of the country's people.

After the conference, the NSA worked the contacts it had made with the federal government and placed a special order with Martin Strand for two pairs of skis. Strand, who was usually aloof from the factory's daily operations, directly oversaw the skis crafted for President Calvin Coolidge and First Lady Grace Coolidge. The skis were made from "extra fine quarter sawed white ash with special nickle plated side irons for the bindings."

On December 18, 1924, a delegation including Senator Peter Norbeck from South Dakota and Congressmen Sidney Anderson, Harold Knutson, and C. J. Kvale from Minnesota presented the skis to President and First Lady Coolidge. The nation's leading couple was dragged onto the White House lawn for a photograph, and then, in the grass of a Washington December, they strapped on the skis, with the makeup man Gustave Lindboe kneeling chivalrously to adjust Grace Coolidge's binding.

The following June, in 1925, President Coolidge traveled to Minnesota and the state fairgrounds for the Norse American Centennial, which celebrated one hundred years since Norwegian immigrants began arriving in America. Martin Strand displayed his skis, and Aksel Holter traveled from Ashland to man an exhibit promoting the NSA. Volunteers from the Twin

President Calvin Coolidge and First Lady Grace Coolidge with a delegation from the National Ski Association, 1924. NSA secretary Gustave Lindboe stands to the right of Grace Coolidge.

Cities were supposed to help Holter with the booth, but they either didn't show or left early, leaving Holter to pack up the exhibit. He was harried by ill-behaved children "constantly tampering with the exhibits," he wrote to the man in charge of the displays at the centennial, Knut Gjerset, a Norwegian-born professor at Luther College in Decorah, Iowa.

Though Holter had been quite frayed by his experience at the expo, he donated a portion of the exhibit to Gjerset's Vesterheim Museum in Decorah. The donation contained a number of old photographs and several skis—including one pair made by Torjus Hemmestveit. The Hemmestveit skis, Holter explained, were used in competitions in Red Wing and La Crosse in 1887. Three others were of the original seven pairs of Hagen skis that Holter had imported from Norway in 1900, from which he based the design of his Holter skis. Although the brand hadn't lasted long enough to become as ubiquitous as Strand skis, the design of high-quality Holter skis had influenced, for the better, how Martin Strand built his own wares. Holter's claim to Gjerset of the historical significance of the imported

Martin Strand advertised his wares in a pop-up shop at the Norse American Centennial, held at the Minnesota State Fairgrounds in June 1925.

Hagens had merit: "These forming the actual beginning of ski interest after many years of earlier efforts having failed. There are no other skis like them in this country."

Although it had been the center of skiing in America, the Midwest, with its high-minded proselytizers of the *idraet*, was losing control of the sport. The U.S. Eastern Amateur Ski Association, a subdivision of the NSA, had formed in 1922. The eastern skiers were not keen on being managed from afar and proposed developing regional groups, over which the NSA would be an umbrella organization. At its 1926 annual meeting in Duluth, the NSA approved the plan. With good snow, a bigger population, and larger hills, the eastern states would soon supplant the Midwest as the nation's skiing center.

Another important development in the governance of the ski sport came in 1924, when the Fédération Internationale de Ski formed to oversee international competitions. Despite its name, the FIS was dominated by Norwegians. Norway's authority over international competition has always been rooted in its abundance of recreational skiers who routinely set off through the mountains for fun. In the United States, Norwegian immigrants began importing this type of adventure skiing.

♣

In 1926, the great Norwegian Minnesotan skier Lars Haugen embarked on a journey with his friend Erling Strom. Strom was broad shouldered and handsome (the fashion photographer Toni Frissell, who spent time documenting the glamorous Sun Valley ski scene that was soon to pop up, claimed Strom was the best-looking man she had ever photographed). Gregarious and warm with an easy smile, he spoke with a stutter. Though never based in the Midwest, Strom was a pioneer in the development of cross-country skiing in North America, and he provided a thoughtful narrative of American skiing in a book he published in 1977 (with help from his friend, the writer Lowell Thomas) that featured chronicles of numerous cross-country adventures the likes of which were rarely recorded. He

Erling Strom with Russian aristocrat Marquis Nicolò delgi Albizzi *(far left)* at one of the cabins near Assiniboine in the Canadian Rockies, 1928.

Seven-time national ski jumping champion Lars Haugen, photographed in 1934 while skiing with the St. Paul Athletic Club.

would partner with Minnesotan skiers on three notable expeditions in the late 1920s and early 1930s.

After immigrating and spending several ski-less years as a cowboy in Arizona, Strom began instructing skiing at the massive Lake Placid Club in the Adirondacks of New York. The club was an autonomously functioning village with two thousand beds and over one hundred miles of cross-country trails. Strom quickly developed a reputation, and fancy ladies from New York City kept his instructing calendar full. He was among the first of the debonair European ski instructors who would become commonplace at swanky resorts in the coming decades. He was, at heart, forever a cross-country skier but would shift to downhill as it surpassed cross-country in popularity. When he wasn't teaching Strom would travel, and as he explored the United States and Canada, his eyes popped at the wealth of untapped skiing potential. With financial backing from wealthy Minnesotans, Strom founded the Assiniboine Lodge, the continent's first backcountry ski lodge, which still functions as a wilderness skiing paradise outside Banff in Canada.

In April 1926 in Estes Park, Colorado, Strom and Lars Haugen decided to ski cross-country one hundred miles to Steamboat Springs. The jumping season was over for the year; Haugen's brother Anders had just won the national Class A title in Duluth. During the tournament, both Lars and Barney Riley, the Wild Irish Rose, had suffered nasty wipeouts caused by the vicious wind blasting off Lake Superior. Both men had been knocked unconscious. By April, Haugen had recovered from his concussion and was in Colorado selling skis for his employer, the Northland Ski Company of St. Paul. Before setting out, he prevaricated a bit and told his boss, C. A. Lund, that he'd be hawking skis a while longer.

Haugen complained that he'd gotten fat, which shortens a jumper's distances, and convinced Strom they should go light on foodstuffs to encourage weight loss. Strom wasn't enthused about the idea, but he worried that if he carried extra food for himself, Haugen would get hungry and wind up eating the goodies he had painstakingly schlepped. In the end, they set off with a large supply of Ry-Krisp crackers (made in Minneapolis), two pounds of butter each, and "some nuts and chocolate bars plus tea and a good supply of sugar."

Strom described the journey as "a cross-country trip such as we both had taken many of back home [in Norway]." This unusual type of backcountry

A ski brigade navigates the wilds near the mining town of Irwin, Colorado, circa 1910, recalling the early ski races held by miners in California.

adventure ski trip wouldn't be common in the United States for decades. The men carried thick blankets, warm clothing, an ax, a shovel, a can for heating water, and a wooden cup each. They didn't have a map, figuring they could navigate from the prominent peaks. The first night they stayed with a park ranger, who was unique at that time in Colorado for knowing how to ski. Barely anyone in the Rocky Mountains skied, and most folks equated skiing with jumping. Strom was often ridiculed by locals for trying to get anywhere on skis. Everyone else used snowshoes, and time and again they had to eat their words as Strom and his compatriots smoked them on their long boards.

The second night, Strom and Haugen tried to find a hermit named Squeaky Bob, but he was away from his cabin, so the men made themselves at home in it. The next day they climbed for eight hours toward the twelve-thousand-foot Lulu Pass before digging a snow cave and spending a wretched night there. They got lost and eventually stumbled on "the loneliest little ranch in all of Colorado," inhabited by a mother and her two sons. The ranchers hadn't seen an outsider since fall and were happy for the company. They had never seen skis before but had recently read about ski jumping and that the best jumper in the country was a Norwegian named Lars Haugen—and here was that Norwegian on their doorstep!

Lars Haugen's infatuation with Steamboat Springs began early in his career. During a tour there in 1919 sponsored by St. Paul's Northland Ski Company, the Haugen brothers were joined by Minneapolis jumper Hans Hansen *(second from right)* and Carl Howelsen *(far left),* the famous Norwegian skier who won the Nordic combined at Holmenkollen in 1903.

Carl Howelsen, a founding member of Chicago's Norge Ski Club, was discovered in 1906 by Barnum & Bailey. Billed as the "Flying Norseman," Howelsen thrilled audiences for three years before being lured west to Steamboat Springs, where he built the town's first ski jump.

Haugen and Strom were warmly hosted and slept two nights in the boys' beds while the children slept in the barn. Haugen's weight loss plan fell apart as he gorged on beef from the ranch. He and Strom gave the sons ski lessons, and Haugen promised to send the boys Northland skis at a discounted price; he was working, after all.

The men left the ranch and hurried on to the coal mining town of Walden. By sheer luck they arrived just as the only train of the week was about to leave. They wanted to take the train twenty miles to skip the flat, densely wooded terrain they found dull. Strom and Haugen ran to flag down the engineer just as the train was pulling away from the station.

The train backed up to the platform to allow the men to buy tickets. The townspeople had never seen skis before, so the train was delayed while the curious onlookers inquired about them. Folks were amazed to hear that the men had traveled from Estes Park. Again, Haugen had an opportunity to expound on the virtues of Northlands. He was ahead of his time, essentially working as a sponsored athlete for an outdoor gear company.

After a full week, they eventually reached Steamboat Springs. Haugen had become snow-blind, so they took a day off before catching a train to Hot Sulphur Springs, from where they skied back to Estes Park. They felt they had to ski back because otherwise nobody would believe they had made the trip. Strom concluded: "We also felt we were promoting cross-country skiing in a small way; little did we know that nearly fifty years would pass before that kind of skiing would really catch on."

Weight loss or no, Lars Haugen won the national Class A jumping title in both 1927 and 1928. The next year, Lars and his brother Anders headed to California to consult on the construction of a ski jump and the possibility of turning the mountains around Lake Tahoe into a skiing mecca. Lars went back and forth between Tahoe and the Twin Cities, eventually retiring in Minneapolis. He died in 1969. Anders led the junior skiing program at Tahoe into his seventies. He died in Southern California at the age of ninety-five.

♠

The Aurora Ski Club hosted the 1928 national championships in Red Wing. Buddy Borgen, whose dad had made him a pair of skis at the dawn of the century, remembered that the weather was mild and the snow was lacking. Volunteers dug snow from ditches and ravines to supply the jump, called Charlson Hill, which was dripping wet under a hot February sun.

Thirty riders, including the Haugens, demanded that the NSA ease its rule on professionalism. "Tired of risking their good health to entertain ski fans for silverware, crockery and other such gifts permissible under the existing rules, the riders demanded that they be permitted to accept cash prizes," wrote the *Minneapolis Morning Tribune*. The Haugens "have won so much silverware, crockery and medals that it has become a perplexing problem as to what to do with their trophies." Despite the jumpers' protests, the amateur rules remained intact.

U. S. NATIONAL SKI TOURNAMENT

AND 50th ANNIVERSARY AURORA SKI CLUB

RED WING MINNESOTA

Saturday, February 1

Cross-country ski race...dog-sled derby in the morning...skiing in the afternoon...the United States' best fancy ice skaters performing in the evening on beautiful Mississippi river...Tobogganing and Skating Parties...A full day culminated with the crowning of the tournament queen at the ball in Red Wing Armory.

ROOM FOR 50,000 CARS

This Is a View Taken at the 1928 National Tournament Held at Red Wing, Minn.

Sunday, February 2

Thrill at the perfect form of the country's best riders as they glide through the air at 90 miles per hour speed...chill at the spills...applaud with the thousands when 60-year-old Carl Ek, the United States oldest skier shoots down the bedding...cheer the daring feminine riders as they take their turn in the jumps.

ROOM FOR 50,000 CARS

SATURDAY SUNDAY FEB. 1-2

CHARLSON HILL SLIDE
UNLIMITED PARKING SPACE

The original Red Wing Ski club, organized by a group of men of Norwegian birth or descent in Red Wing 50 years ago. This organization introduced the ski sport to America.

Organize your party now and follow the "Snus Box Trail" to the world's most natural ski slide at Red Wing, Minn., for the grandest two-day winter sports carnival anywhere — On these two days Red Wing's Aurora club, the oldest ski organization in the country is celebrating its 50th anniversary — come and join in the winter fun of this golden jubilee.

The famous Hemmestveit Bros.-Hemingstad-Hjarnstad combination which brought fame to Red Wing in the early days with their prowess as performers on skis.

ADULTS   SATURDAY, 50 Cents
SUNDAY, $1.00
SEASON TICKET, $1.25   :-:   **CHILDREN**   **25c**

Red Wing Printing Company

Boasting the event's proud heritage, the poster for the 1928 national championships in Red Wing featured photographs of the Aurora Ski Club's first lineup, led by Torjus and Mikkel Hemmestveit.

Twenty-five thousand spectators watched the event, brought in on special trains and buses from Milwaukee, Chicago, the Iron Range, and Canton, South Dakota, which was home to a thriving ski scene. Police and National Guardsmen directed traffic down the narrow country lane that accessed the new Charlson Hill. Designed by Lars Haugen for the tournament, for a time, the Charlson Hill slide was known as the best in the nation. The first round consisted of 120 jumpers. Those who fell on their first jump didn't get a second. A newspaper chronicled the flurry of leaps:

> It was about 2:30 when the first of the Class A jumpers stepped up on the wooden scaffold, perched on the top of the world, and nonchalantly gazed off into space, looking down a precipitous white cliff, where far below a black mass moved in impatience. He gave a half-conscious tug at his ski straps, gazed indifferently at the glistening stretch of snow before him and shuffled off. Two steps with the skis and he was on his way, while the voice of the announcer boomed to the crowd, "Hans Hansen of Hammond, Ind., now jumping."
>
> Down the slide he slid gathering speed as he went, crouching low over his skis, hands almost on his cramped knees. With a swish he hit the bottom of the slide, started upward and shot off into space. There was a sudden, yet graceful, straightening of his body. He rose erect, skis tilted up before him, and waggled his arms for greater distance.

Halvor Walstad, from Racine, Wisconsin, jumped 151 feet. Lars Haugen, the defending champion, answered. "He slipped down the slide without apparent effort, rose high into the air and volplaned down the hill." An "involuntary cheer" rose from the crowd as Haugen nailed a jump of 151 feet, tying Walstad. The big surprise was when Class B jumper Earl Aakers, "a young Minneapolis boy," jumped 156 feet, surpassing the Class A studs. But poor Aakers suffered a massive wipeout upon landing, so his jump didn't count. The judges convened and declared Haugen the winner. Walstad wound up in third place. Haugen even received the trophy for the longest jump because the judges declared he had better form. This may have been true, but a common complaint in jumping was that in a toss-up between a star and an unknown, the star always came out on top. La Moine Batson, the Olympic "Bonny Scotchman," came in sixth and Barney Riley ninth. Riley, who would never win a Class A national title or compete in the Olympics, was, nonetheless, the country's most loved yumper of the 1920s.

A lone woman, Lorraine Madsen with the Norge club of Chicago, jumped at the tournament. The *Red Wing Daily Republican* featured a picture of Madsen standing next to Lars Haugen, both wearing big grins. Whether Madsen jumped as a competitor or in an exhibition is unclear. The very few women jumpers of the era were almost always relegated to exhibitioner status and not allowed to compete. The Norge club had a track record of encouraging female participation. Back in 1916, it permitted women to compete in a tournament, despite the male jumpers' threats of striking in protest. Two years later, the club invited women to compete in the national tournament: "If any of the fair sex feel brave enough to try the giant slide at Cary they will be allowed to compete." This early attempt at jumping parity was highly unusual.

A jumper appears on the verge of falling during the 1928 National Tournament in Red Wing. Known for a time as the "greatest natural ski hill in America," the Charlson Hill jump was designed by Lars Haugen for the tournament.

Red Wing's national cross-country championship was scheduled for 10:00 a.m. on Saturday, February 4. The cross-country race reportage occupied only a small niche of the tournament's extensive media coverage. In one amusing snippet, titled "Chur Doesn't Mean Cheer," a reporter chronicled an embarrassing incident in which the race officiant, one Edward C. Bryan, commenced the race while shouting "chur, chur!" Spectators laughed like rubes at this display of foreignness, though the reporter, wishing to be a good sport and mistakenly thinking Bryan was instructing onlookers to *cheer,* began cheering on the racers. Later, Bryan took the reporter aside and explained that "chur" meant "speed up" or "start quick." Only twelve cross-country skiers competed in the national race. Three of the dozen were brothers who had traveled from Connecticut. Between 1927 and 1935, the trio of Norwegian-born Satre brothers took turns winning the national cross-country title six times out of nine. In Red Wing, Karl Magnus Satre took the title from the defending champ, his brother Johan. Johan finished second, and the third brother, Paul Ottar Satre, took fifth.

Chicago's Norge Ski Club was unusual in its inclusion of women in competition. In this photograph from 1923, club members Margaret Thompson *(right)* and Carl Nelson pose with their long wooden jumping skis.

The top Midwesterner was Carl Sundquist, in third place. Sundquist had immigrated to the Twin Cities from Sweden and skied with the Swedish-American Club of Minneapolis. Later, he would help build a trail network south of Lake Minnetonka and would eventually claim the national title for his own.

The skiers raced over eight miles "of wooded hills, swamps and open country, picking out threads of snow to hasten their flight over the almost bare countryside." The winning time in the awful conditions was one hour, seven minutes, and ten seconds, with Sundquist two and a half minutes back.

An old-timer named John Hjermstad watched the race with interest. Hjermstad questioned the skiers' use of two poles. "We used only one in my days," he said. "We

An unknown *langlaufer* (or "long run") races in the 1928 national cross-country championship on the frozen Mississippi River in Red Wing. Karl Magnus Satre, a twenty-four-year-old Norwegian immigrant who had settled in Connecticut, won the race.

handled it like a boatman does his boatstick. A two-handed push sent us speeding for many feet."

Despite the poor weather, the tournament was a success. Red Wing hadn't seen such a crowd since the visit of Prince Gustav from Sweden three years earlier. The tournament turned a profit of between six thousand and seven thousand dollars, half of which went to the forty men who had contributed a combined four thousand dollars necessary to land the contest. One quarter of the profits went to the Aurora club and the rest to the local chamber of commerce.

🌲

Only two weeks after the Red Wing tournament, the second Winter Olympics took place in St. Moritz, Switzerland. The United States sent only three skiers for jumping, cross-country, and Nordic combined. The U.S. team consisted of Rolf Monsen, who was Norwegian born and had settled in New England; Charles Procter, who had learned to ski in Hanover, New Hampshire; and Anders Haugen, the only Midwesterner.

Evidently, New Englanders were taking cross-country seriously in a way that Midwesterners were not. By the 1932 Lake Placid Olympics, no Midwesterners skied on the eight-man cross-country squad, but seven of the men were New Englanders. Julius Blegen of Minneapolis, the two-time national cross-country champion, was head coach. Jumping, on the other hand, maintained a strong Midwestern presence, with North Dakotan Casper Oimoen taking an impressive fifth place.

North Dakota's Casper Oimoen placed fifth in the 1932 Winter Olympics at Lake Placid before being lured west to the thriving ski jumping scene in Utah. *From left:* unidentified, Einar Fredbo, Casper Oimoen, Alf Engen, Corey Engen, and Sverre Engen, circa 1935.

The third Winter Olympics would be the last without downhill skiing, which was advanced in 1929 when Guido Reuge, a Swiss ski racer and engineer, invented the Kandahar binding. The Kandahar used a cable to lock the heel in place, allowing the skier to turn easily just by rotating a leg. No longer would skiers need to master the technical Telemark turn. The Kandahar binding would become standard for downhill skiers for the next forty years. In the early 1930s, the chairlift had yet to be invented, so skiers still had to trudge back up the hill. This was accomplished by unhooking the cable from a couple of clasps on the binding alongside the foot. Without the binding cable around the hooks, the cable remained sufficiently slack to allow the boot free-heel movement. For cross-country racing, the Kandahar was too heavy. The binding also had serious safety drawbacks. When the cable was tensioned tightly to the skier's foot, wipe-outs were gruesome, resulting in countless broken legs and the binding's nickname—the beartrap binding.

♠

At the end of March 1930, four years after Strom and Haugen's Colorado jaunt, Erling Strom set off on another cross-country ski adventure, this time with a quartet of Minnesotan swells he had previously guided at his Assiniboine Lodge (they not only were clients but had also financially invested in the lodge's opening). The Minnesotans were young WASP lords from the Midwest's upper class who liked adventure and had the funds to indulge in it, despite the Great Depression gripping the country. These men, and one in particular, would go on to promote cross-country skiing in their home state to a crowd quite different from the working folk of Scandinavian heritage who had been cross-country's traditional practitioners.

Strom's skiing companions were all born around the turn of the century and included Henry Kingman, a prominent banker, and Russell H. Bennett, who would become a bigwig in the mining industry and eventually help found the Eloise Butler Wildflower Garden in Minneapolis's Theodore Wirth Park. Richard Pillsbury Gale was grandson of the former Minnesota governor and founder of the Pillsbury Company. In the 1940s, Gale would serve two terms as Minnesota's Third District U.S. congressman. He had a farm near Lake Minnetonka where he would host informal cross-country ski

Under the guidance of Erling Strom, Minnesotan expeditioners Al Lindley, Russell Bennett, Richard Gale, and Henry Kingman ski en route to the Columbia Icefield in Jasper National Park, Alberta, Canada, circa 1930.

races in the coming years. The fourth man, and of most importance to the development of skiing, was Alfred Damon Lindley, a cousin to Richard Gale.

Al Lindley was born in 1904. His Quaker grandfather, whose abolitionist views forced him to flee his home in North Carolina, became one of Minneapolis's first public health physicians and had a fine home built for his family at 1920 Stevens Avenue. The Minneapolis Lindleys were respectable but not exceedingly wealthy, though Al's father, Clarkson Lindley, married Anna Gale (Al's mother), of the very rich Gale family, the namesake of the Minnesota Historical Society's research library. The Gales had homesteaded property on the rural shores of Lake Minnetonka, which, aside from proving to be an excellent investment, was the backdrop for much of Al Lindley's active boyhood.

Good looking, confident, and standing six foot one, Lindley was a natural athlete. Lindley excelled in Minnetonka's thriving tennis and sailing scene, a community that had been fostered by the Burton family, who were members of the same rarefied social class and whom Al's sister Ella eventually married into. This union would produce two national-caliber skiers. In 1920, when Lindley was sixteen, he climbed Jungfrau, a major mountain in Switzerland. As an undergraduate at Yale University in 1924, he won a gold medal in the Paris Summer Olympics with his eight-man rowing team. The team included two other Minnesotans and a pediatrician in training who would be known to a generation of parents as Dr. Spock.

Where and when Lindley started skiing is unclear. At some point, he became acquainted with Carl Sundquist, the Swedish immigrant who took third place in the 1928 Red Wing cross-country nationals. Sundquist would eventually lay out a trail system in Deephaven, where Lindley and his Burton nephews skied, but what role, if any, Sundquist played in getting Lindley into skiing is clouded. Lindley loved the mountains, liked adventure, and had money, and in the late 1920s he found his way to Mount Assiniboine under the guidance of Erling Strom. Lindley was mountain skiing decades before regular Americans discovered its joys.

The 1930 adventure of Strom and the Minnesotans involved skiing 125 miles through the Canadian Rockies wilderness, making the first winter crossing of a major mountain pass and culminating in the first winter ascent, by Strom and Lindley (the others having turned back), of Snow Dome, a prominence in the Columbia Icefield. The trip not only further developed the use of skis in winter adventure travel but also fostered the partnership between Lindley and Strom, resulting in another trip of even greater significance.

For some years since Strom first laid eyes on Mount McKinley (as Denali, North America's highest peak, was then known), he had been trying to recruit cohorts to join him in skiing the mountain. Later in 1930, Lindley was sightseeing in Alaska and caught a glimpse of the mountain. He concurred with Strom: the massive snowy flanks of Denali appeared loaded with sweet powder. The men would be incorrect in this assertion—the wind- and sun-hardened snow would make a mockery of their wooden skis and leather boots—but Lindley and Strom would endure one hell of an adventure to learn this.

By April 1932, Strom and Lindley were on Denali. Lindley had paid for the entire expedition. He'd saved money by completing the four-person team with two rangers from Mount McKinley National Park. One of those rangers was Harry Liek, the park superintendent. By recruiting Liek, the

Erling Strom's Minneapolis ski party pauses at Maligne Lake narrows on their way to the Columbia Icefield in Jasper National Park, 1930.

expedition gained free use of the park's dogsled teams for transporting gear. Liek would prove to be the party's weakest member (after one long day, he passed out in the tent still wearing his pack). The other park ranger, Grant Pearson, was an indominable asset to the team. They had to ski one hundred miles just to reach the base of the mountain. Sled dogs hauled hundreds of pounds of gear as far up as eleven thousand feet. It was a grand, old-style mountaineering expedition, with literally tons of gear and well-appointed camps that became more spartan as they neared the summit.

Denali had been successfully climbed only once before, in 1913. No mountaineer had given it any mind in the ensuing nineteen years. Oddly enough, that spring, a scientific expedition led by a highly regarded mountaineer named Allen Carpe aimed to climb Denali while studying a subject of fascination at the time, cosmic rays—charged matter from distant space. Carpe asked Strom and Lindley to haul some of his expedition's gear via dogsled. Lindley agreed. Carpe and his team would be flying into the glacier at the base of the mountain. (Today all climbers reach Denali by plane, but back then it was a new timesaving technique.) For the rest of his long life, Strom would regret accommodating Carpe's request.

Skis had never been employed before on a major mountaineering expedition. Strom and Lindley pioneered their use. Skis can be particularly valuable for traveling on glaciers. By more widely distributing a climber's weight, skis glide across weak snow and over hidden crevasses that a climber on foot would plummet through.

Before starting the climb, neither Harry Liek nor Grant Pearson had ever skied. Lindley and Strom figured they would learn on the way up. Lindley had ordered each man a pair of short, lightweight Northland skis to be carried up the steep ridge they planned to ascend by, so that they could ski the gentler upper slopes of the mountain. They would jettison the short skis on high, downclimb the ridge, and near the bottom reclaim their heavier touring skis for crossing the crevasse-ridden lower glaciers.

The men spent six weeks climbing. They slowly worked their way up Karsten's Ridge, establishing camps and taking numerous trips up and down the mountain to haul gear. Leaving the ridge for the upper slopes required a dicey move through a steep icy corner, but all men passed

Members of what was known as the Lindley–Liek expedition pose on the way down from Denali's summit in 1932. *From left:* Al Lindley, Harry Liek, Grant Pearson, and Erling Strom.

Flanked by skis and snowshoes, the Lindley–Liek team stands with their gear for expedition photographer Merl LaVoy during their 1932 ascent of Denali.

through, and the slopes eased. Beneath a distinctive rock outcropping, they found a wooden box left by the first party to climb Denali. The box contained a thermometer that had a feature of recording the lowest temperature reached. The thermometer's lower limit of ninety-five degrees below zero had been exceeded, and the men estimated the reading to be one hundred degrees below zero. They left their own cache, containing food, in case they needed it on the way down. Ten years later, the famed mountaineer Bradford Washburn found this cache, ate a chicken dinner from it, and passed on his thanks to Lindley and company.

They made a high camp at seventeen thousand feet and proceeded to the summit the following day. The snow on high was, alas, hard and icy, not the oasis of great skiing that it appeared to be from sea level. Still, after a day of rest, and as the crew made their way to the shorter north summit of the mountain (thus becoming the first party to climb both summits), Strom and Lindley strapped on their wooden skis in the gentle saddle between the summits and skied for the sake of skiing at such a rarefied elevation. They had lugged the skis all that way, after all.

Strom had made a decision that put him in a tight spot. Instead of taking the short Northlands, he'd lugged his regular skis. "I had seen the most beautiful snow-covered slopes high between the two peaks, promising wonderful skiing which I did not want spoiled by some miserable short skis," he wrote. Unlike his three compatriots, who would leave their disposable Northlands high on the mountain, Strom would have to carry his several-feet-long hickories down the treacherous Karsten's Ridge. He had no other pair, and they would be essential in crossing the heavily crevassed glaciers below the ridge.

After eighteen hours of downclimbing, the party reached the base of Karsten's Ridge, where they had planned on taking a rest day. Here, though, they made a horrible discovery that nearly led to more tragedy. They found empty tents of the Cosmic Ray Expedition. In the tents were the journals of Allen Carpe and another climber named Theodore Koven. Food sat on the stove, but fresh snow covered the tracks of the tents' inhabitants, making it clear that the Cosmic Ray men had stepped away briefly and not returned. The foursome set off to lend assistance. On the glacier below they found Koven's frozen body. He had fallen into a crevasse and managed to climb out but succumbed to his injuries and the cold. They loaded Koven into a sled and set out looking for Carpe. Pearson meanwhile had swapped his skis for snowshoes and soon fell into a hidden crevasse. In an epic struggle, the remaining team helped Pearson free himself without serious injury. Thirty hours had passed since they'd left their camp on top of the mountain, so they were forced to abandon Koven and press on. After another ten hours, the men finally reached their base camp. Carpe, they concluded, had traveled onto the crevassed glacier in his boots and fallen to his death. Strom blamed himself, thinking that had Carpe and company gone through the struggle of skiing up with their gear themselves, they would have known not to take the glaciers so lightly.

The tragedy notwithstanding, the Lindley–Strom expedition had been a success. The *New York Times* ran a large spread of photographs from the climb. Back home in Lindley's Twin Cities, his adventure was front-page news. In the weeks after the trip, Strom's fingers turned black with frostbite. A number of doctors suggested he get his fingertips amputated. Strom demurred; he doubted doctors. Once, in South Africa, a physician had told him the "bumps" on his stomach were cancer and wanted to operate. Strom, who in his years of guiding had developed six-pack abs as well as the flair of a raconteur, noted that white men in South Africa were

The camp where Theodore Koven's body was found by the Lindley–Liek crew near the Muldrow Glacier, 1932.

unfamiliar with physical labor and that the doctor had never seen a man with a well-honed core. Strom's blackened fingers healed.

Later that year, Lindley founded the Bush Lake Ski Club and enlisted the financial help of his friend, Louis Hill, who was a son of the railroad tycoon James J. Hill and president of the Great Northern Railway, to construct the Bush Lake ski jump in Bloomington, Minnesota. The site is known today as Hyland Lake Park Reserve and is home to three new jumps operated by the Minneapolis Ski Club, which the Bush Lake club would eventually become.

Lindley competed in 1935 for the NSA's national cross-country title in Canton, South Dakota. He took fifth place; Paul Ottar Satre won. The following month, at Bush Lake, Lindley finished third in the Central Division cross-country championship. Carl Sundquist won, followed by Peter Fosseide from Duluth. Lindley's young nephew Gale Burton finished fifth, and another Duluthian, Erik Judeen, placed sixth. Judeen and Fosseide were beginning to cultivate Minnesota's most venerable, ongoing cross-country legacy and would soon become the region's prominent practitioners of the quieter side of the *idraet*.

Even in the midst of the Great Depression, Twin Cities ski manufactures continued to churn out the boards. Martin Strand, in his usual and delightful lack of self-awareness, stated in early 1932, "You know, it's a peculiar thing about periods of so-called depression. People have more leisure for recreation, and, somehow, more money to spend for things to help them enjoy it." Strand's idea of depression sounded fantastic. Fortunately for him, his company proved resilient to the "so-called" depression, and Strand's son, Martin E., prepared to take over operations. With steady-handed daddy at the helm, Martin E. didn't have to worry about heading off to a Civilian Conservation Corps camp to earn money, as many men of his generation did. Strand ran an advertisement in 1935 stating that his skis could be purchased "At Prices to Suit Any Pocketbook." A person could pick up a pair of Strand skis from the New Richmond factory store for a dollar and a half.

A skier rockets off the jump at the Bush Lake Ski Club in Bloomington, Minnesota, 1936.

Christian Lund's Northland Ski Company was also growing. In 1927, Lund started a sister company called the C. A. Lund Company and opened another factory outside the Twin Cities, in Hastings, for the production of Lund skis. Lunds were cheaper and sold wholesale to retailers like hardware and department stores. A hardware store would order skis from Lund, and Lund would slap a label on the skis bearing the store's name. In 1938, Lund opened yet another Northland factory, this time in Laconia, New Hampshire.

Lund, who was younger and shrewder at advertising than Strand, was on his way to usurping his competitor as the self-acclaimed biggest manufacturer of skis on the planet. While Strand stuck with his wonderfully stodgy slogan "Everyone tells me: 'I am very much pleased with your goods'" and used simple, old-fashioned drawings on his advertisements, Northland employed hip artwork in bright colors, often featuring women and idyllic winter scenes. Northland also more aggressively recruited top athletes—for example, turning Anders Haugen, who had previously been sponsored by Strand, into not just a Northland-sponsored athlete but an employee, a career shift that garnered Haugen's loyalty to the brand through the increased freedom it gave him over his earlier work as a bricklayer.

With a measure of chivalry, the always canny Christian Lund captured the spirit of the *idraet* in promotional material produced by Northland in the 1920s.

Workers at the Gregg Ski Manufacturing Company finish a batch of skis to ship out just before Christmas in 1937.

Northland's Hampden Park neighborhood was also home to the Gregg Ski Manufacturing Company. Founder Henry S. Gregg initially made farming equipment but got into skis after 1919, when the Dartmouth Co-op of Hanover, New Hampshire, contracted Gregg to produce them. The Dartmouth Co-op provided gear to the Dartmouth Outing Club, which was the outdoor adventure club for the Ivy League university and at the center of the NSA's Eastern Division. Dartmouth produced many of the nation's best skiers, and its Outing Club was emulated at other universities around the country, including the Hoofers Club at the University of Wisconsin–Madison. By the 1930s, Gregg had moved away from farm equipment entirely and focused on skis. The Twin Cities ski industry would continue to do well through World War II but then ironically would stall in the booming economy that followed.

In 1940, William Sautbine of Walker, Minnesota, leads a family outing on the ski trails of the Shingobee Winter Playground in the Chippewa National Forest.

4

High Times for the Ski Sport

1930s–1940s

In rural Minnesota, cross-country skiing continued to be a practical mode of transportation into the 1930s. Born in 1911, Harold Moe, from Brainerd, was the son of Norwegian immigrants. To raise money for his tuition at the University of Minnesota, Moe competed for prizes in running and skiing races, as well as by playing violin. Once, for placing well in a running race, he won a supply of coal, which he gave to his parents for heating their home. Moe was working toward a degree in engineering when he ran out of money and left college. By 1934 he had joined the Civilian Conservation Corps and moved to Spruce Creek CCC camp near Lutsen, Minnesota. After building the Cascade River State Park Wayside with the CCC, he began a career in log cabin construction on Minnesota's North Shore.

Later in the decade, Moe moved to Brule Lake (now in the Boundary Waters Canoe Area Wilderness) to build a cabin for a client. Moe lived on-site as construction continued into the winter. The Caribou Trail, the road linking Brule Lake to the nearest grocery store in Lutsen, became impassable by vehicle as snow piled up. Every week, Moe skied thirty miles into town for supplies at Jonvik's Store. One day, he noticed a new face behind the counter, a young woman named Eleanor Atkins. Miss Atkins had arrived on the mainland after spending the summer working in the fish camps on Isle Royale, Lake Superior's largest island, which before

Harold Moe was enrolled in the Spruce Creek Civilian Conservation Corps camp near Lutsen, Minnesota, in 1934.

becoming a national park in 1940 was home to commercial fishing operations run by mostly Scandinavian immigrants. Moe began skiing the sixty-mile round trip to Lutsen more frequently. The couple courted for seven years, until the night before Moe shipped out for World War II with the Army Corps of Engineers, when he and Atkins rousted the local judge from his bed to marry them. After serving in Italy and Tunisia, Moe returned to Minnesota and built many cabins and homes along Lake Superior. Before he left for war, though, he had a few moves to make in the ski world.

🌲

In 1936, the National Ski Association's annual tournament moved back to Red Wing. Despite the prestige of putting on the country's biggest ski contest of the year, this marked the beginning of the end for the Aurora club. Local interest in jumping would occasionally flare up in the coming decades, but the championship that year would be Red Wing's last grasp at competitive relevancy on the national level—and at that, it fell short. The timing was bad: the fourth Winter Olympic Games in Garmisch-Partenkirchen, Germany, were to begin three days after the Red Wing meet. The defending national cross-country champion, Karl Magnus Satre, who had also won the cross-country title the last time the nationals were in Red Wing, was in Germany for his second Olympics. The U.S. Olympic teams for cross-country and Nordic combined were dominated by New Englanders, but the jumping squad was exclusively Midwestern, made up of defending national champ Roy Mikkelsen and team captain Casper Oimoen, both from Canton, South Dakota; Walter Bietila, from Ishpeming; and Sverre Fredheim, from St. Paul. The local heroes weren't home to jump in Red Wing.

In a further blow to the hosting city, the lone superstar present wasn't able to compete, instead spending his time in Red Wing in the hospital for treatment of influenza. This was Alf Engen, who was born and raised in Norway but moved to Chicago, where he tore up the competition before moving to Alta, Utah. After World War II, Engen would transition from his success in jumping to take a place at the center of the golden age of downhill skiing. He'd occasionally venture back to the Midwest for a spell of ski instruction.

The Aurora Ski Club got stuck with this bill for a shoulder X-ray for a Chicago skier injured during the 1936 national tournament. The club never fully recovered from the debt it incurred for hosting the tournament.

At the 1936 tournament in Red Wing, George Kotlarek reclaimed the Class A title for Duluth and inspired a generation of Chester Bowl boys who would go on to be among the nation's best.

The Red Wing tournament drew fifteen thousand spectators (compared to twenty-five thousand onlookers eight years earlier) and more than two hundred competitors. Paul Bietila, seventeen years old, won the boys' division with jumps of 173 and 176 feet. The next day, George Kotlarek broke a twenty-seven-year dry spell for the Duluth Ski Club by winning the Class A title. At 164 and 169 feet, Kotlarek's Class A jumps were shorter than those of the winner of the boys' division. This was another embarrassment to the hosting city, which had claimed that their Charlson Hill jump would produce leaps of more than 200 feet. But NSA officials had determined that a portion of the jump was too dangerous and ordered that 12 feet be cut off from the jump's bump. Between the opening and closing days of the tournament, workers cut 8 feet (refusing to remove the full 12 feet) off the ramp at the end of the jump. As a result, the Class A jumpers had shorter jumps than the best boy jumpers. Aurora's top skier, Harry Tregillis, finished a disappointing fourteenth in Class A. The value placed on jumping versus cross-country was evident from the prizes allowed (per NSA amateur regulations) to the winners: for capturing the Class A jumping title, Kotlarek received a twenty-six-piece silver set, while the cross-country champ took home a four-piece one.

The cross-country race started at Levee Park along the Mississippi River and, as the newspaper reported, "transcribed a six-mile irregular circle which took them across the hills and valleys of Sorin's Bluff and College Hill and along the fields and woods skirting Spring Creek back to Levee Park." The racers would ski two laps. Peter Fosseide from Duluth finished the first lap in the lead, with Carl Sundquist, now skiing with Al Lindley's Bush Lake Ski Club, thirty seconds behind. On the second lap, Sundquist overtook Fosseide and won the national title with a time of 1:10:15. Fosseide's time was 1:11:30. In third place was Duluthian Erik Judeen.

Unlike the 1928 tournament, there were no profits to divvy up between sponsors. Aurora came out of the national meet in debt to a number of local businesses as well as to the NSA. This ignominious conclusion to what should have provided the once stalwart Aurora Ski Club a much-needed boost marked the beginning of a slide into desuetude from which there would be no return. Four years later, its debts still unpaid, the Aurora Ski Club was expelled from the NSA.

The Winter Olympics of 1936 marked the first time the games included downhill skiing events, and not just for men. Al Lindley turned away from cross-country and tried to make the inaugural U.S. Men's Alpine Ski Team. At thirty-two years old, he did well enough to be named an alternate. The tryouts had been held a few months before on Mount Rainier. Lindley met a woman there, Grace Carter: she was twenty years old, gorgeous, and effervescent, and raced her way into a spot on the Olympic squad.

The U.S. Men's Alpine Ski Team for the 1936 Winter Olympics in Garmisch-Partenkirchen, Germany. *From left:* Link Washburn, Al Lindley, Alec Bright, Tony Page, Darroch Crookes, Dick Durrance, and Bob Livermore.

Carter lived in Seattle but had Midwestern roots. Her father, who had long since passed away, had been a Rough Rider with Teddy Roosevelt and a lawyer in Chicago. Traveling to Ashland, Wisconsin, for work, Carter's father became acquainted with a local woman, married her, and brought her back to Chicago, where Grace was born. A predisposition to alcoholism ran in the Carter family genes, and Grace's father was no exception. One night he was walking the streets of Chicago when a vehicle struck and killed him. Carter's mother contracted tuberculosis, and a doctor advised her to move to a western climate to improve her chance of survival. She moved to Seattle and lived with her sister on a houseboat (it's hard to imagine the dank air of the Seattle harbor is what the doctor ordered). At the age of seven, Grace was sent to the Illinois Soldiers' Orphans' Home in Normal, Illinois. The state had opened the home for Civil War orphans, and by the time Grace was there the kids earned their room and board by doing domestic chores and farmwork for area families. The children spent a lot of time outside, and Grace discovered she had talent for sports such as gymnastics and riding horses. She ran away from the orphanage once, but the police caught her, and she spent the night in jail.

Her mother eventually recovered. When Grace was fourteen, she left the orphanage and moved to the houseboat with her mother and aunt. They were quite poor, driven by necessity to steal logs from Weyerhaeuser company log drives in the harbor. They'd finagle a log back to their houseboat and chop it up for stove wood. Grace Carter was strong and wild. Whenever she saw horses, which were still common around Seattle in those days, she had to jump up on one. For kicks, she once dove off the high bridge spanning the harbor. One night she

Grace Carter Lindley, 1930s.

and a friend paddled a canvas canoe in the dark and raided an anchored schooner that was to be scrapped. Carter climbed aboard the ship, stole its steering wheel and bell, and carefully lowered the liberated objects into the canoe bobbing below in the black water.

Carter learned to ski on Mount Rainier and had been at it only a couple of years when she made the Olympic team. She and Lindley shared an adventurous streak. Although Lindley wasn't fast enough to make the team and was a dozen years Carter's senior, he was wealthy, well traveled, and suave. When Lindley told Carter about the polo ponies he owned and stabled at Fort Snelling, well, for Carter the horse lover, that wasn't exactly a turnoff. They married in 1937.

🌲

Minnesota became the first state in the nation to sponsor skiing as an official high school sport, in 1932, when the large Scandinavian population in the state's northeastern corner, a region of boreal forest and rocky lakes dubbed the Arrowhead for its angular southern border made by the shore of Lake Superior, prompted the first regional Arrowhead High School Ski Meet. The tournament was held in Duluth's Chester Park and offered jumping only and included teams from Duluth, Coleraine, Virginia, and Cloquet. Chester Park, also called Chester Bowl, was situated in a notch

GRACE CARTER'S OLYMPIC VOYAGE

Grace Carter left Seattle onboard an apple freighter on November 30, 1935, bound for the 1936 Winter Olympics in Garmisch-Partenkirchen, Germany. The *Oregon Express* was a 338-foot-long Norwegian vessel heading for Europe via the Panama Canal. In this era before transatlantic flights, Carter and three other members of the U.S. Ski Team had a month's journey to Europe. Woebegone Seattle of the 1930s bore little resemblance to the monied metropolis it is today. After months of fundraising for her alpine racing efforts, Carter still needed more money, so she mailed dispatches to the *Seattle Star* from ports along the way.

"The chic imp of ski-dom," as the *Star* described Carter, slept alone on the ship's deck. She did calisthenics and jumped rope in the morning with her fellow skiers, Don Fraser and the sisters Ellis and Ethlynne Smith. After a week they reached the tropics. Carter ran laps around the deck and climbed the ship's rigging. She spent her days on ship barefoot and put on an old pair of blue cords and a ragged kerchief.

Grace Carter and her teammates rode the *Oregon Express,* a Norwegian fruit freighter, from Seattle to Europe in 1935. The ship was sunk by a German U-boat in 1943.

in the hills above Lake Superior on Duluth's east side. The Duluth Ski Club had been jumping here since the first decade of the century. Greenway High School in Coleraine won the meet, led by Harry Tregillis, who would soon move to Red Wing and participate in the 1936 national tournament with the Aurora.

At the next year's tournament, the Minnesota State High School League, the governing body of the state's high school sports, added a cross-country race. Coleraine again won jumping, this time led by Gene Wilson, who would go on to have a long national career, but Duluth Central won the cross-country race and edged out Coleraine to win the overall tournament. For the next twenty years, Duluth Central would be the state's winningest team, with Coleraine a distant second.

The MSHSL reported in its 1934 annual yearbook: "Due to the increased interest in Skiing, the First State Meet will be held at Duluth on Saturday,

She knit herself a sweater and helped the crew ("good-natured, blue-eyed, tow-headed Vikings. But so very painfully bashful") scrub and paint the decks. The nights were warm and breezy. Carter sat in the bow with "moonlight simply drenching everything." A white silver path led from the moon to the ship. "Wish I could sing like a prima donna!" Carter said, before putting on a lacy pink satin nightgown. The poor girl from the houseboat felt like a queen. "Hurrah for skiing!" she extolled.

On December 30 the *Express* docked in La Havre, France. Carter continued overland to Germany. Ultimately, she was left off the four-woman racing squad and didn't compete in the Winter Games. She sold the expensive pair of skis that her beau Al Lindley had given her and used the proceeds to prolong her stay in Europe. She bought herself a pair of cheaper skis, raced in the European circuit, and placed well. When she returned home to Seattle, the editor of the *Star* refused to pay her for her dispatches, claiming that her amateur athlete status precluded her from earning money from skiing. ⚶

After the 1936 Olympics, Grace Carter lingered in Europe to race on the European circuit. Here she wears her Olympic team sweater in Austria.

February 17." This motion transformed the regional Arrowhead meet into the state meet.

Two years later, Reuben Silvola from Virginia was the first non-Duluthian to win the cross-country run. Just a couple of weeks earlier, Silvola had taken sixth in the cross-country nationals at Red Wing. He would go on to ski with the Wisconsin Hoofers, the venerable outdoors club at the University of Wisconsin that had been modeled after the Dartmouth Outing Club. Even after the meet had been expanded to include the entire state, all participating schools were from the northeastern corner of Minnesota, with Hibbing, Ely, and Grand Rapids joining the roster of competitors in 1937.

1932 COLERAINE SKI TEAM

This squad from Greenway High School won the first Minnesota high school state ski meet, which involved jumping only. Harry Tregillis stands at right. Eugene Wilson (*seated right*) had first honed his skills while homebound during a flu pandemic in 1923. Coached by Ole Mangseth, Wilson would win the national Class B title in 1936, make the U.S. Olympic Ski Team in 1940 (though the Olympics would be canceled for war), and be named captain of the U.S. Ski Team in 1950.

Coached by the legendary Victor Dunder, Duluth Central took top honors in cross-country and jumping during the 1933 Arrowhead High School Ski Meet.

By 1939, fifteen schools, including Minneapolis Washburn and Minneapolis North, Red Wing, and St. Paul Mechanic Arts, competed. Washburn did well for a downstate school by taking second in jumping. One hundred boys competed in the jumping portion of the meet, while eighteen signed on for the cross-country race. For the first time, the new sport of slalom was included, completing the three-way ski lineup that would last at the state meet for almost forty years. Duluth Central won the jumping title back from Coleraine. In twenty-first place, jumping for Ely, was Sigurd Olson Jr., son of the famed writer and conservationist. Duluth Central skiers swept the top five places in the cross-country race.

In 1940, the state meet left Duluth for the first time and moved to Theodore Wirth Park in Minneapolis. The top two finishers from each school determined the team's score in a particular event. Minneapolis North placed first in slalom, followed by Duluth Central, which was led by a sophomore named in MSHSL records as Charles Bankii. Bankii placed sixth in cross-country that year. The next year, back at Theodore Wirth Park, the results listed Bankii as Charles Bankui, when he took second in cross-country. In 1942, his senior year, Bankui won the state cross-country title. Minneapolis North won the overall meet. This was the first time a non-Arrowhead school won the state title. Thirty years would pass, with the world a very different place, before greater Minnesota would reclaim the state ski title.

Charles Bankui joined the navy after graduating from high school and shipped off to the Pacific. Following World War II, he settled in Clover Valley, north of Duluth, and cleared his own ski trail system with an ax.

Wisconsin Hoofers
15th
Annual

Ski Meet

Official Central Ski
Association Meet

Jumping Tournament-Muir Knoll
2:00 p. m. Sunday, Feb. 2
Admission 50c.

DOWNHILL SLALOM AT CROSS PLAINS
10:30 a. m. Sunday, Feb. 2

Cross-country skiing over an 8 mile course, starting at the Union.
2:00 p. m. Saturday, Feb. 1

Some of the best skiers in the nation competed with the University of Wisconsin Hoofers club. The club hosted jumping contests on its ski slide in Madison, named Muir Knoll after the pioneering conservationist John Muir, who attended the school.

He would become known and loved by generations of skiers as Charlie Banks, and today a relay race at the state meet bears his name—but much was to pass before then. Charlie Banks came up as a boy in Duluth learning to ski by chasing after the founders of the Midwest's richest and oldest enduring cross-country legacy.

Neighboring Wisconsin took note of Minnesota's high school league and held its first state skiing meet in 1939, in Rosholt, a village east of Stevens Point. Sixty-four skiers competed. "A very fine start had been made to introduce skiing into the public schools in Wisconsin. It is expected many schools will hold meets next year," reported the NSA's regional mouthpiece, the *Central Ski Sport*. The Wisconsin Interscholastic Athletic Association, the governing body for high school sports in the state, did not oversee this tournament, so it is unclear which entity executed the Stevens Point meet and for how many years, if any, it continued. Wisconsin would sanction high school skiing, and only downhill at that, for a relatively brief window beginning in 1958. Michigan schools had yet to foray into organized skiing competition, though they would, beginning in the late 1940s.

🌲

Duluthians Peter Fosseide and Erik Judeen, who respectively took runner-up and third place in the Red Wing 1936 national cross-country championships, became friends in Duluth in the early 1930s. Their skiing rivalry would push Midwestern cross-country to new levels. Finding no cross-country trails in Duluth, they made their own around Hartley Park, St. Scholastica University, and Chester Bowl. The *Duluth News-Tribune* dubbed them the "Damon and Pythias of the ski trails,"

Washburn High School skiers Gordon Egsgaard *(left)* and Henry Hansen (son of famous jumper Hans Hansen) took top honors in the 1940 Minneapolis high school ski championships.

referring to an ideal of friendship stemming from a Greek myth. They were both Norwegian immigrants who loved to ski, but their personalities could not have been more different.

Judeen was born in 1902 in Oslo and lived near Holmenkollen hill. His father was an illegitimate child who came from Sweden to escape the condescension that was his birthright. Judeen's family didn't ski, but he took it up as a boy. When he was twenty-six, he immigrated to Duluth, where his older brother lived. He later told his family that he left Norway because he was in financial and legal trouble. Judeen was about five foot nine, had dark wavy hair that he wore a little long, and liked to dress sharp. A Duluth newspaper once referred to him as "Brother Curley Judeen." Initially he worked in the shipyards before becoming a union heat and frost insulator

Peter Fosseide *(left)* and Erik Judeen at the top of Chester Bowl with their jumping skis.

with the Walker Jamar Company, an extant century-old construction company that built much of Duluth. His job was wrapping pipes in asbestos.

A widow named Olga Olson ran a boardinghouse where Norwegian immigrants lived. Her husband and son had both died at the Nopeming tuberculosis hospital south of town. Her daughter, Doris, had the disease, too, but refused to go to the hospital where her father and brother had perished. Doris stayed home with her mother and would live until 1986. She was a junior in high school when she met the dapper, hard-drinking Judeen, nine years her senior. Doris had emigrated from rural Trondheim when she was just two years old and spoke Norwegian in an older, countrified style compared to the urbanite Judeen. Judeen found this funny, and after the couple married, had three daughters, and quit speaking Norwegian in their home, Judeen still sometimes teased Doris about having what he considered a farmer's accent.

The Judeens lived on First Street, beneath Enger Hill, a prominence on the basaltic ridge that framed Duluth. Judeen worked long hours during the week and trained on the weekend. He'd ski up Enger Hill and then to a golf course on the other side, where he would ski a couple of laps. Enger Hill was rugged and mostly treeless, with stone outcroppings and cliffs. The Judeen home had a view of the hill from its living room window, through which Judeen's youngest daughter, Julie, liked to watch her father ski home. Judeen picked his way down the precipitous slope, carving Telemark turns and jumping off ledges on his hickory Northland skis with simple metal and leather bindings. His leather boots were uninsulated, and Julie remembered her father returning home and warming his feet in the kitchen. Here he'd apply pine tar to the bases of his Northlands, and the piney scent would linger for days.

When Julie was just a few years old, she and her dad walked together all the way to a ski competition at Chester Bowl. Judeen was fun to be with, except when he was in his cups, and as he got older, his drinking worsened. By the time Julie was growing up, his best racing days were behind him, and he didn't take her out skiing like he had done with his older girls. When Judeen was drunk, he'd get a nasty mouth. He might pick a fight in a bar with someone bigger than him and get beat up. Occasionally, he'd get arrested. Julie believed her father drank because he missed Norway. He would spend more of his life in Duluth than in Oslo, but he always longed to return. Skiing was an element of his homeland that he could live out in Minnesota. He'd tell his future son-in-law, who would marry the daughter

Tournaments at Chester Park were a leading attraction in Duluth in the decades before World War II. Erik Judeen and Peter Fosseide were at the heart of the thriving Chester Park scene, shown here in the 1940s.

who inherited Judeen's pure athleticism, that when he was cross-country racing, he wasn't satisfied with his performance unless he was coughing up blood by the end of the race.

Judeen's friend and competitor Pete Fosseide was in many ways his opposite. Fosseide was born in 1906 in Rindal, south of Trondheim. Even for Norway, Rindal was a skiing hot spot, with Landsem and later Troll ski companies operating in the town. Fosseide started skiing when he was four and regarded himself an average skier by Norwegian standards. He left Norway for Duluth when he was seventeen or eighteen. While Judeen washed off the flecks of asbestos after work and changed into something snazzy, Fosseide often kept on his white housepainter's suit when the families socialized. Fosseide had two daughters about the same age as Judeen's two older girls. While Judeen was smaller and wiry, Fosseide was five foot ten and weighed more than two hundred pounds. With softer features and an aw-shucks grin, Fosseide wasn't dashing like Judeen. Whereas Judeen's temperament went dark, Fosseide was light-hearted and positive. It's no surprise which of the friends would outlive the other by nearly forty years.

In the late 1930s, Fosseide and Judeen were in their prime, usually claiming the top two spots in ski tournaments as they traveled the Midwest with the Duluth Ski Club. The ski scene in Duluth was booming. George Kotlarek had brought Class A glory back to the city for the first time since the era of the yumping Oles. Most every Saturday and Sunday at Chester Park, one hundred or more boys would walk to the bowl in the morning and spend the day jumping. There was little organization or formal coaching, and adult supervision was minimal. The rich kids came from the east side of town and the poor kids from Central Hillside. They'd ski all day and return home for dinner exhausted.

Skiing cross-country, though, was not a motivator for these young jumpers. Flying one hundred feet off a jump was doubtlessly cooler than scooting around the woods at a few miles per hour. Fosseide and Judeen were skilled jumpers but practiced cross-country with at least as much discipline, a highly unusual approach. They had developed a loop trail out of Chester Bowl that followed Chester Creek upstream, crossed under Kenwood Avenue through a culvert, and looped around St. Scholastica.

George Hovland grew up as a Chester Bowl boy emulating Fosseide and Judeen. Born in 1926, the future Olympian could tell when Judeen had skied the loop recently because Judeen always marked the trail with dark splashes of spit stained from the wad of tobacco he packed in his cheek. "You had to be careful trying to pass Erik," Hovland said; Judeen was not only skiing fast but frequently spitting. Hovland remembered Fosseide as a big man. "Never heard a cross word uttered by that man. Everything about him was fun." Hovland told Duluth outdoor writer Sam Cook, "I remember learning how to ski by skiing along behind him. I looked to see where his poles went in the snow and tried to put mine in the same holes. If he skated around a turn, I thought that must be the way to do it." Hovland described Fosseide's technique as musical. "He just kind of floats along—his whole body. The way he moves is kind of a rhythmic, swinging kind of singing thing."

Hovland grew up a block from Chester Bowl and was inevitably drawn to its ski contests. Unbeknownst to him, the skiers were often handed cups of blueberry soup as a refreshment as they raced, some of which splashed on their clothes. Hovland figured the soup stains were blood. "Oh, what a terrible sport," he thought. "I'm never going to do that."

In the 1930s and 1940s, a day at Duluth's Chester Bowl promised skiing thrills for competitors and spectators.

♣

In January 1937, Fosseide and Judeen traveled to Minneapolis to the Bush Lake Ski Club's home course for a rematch with reigning national cross-country champion Carl Sundquist. Judeen won the twelve-mile race with a time of 57:28. Fosseide was less than a minute behind, and Al Lindley finished in third place, with Sundquist in fifth.

A year later, on January 22, 1938, Fosseide and Judeen were back in Minneapolis for the national cross-country championship race, again hosted by the Bush Lake club. David Bradley, from Madison, trounced the competition. A promising young jumper, Bradley had left the Midwest to go off to college at Dartmouth, where that year he was captain of the Dartmouth Outing Club's ski team, leading phenomenal skiers like Dick Durrance and Warren Chivers, who skied on the 1936 Olympic team and won the national cross-country title in 1937. Although Bradley remained in New England, where he graduated from Harvard Medical School after Dartmouth and became a surgeon, best-selling author, and U.S. congressman, he would stay involved, along with his father and brother, with the Central Division. Adrian Watt, a future Olympic jumper who came up as a Chester Bowl

Members of Al Lindley's Bush Lake Ski Club race on their home course in 1937.

boy in the 1950s and 1960s, recalled traveling to Madison as a kid and congregating with other skiers in a dark old house where they were hosted by an older, absent-minded-professor-type man who wore a tweed jacket and goofy beaded belt that looked like it'd been made at summer camp. Only upon reflection later in life would Watt note the significance of having hung out with David Bradley at the family's Louis Sullivan–designed mansion, which was later designated a National Historic Landmark for its architectural significance.

Bradley beat Fosseide in the 1938 cross-country national competition by a full five minutes. Sundquist was four minutes behind Fosseide, with Judeen in fourth. Two of Al Lindley's nephews finished in the top ten, Lindley Burton in fifth, and fifteen-year-old John Burton in tenth place. That a fifteen-year-old placed so high in the national championship race speaks to the shallow pool of competitors.

Skiing aces Warren Chivers (left) and Dick Durrance of the Dartmouth Outing Club in Minneapolis in 1937 before a competitive meet at the Bush Lake jump.

John and Lindley Burton were the sons of Al Lindley's sister. Lindley would give up competitive skiing for academia, but John would eventually represent his country with George Hovland in the Olympics. A friend of the Burton boys, Bradley Board, finished just ahead of John. Unlike the wealthy Burtons, Board grew up on a small farm in Deephaven (the town had been named by the Burton family). Board's father was too busy, in the words of a grandson, planting crops and butchering chickens to indulge in something as frivolous as skiing, so Board hung out with the Burton boys and joined them for Sunday races put on by the Bush Lake club. Board won one of these races and received a new pair of skis as a prize. He would go on to spend his career in the ski industry. After flying a P-38 reconnaissance plane during World War II, Board settled in Squaw Valley, near Lake Tahoe. He almost certainly would have known Lars and Anders Haugen. He bought a surplus World War II M29 Weasel, a tracked vehicle designed for snow travel, and used it to become a pioneer in ski trail grooming.

🌲

Representing the Wisconsin Hoofers, former Minnesota state champ Reuben Silvola had finished in sixth place in the 1938 national cross-country race, just behind Lindley Burton. Less than a week later, Silvola and Fosseide faced off again, this time in one of the Midwest's most unusual and ambitious ski races. The Arrowhead Derby of 1938 happened in conjunction with the St. Paul Winter Carnival and ran 153 miles from Duluth to St. Paul over five days. The winner would receive $150, while the runner-up and third-place finisher would take home $75 and $50, respectively.

Eleven-year-old George Hovland was in the crowd of three hundred spectators who had gathered in front of the Duluth Civic Center at noon on January 28 to watch the fifteen Arrowhead Derby racers set out. The local paper claimed it was the "longest jaunt in the history of the sport." The Arrowhead Derby was decisively not a jaunt, but the word accomplished the effect of making the racers seem extraordinarily savvy. The derby would be front-page news for the *Duluth News-Tribune* for the next five days.

A bizarre story soon appeared in both the Duluth and Twin Cities papers, headlined in the *Duluth News-Tribune* as "Wanted to Enter Arrowhead Derby; Buys Skis with Forged Check; Youth is Held in St. Paul Jail, Identity Unknown." Dubbed "Nells of Norway," a young man told police a story that seems the product of a manic episode. Claiming to be Nells Jorhenson of Norway, the man told a delusional story of jumping ship in Kentucky as a four-year-old to obtain an American education. Nells had no Norwegian accent and spoke proper English with a slight southern drawl. He claimed he roamed the country, attending aviation school and working at a logging camp, as an orderly in San Francisco, and as a farmhand. His dream was to become a bacteriologist. He also wanted to ski the Arrowhead Derby. After using a forged check to successfully buy a diamond ring in St. Cloud for a girl he was courting in Minneapolis, he was caught in the latter city using

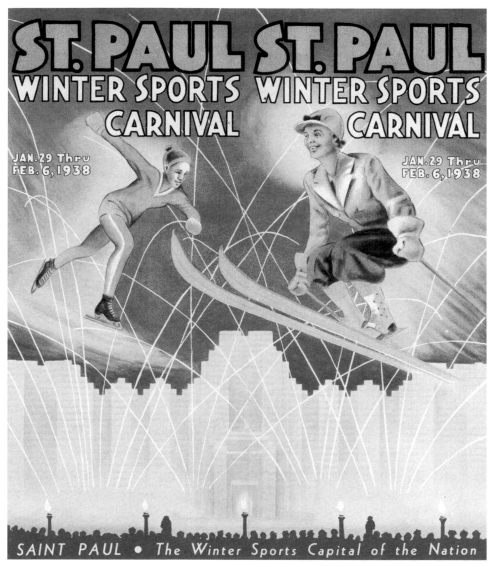

Winter thrills on skis and ice skates adorned the program of the 1938 St. Paul Winter Carnival. A much-anticipated carnival highlight was the Arrowhead Derby, a cross-country race of 153 miles held over five days.

a bad check to buy a pair of skis. "He is confident," the article stated, "that if his arrest had not interfered, he would have been a winner in the derby."

The skiers strode away from Duluth's city hall and made their way west to Skyline Parkway. The plan had been to ski through Jay Cooke State Park before reaching the hamlet of Carlton, where they would stay the night before embarking on the second stage of the race. Skiing along the rugged

Entrants in the 1938 Arrowhead Derby left Duluth for St. Paul at one-minute intervals. Here, Billy Anderson departs the Zenith City as mayor C. R. Berghult fires the starting gun under the watch of King Boreas and Winter Carnival officials.

St. Louis River in Jay Cooke would have been a more picturesque course, but, as Fosseide recalled, recorded in his Norwegian brogue by Sam Cook in the 1980s, "Der was supposed to be a trail in Yay Cooke Park, but it wasn't open. Den dey told us to take de road." Fosseide was fifth to start the race but soon took the lead. He reached Esko and stopped to have a cup of coffee. "Aren't dose guys coming?" he wondered. He was using a new pair of hickory Northland skis with a deep groove running down the middle of its base. According to Hovland, the Northlands were not light but they were strong.

The only non-Minnesotan racing was Joe Maurin, a Finn from Iron-wood, Michigan, who skied with the Gogebic Range Ski Club. On the front page of the *Duluth News-Tribune,* plastered with Arrowhead Derby stories, one dispatch titled "Skier Battled Big Drifts to Succor Stranded Pair" detailed how, just a few days earlier, Maurin had skied through a blizzard to bring food to stranded Works Progress Administration workers. As the countdown drew down on the noon start of the derby, the paper reported that Maurin "was more interested in testing his skis and getting ready for the start than in telling of his hour and a half battle against the storm to reach the men." Yet Maurin managed to relate how he'd struggled through fifty-mile-per-hour wind and two miles of heavy snow to deliver food to the WPA workers stranded succorless on a small ski hill called Mount Zion. Then, like any good gearhead, Maurin spent the rest of the interview talking about his skis, which were made of birchwood imported from Finland. His specially made boots featured leather horns on the toes that fit into apertures in his customized binding straps.

Racers from the St. Paul and Bush Lake clubs also participated in the derby. There was a lone skier from Chisago City and another listed as being from Brainerd. The Brainerd skier was Harold Moe, the cabin builder and suitor by ski, who by this time had moved permanently to Lutsen.

Fosseide arrived first in Carlton, followed by Hartwig Strand from Bush Lake and Hilding Swenson, another Duluthian. The field narrowed to twelve skiers. Bob Miklya, an eighteen-year-old from Chisago City, dropped out because of a broken binding. Charles Bauer, of the St. Paul Ski Club, got lost during the day and didn't make it to Carlton. Another St. Paul skier, Louis Soukup, apparently stopped to color the snow shades unnatural, ending his derby run short of Carlton due to what the paper labeled "only a minor stomach ailment."

The next day's leg to Willow River was longer, a little over thirty miles. Skiers left Carlton at 9:40 a.m. Reuben Silvola edged out Fosseide for the day by exactly three minutes, though Fosseide remained in the overall lead. "I got tired of breaking trail, so I waited for dose udder guys," Fosseide said. Another St. Paul skier, Harold Runyan, dropped out with a bad back.

The third day was a tough one. Skiers struggled through fresh snow and subzero temperatures for the thirty-nine miles to Pine City. Fosseide came in sixth for the day. "Even if you don't ski hard," he said, "if you ski fifty miles in a day you take out a lot of stuff. Like wearing down a battery." St. Paulite Harold Raak won the day with a time of seven and a half hours, cutting Fosseide's overall lead to six minutes ahead of Hilding Swenson. Raak's clubmate Joe Gould dropped out in the morning, leaving ten racers. Erwin Gerald, another St. Paul skier, complained of a frozen neck. "However," the paper reported, "it was only frostbite."

While Peter Fosseide blew past the competition during the 1938 Arrowhead Derby, his cousin, Magnar Fosseide, was tearing up cross-country races around Europe.

The snow cover thinned as the skiers neared St. Paul. "The conditions were, in a word, shitty," George Hovland said. But Fosseide came alive on the thirty-five-mile stretch to Wyoming, Minnesota, and doubled his lead to twelve minutes. The snow was patchy, and skiers looked for unbroken expanses in the ditches, shoulders, fields, and yards. That night in Wyoming, the racers were given a big dinner and a chance to shower. "We had to look good coming into Saint Paul," Fosseide told Cook. Indeed, in photographs of the final day, Fosseide raced sporting a clean-shaven face and a tie. The *Pioneer Press* featured a photograph of Fosseide leading, followed closely by Hilding Swenson, Hartwig Strand, and Reuben Silvola, as they skied down a spectator-lined Highway 61 in White Bear Lake. A police escort met the racers as they entered St. Paul and led them over the Third Street Viaduct to Kellogg Boulevard and the finish line at Washington Avenue. Fosseide maintained his lead to win the first and only Arrowhead Derby. Greeted by the St. Paul Winter Carnival's King Boreas and his entourage, the ten finishing skiers headed to a party at the St. Paul Auditorium.

The poor snow had taken its toll—the base of Fosseide's new hickory Northlands had been worn to the quick, with the deep central grooves completely worn away. He'd skied twenty-eight hours and forty-four minutes over five days, or a little less than six hours a day.

Interestingly, the Duluth morning news had reported that a woman, Mae Lundsten, with the Oconomowoc Ski Club of Milwaukee, would be racing the Arrowhead Derby, though nothing more was mentioned of her. It is unclear if she was prohibited from participating because of her gender or if the report was erroneous to begin with. In a singular turn of events that same winter, the state of Wisconsin hosted a smattering of women's cross-country and jumping contests. The Chippewa Falls Ski Club hosted a women's race won by Ruth Frankenberg from Cameron, Wisconsin, followed by two women from the Eau Claire club, Lucille Loken and Mae Roach. The Hayward Out Door Sports Club held a girls' race won by Donaldeen Hovland; Frankenberg took second and Tootie Severson third.

In the mid-1930s, the Norge Ski Club of Chicago continued its history of gender progressivism when it invited a Norwegian woman named Johanne Kolstad to demonstrate her jumping skills on a national tour. Women were not allowed to jump

A victorious Peter Fosseide grins for the camera after winning the first (and only) Arrowhead Derby.

Bert Strong (*left*) and Spencer Snaith prepare for a day of skiing at a small ski club in Rhinelander, Wisconsin, 1940.

competitively in Norway either, but for a few seasons Kolstad traveled the United States to give exhibitions. She performed in front of twenty thousand people at Fox Hill, the Norge club's jump near Chicago, and jumped Suicide Hill in Ishpeming, but never as a competitor. Kolstad jumped the Hoofer club's Muir Knoll as well. The Hoofer club notably had several female jumpers. Wisconsin politics at the time, fueled by Fighting Bob LaFollette, were among the most progressive in the nation, and perhaps this climate enabled women's competitive jumping when it was discouraged, if not expressly prohibited, elsewhere.

Natalie Bailey, born in Minneapolis in 1916, was an ambitious jumper who struggled to enter tournaments. She was an athletic child who endlessly irritated her mother by doing physical stunts like jumping with her ice skates over kids lying prostrate on the ice. She did not come from a skiing family, but when she was seven her father made her a pair of skis.

By the mid-1930s Bailey was jumping with the Bush Lake Ski Club. In 1936, she sent a letter to Lloyd Ellingson, a former Olympic skier from Colfax, Wisconsin, who was teaching at St. Olaf College and managing the annual Northfield ski tournament. Bailey announced her intention to jump in the upcoming tournament. She sent a similar letter in advance of a tournament in Devil's Lake, North Dakota, where she became the first woman to jump the Devil's Lake Hill. She

Bush Lake Ski Club member and aspiring Olympic jumper Natalie Bailey lugs her skis up the hill at Glenwood Park in Minneapolis, 1937.

also jumped in tournaments at Coleraine and Duluth. Her longest career leap was 135 feet. Bailey, however, was relegated to jumping as an exhibitioner and was never allowed to compete. Her dream was to jump in the Olympics, but this would not be a possibility for women for a surprisingly long time.

In 1938, at a tournament at Chester Park, Bailey met a spectator from Wisconsin named Joe Gammey. The pair married before Gammey went to war. Upon his return, they had a daughter and moved to Southern California. Bailey made her last jump there in the 1950s and became an avid downhill skier at Big Bear resort.

🌲

Later in 1938, the Central Ski Association, the regional division of the NSA, formed a committee to increase interest in cross-country skiing. Peter Fosseide was the Minnesota representative on the committee, which included a man from each of the three other Midwestern states that made up the Central Division: Harold C. Bradley of Madison; A. M. Gimse of Minot, North Dakota; and C. L. Peters of Munising, Michigan. Bradley, a prominent physician, was father of the reigning national cross-country champ, David Bradley, and had founded the Hoofers club as well as building a ski jump on his property in Madison.

The committee sent questionnaires about cross-country skiing to its fifty-five Central Division clubs. Only four of the fifty-five had been active in cross-country. The St. Paul Ski Club had held a short race in which several boys and girls participated, as well as a longer twenty-five-mile race. In Munising, the local club conducted a youth Nordic combined tournament, in which three of the twenty-eight contestants had been girls. The Bush Lake Ski Club, which had fostered a relatively thriving cross-country scene, staged six Sunday morning races with between fifteen and twenty racers. "In spite of general lack of interest in this form of skiing in the Midwest," the committee reported, "we feel . . . that increased interest is certain to follow."

The *Central Ski Sport*, the publication of the Central Division, laid out the cross-country committee's

Wearing standard ski attire for the era, Erik Judeen and Pete Fosseide stand in front of Fosseide's cabin in Finland, Minnesota. The men were likely grooming a ski trail, with Fosseide on snowshoes tamping down the snow and Judeen following behind on skis and putting in the track.

strategy to turn their athletes into contenders: "The
purpose is to . . . give us better representation in international competition, based on
a sound foundation of wide
participation at home." The
committee went on to state
that American jumpers and
downhill skiers could compete internationally, but "Our
langlauf men are few and lag
far behind the competence
of their European competitors. And in the Central Division there are practically no
langlauf runners except in
the northern part." *Langlauf,*
or *langlaufer,* was a German
word that literally meant
"long run" and, in the 1920s,
had become a synonym to
denote cross-country skiing
or a cross-country skier.

An unknown skier competes in the national cross-country championship hosted by the Bush Lake Ski Club in January 1938. The rough
track through thin snow cover and unkempt vegetation made for a
slow course.

Early in 1939, Fosseide and the Duluth Ski Club put on a cross-country
ski school that attracted 150 students. The school's culmination was a sort
of gonzo circuit—a local businessman had bet Fosseide to ski through the
night. Fresh off his prior year's win at the Arrowhead Derby, Fosseide carried a well-earned mythology about his endurance. He was joined by a Professor Nilsen and Harold Grinden, president of the Duluth Ski Club. The
trio set out skiing through the night, navigating initially by moonlight and
then switching to flashlight and gas lamp after the moon set. As they skied,
Grinden reported, Fosseide and Nilsen argued in Norwegian. Grinden was
American born, and though he could follow the gist of the conversation
(Fosseide and the professor were debating whether they should follow
through with the nighttime ski), the details were beyond him. Halfway
through the ski, the flashlight and gas lamp both died. Well into the long

ski, Nilsen began loudly singing a song about Holmenkollen. Nilsen's "song reverberated from crag to crest, the wolves ceased their howling and broke for the deep timber," Grinden joked. A kernel of some greater truth about skiing lay in this anecdote—that is, skiing through the cold woods at night, tired and lacking light, these skiers did not despair but took to song, in an example of the alchemy that skiing can be; it turned the cold dark woods into something warm and humorous. Though the three skiers were Norwegian, this was pure *sisu*, the Finnish concept of mental perseverance.

♠

Paul Bietila from Ishpeming was one of six brothers known as the Flying Bietilas. A family of Finnish miners, the Bietila boys were all skilled jumpers. One of the brothers, Walter, would go on to make three Olympic teams, but in 1939, Walter's little brother Paul was the one everyone was watching. In 1931, at the age of twelve, Paul had jumped 185 feet and set a

new record for youth jumping. In 1938, representing the University of Wisconsin Hoofers, he'd won first place in the International Intercollegiate Ski Meet in Brattleboro, Vermont. That same year he came in third behind another set of famed ski jumping brothers, Norwegians Sigmund and Birger Ruud, the latter of whom had twice won Olympic gold. Paul Bietila had the potential to win on an international scale.

At the 1939 national jumping championships in St. Paul on February 5, during a warmup off the Battle Creek jump, twenty-year-old Paul Bietila crashed into a metal object—either a post or a barrel—demarcating the edge of the landing area. Rushed to a nearby

The Flying Bietilas of Ishpeming at Iron Mountain, Michigan, in the 1940s. *From left:* brothers Len, Roy, Ralph, and Walter.

Norwegian-born Minneapolis resident Hans Hansen had a storied jumping career by the time he turned forty in 1930. Instead of settling into middle age, he began wowing spectators at tournaments with flips. In 1938, before a crowd of fifteen thousand, he executed a forward somersault at Glenwood Park.

hospital, Paul hung on for three weeks before dying from pneumonia on February 26.

The national tournament marked the demise of another jumping icon. As Barney Riley, the Wild Irish Rose, was leaving his hotel in Grand Rapids, Minnesota, to drive to St. Paul to watch the contest, he steered twice into some snowbanks adjacent to the parking lot. A bystander was curious and went to

assist. Riley was fallen over the wheel, gasping and struggling for breath. The bystander found help, and the men dragged Riley into a neighboring building and summoned a doctor, but Riley was dead. He'd had an earlier heart attack just two weeks before. He was forty-nine years old. The local paper's headline mourned: "Barney Riley, Only Irish Ski Rider, Will Never More Watch Great Sport In Which He Became Famous."

Dressed in impeccable ski couture, Minneapolis jumper Natalie Bailey poses while on a touring excursion in the 1930s.

As cross-country boosters worked on advancing their sport, jumping continued to be a mainstream popular sport throughout the northern United States. In addition to jumping for the University of Wisconsin Hoofers, Olympian Walter Bietila was a star baseball player for the university team. In June, he turned down an offer to try out for a major league team in New York so that he could focus on jumping.

Downhill skiing was coming into its own and before long would displace jumping at the top of the skiing hierarchy. The world's first chairlift had begun hauling skiers up Proctor Mountain in Sun Valley, Idaho, in 1936. For the first time, in early 1939, a European women's ski team traveled to the United States to compete in the NSA's downhill and slalom championships on Mount Hood. Women's skiing, however, would not progress in a clean upward arc. Women would continue to be excluded from the jumping scenes that thrived throughout the Midwest. Girls and women would also be absent from cross-country racing, which would continue to putter along as a niche activity until the late sixties. Even in downhill skiing, with its luxurious ethos more in line with society's ideas of what was suitable for females, women athletes would see pushback in the era of post–World War II America.

Improved technology was advancing all aspects of skiing. In October 1935, Norwegian Bjorn Ullevoldsæter patented a new design for a laminated ski. Laminated skis had been around since the early twentieth century, including one that consisted of a strip of ash for the gliding surface topped by a strip of willow or alder. These early laminates were prompted by a shortage of ash wood but serendipitously proved to be stronger, lighter, and faster. They had significant problems, however. With one strip of wood layered over another, the strips didn't match perfectly. Of greater concern, traditional carpenter's glue was not strong enough to withstand the wetness and rigorous flexing that accompanied skiing. Kaurit glue changed all that. Developed by Dr. Hanns Klemm, a German plane builder who had worked on zeppelins, the synthetic resin made the modern wooden ski possible.

In Ullevoldsæter's patented design, the ski base consisted of eight vertical strips "standing on their edges like miniature beams," wrote ski historian Roland Huntford. A single layer of thin hardwood made the top of the ski. Coats of Kaurit fused

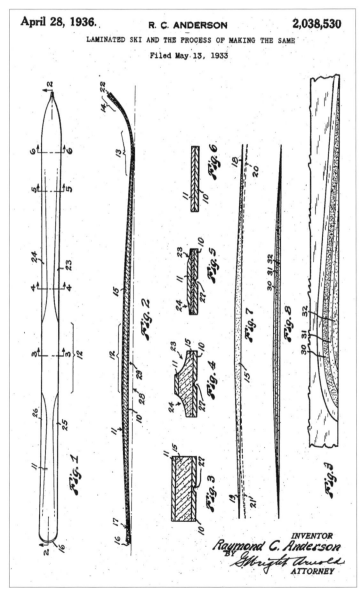

The new patented process of laminating vertical strips of wood revolutionized ski making in the 1930s.

VISIT **IRON MOUNTAIN - KINGSFORD**
NORTHERN MICHIGAN'S WINTER PLAYGROUND

This advertisement for popular Flexible Flyer skis appeared around the country and was customized for ski areas like Iron Mountain, Michigan.

the combined pieces into a ski that was lighter, stronger, more flexible, and more uniform than a traditional solid wood ski.

The ski that became the standard came in 1937 from another Norwegian, Peter Østbye. Østbye had been licensing Ullevoldsæter's design until he furthered it by making the individual elements of the composites into composites themselves. The product was called Splitkein. American ski magazines of the late thirties were filled with ads for Flexible Flyer skis. Flexible Flyer was a snow sled company in Philadelphia that branched out into skis and licensed Østbye's Splitkein for sale in the United States. Flexible Flyer skis would remain popular until metal skis supplanted them in the 1950s.

These advancements were the death knell for old-fashioned ski makers like Martin Strand. In late 1940, Strand sold his ownership of the Martin A. Strand Ski Company, and the manufacturer incorporated as the Strand Ski Company. His sons were apparently out of the picture. Shortly before Strand's retirement, the *Milwaukee Journal* ran a delightful hagiography on him. He was seventy-seven years old and full of vigor. The article extolled: "Out of the sizzling steam of the 101 degree heat the other day strolled a dapper old fellow, looking unbelievably cool and immaculate in spite of his wing collar—or because of it. Such sartorial magnificence. . . . 'So it's 101,' he said. 'Poof! I want to talk about skis!'"

That Strand would use the word *poof* is both unfathomable and perfectly fitting for the eccentric Norwegian. The heat and humidity came from the steam boxes in the factory for bending wood, a technology made obsolete by laminates. With laminates, thin strips of wood could be placed in a press with Kaurit glue, and the resulting ski camber and tips would be forever bent, unlike the steamed solid wood skis, which required special storage techniques and would still lose their perk with time. The article went on to claim two falsehoods: that Strand opened the first ski factory in the United States and introduced the word "ski" to American English.

"Ski should be pronounced 'she,' but that sound is too much like the feminine personal pronoun," Strand told the reporter. "So I made it sound like it looked, simply 'ski.' I know I'm absolutely positive about it—I'm the man who put 'ski' in the English language!" He didn't. Still, the changes Strand experienced in his lifetime were dizzying, both in his own world and as a witness to the transformation of the Upper Midwest from a series of wilderness outposts to established towns and cities in the grip of industrial fervor. "So I have seen the virgin forests when they stood as God had created them," he wrote in his autobiography. "When I drive through that same country now, after commercialism has destroyed them, I have to admit it makes one sad . . . the beautiful trees all gone. . . . They [the lumber barons] cared nothing for the future generations, and simply destroyed everything."

Old Strand was a Norwegian original, full of industry and frugality yet riddled with contradictions. On the one hand, he was the classic American capitalist: he identified a market and supplied

A factory worker sands the surface of a ski at the Strand Ski Company in 1942.

Martin Strand's ski-making empire began to lose steam as changing technology brought new competition to the business, most notably in Christian Lund's Northland company, which by the mid-1930s was churning out highly fashionable and stylized advertising.

it, with skis he himself identified as cheap. On the other hand, what kind of capitalist would say, as he was quoted in his hagiography, "Some ask for flat top skis, some ridge top and others for slalom skis. We give them what they want, but honestly, there isn't any difference in the long run. Some are just fancier than others, that's all"? Perhaps he was jaded from slinging skis, because to say that one ski is as good as another is demonstrably false, but Strand was working toward expressing a pure concept, unsullied by the inescapable financial context of American life. He went on: "Those ski jumpers, too, have given people the wrong idea of the sport. Jumping is to skiing what the Indianapolis race is to automobiling. The real ski enthusiast glides uphill and downhill across country. That's really skiing!"

Strand rang strong that *idraet* bell, in the tradition of his old friend Aksel Holter and all the other Norwegian purists who bemoaned the lack of virtue in the sport's current state. From Strand's perspective, things would worsen at an increasing rate in future decades, as more skiers relied on tow ropes and chairlifts for uphill progress, yet Strand presaged the skiing renaissance that was drawing nearer.

Strand died in the final days of 1947 at age eighty-four. Within months, the Strand Ski Company, which had continued strong through the war before flagging in peacetime, would declare bankruptcy. Many individuals would attempt to reopen the biggest employer in New Richmond, but all would fail.

♠

The 1940 Central Division cross-country and Nordic combined championships took place in St. Paul the first weekend in February. Those who qualified would be eligible to compete in the national tournament later in the month in Land O'Lakes, Wisconsin, a tiny town near the border with the Upper Peninsula of Michigan. Land O'Lakes was home to the Gateway Hotel and Inn, whose brochure advertised "clean and scintillating snow under the bright sun." The defending national cross-country champion was George Gustavson, from Placerville, California, who had won the preceding championship in Salt Lake City and would be traveling east to defend his title from whichever upstarts the Central Division sent.

While Central Division skiers vied for the jumping title on the Battle Creek jump, the langlaufers raced on a 10.4-mile course that wound through

Erik Judeen and Pete Fosseide at a ski race in the 1940s, likely in Thunder Bay, Ontario.

the Highland Park golf course. Erik Judeen was the defending Central Division cross-country and Nordic combined champ, having edged out Fosseide the year before at a race held in Chester Park during a blizzard. Twenty-six langlaufers started the race, the same number as the year before, which had been a record high for a Central Division cross-country race. The division's efforts at recruiting more skiers appeared to be working. Precursors to modern Nordic racers, a diehard lauglauf crew willing to travel hours for a race had coalesced.

One racer crashed while descending a hill and was rushed to a hospital with a dislocated shoulder. Three others dropped out before the finish. Pete Fosseide came out on top, besting second-place Erik Judeen by just under two minutes. Judeen finished nearly three minutes ahead of Bradley Board. Board's fellow Bush Laker (and brother to John and Lindley) Gale Burton took fifth place. The University of Wisconsin Hoofers did well, with Edward Bradley (brother of the national champion) in fourth and Reuben Silvola in sixth. Arrowhead Derby vets Harold Moe and Joe Maurin both finished in the top ten. Maurin had moved to Land O'Lakes to work as a ski instructor. Nobody from Saint Paul finished in the top ten, no doubt a disappointment for the home club.

In another blow to the St. Paul club, its former Class A jumping champ and Olympian Sverre Fredheim had moved to Land O'Lakes and returned to win the Central Division title with jumps of 190 and 197 feet. Right behind Fredheim was Gene Wilson, a former Minnesota high school jumping champion from Greenway High. Wilson had followed the siren song of the mountains that had beckoned to many of the best Midwestern skiers and settled in California. St. Paul's top finisher was Len Soler, who finished third in Class A.

The national cross-country championship was on February 17 at the Gateway Lodge, which had been modeled after the Lake Placid club in New York. Gateway offered all the winter activities a person could shake an icicle at, with miles of ski and snowshoe trails, a skating rink out front, a large ski jump, and a hill with a tow rope for downhill. Gateway had a toboggan run and offered sleigh rides and skijoring by horse. The log-hewn lodge had a massive fireplace and a ski waxing room, fully equipped with irons, waxes, and blowtorches for applying pine tar to wooden ski bases. The Chicago and North Western Railroad ran in special overnight Pullman car service. Gustafson arrived from California to defend his title, and the NSA president, Roger Langley, came from Massachusetts.

On race day, the temperature climbed to thirty-six degrees and the snow became sticky and slow. The course was laid out in a figure eight and wended along the border between Wisconsin and Michigan. Early in

At the height of its popularity, Gateway Lodge offered an impressive array of recreational offerings. In addition to a ski slide and cross-country course, the multiacre property boasted a tap room, cocktail lounge, swimming pool, and bowling alley.

the race, George Gustafson broke a ski pole. He struggled on with a single pole until someone gave him a new one two-thirds of the way through the race, but he was out of contention. Fosseide dominated the race, beating Judeen by nearly three minutes. Gale Burton finished third, and Joe Maurin came in sixth. Gustafson finally finished a disappointing ninth. Peter Fosseide was the new national cross-country champion. He was the fifth Minnesotan to hold the title and would be the last Midwesterner to do so for almost fifty years. The route had been quite flat, NSA President Roger Langley demurred, but then conceded that the rolling hills of the course had offered a good test of cross-country technique. He noted that Fosseide was "in fairly fresh condition" after the race, reflecting well on the Norwegian's endurance.

The next day, in the jumping portion of the Nordic combined competition, the riders leaped against a strong wind that resulted in paltry distances. Reuben Silvola pulled himself up from a mediocre cross-country showing with the day's longest jump, placing him in third in the Nordic combined finals. In second was young Gale Burton. And in first, with the second longest jump of the day, a measly sixty-nine feet due to the wind, was Fosseide. Where was Judeen? While launching off the jump, his left ski had fallen off, perhaps torqued by the wind. But he did not panic: he sailed through the air and landed one-legged on his right ski with his left foot braced tightly behind. He skied down the slope on the single ski and, to stop, rolled to one side in what was technically a clean landing. He'd still managed to get enough points to finish seventh, while Fosseide picked up the national Nordic combined title.

♠

By 1940, brothers Gale and John Burton already had their sights on the Olympic cross-country team, inspired by their gold-medal-winning uncle, Al Lindley. Youthful dreams, however, would hold no sway against the vicissitudes of war. For his part, Al Lindley was spending less time skiing cross-country in the Midwest and more time skiing downhill with Grace Carter Lindley in Sun Valley. The Idaho resort was glamourous. Ernest Hemingway had finished *For Whom the Bell Tolls* while renting a room in the lodge. He and Martha Gellhorn lived there for part of the year. Gary Cooper, Marilyn Monroe, Errol Flynn, and Lucille Ball hung out at the resort. A 1941 film, *Sun Valley Ser-enade*, starring Glenn Miller and Sonja Henie, showed the rest of America what they were missing.

When Al Lindley took third place in a regional 1940 down-hill tournament at Sun Valley, Grace won first. A stylish book from the Derrydale Press that profiled prominent alpine skiers described her as "formerly Grace Carter, now Mrs. Alfred Lindley." Grace now ran in rarefied cir-cles, having grand adventures like climbing Wyoming's Gannet Peak, the highest point in the state, with Lindley and famed mountaineer Paul Petzoldt; the year before, in 1939, Lindley had backed out of the ill-fated U.S. expedition to climb K2, on which four members had died. She'd left her matrilineal houseboat on the Seattle harbor for a grand home on Lake Minnetonka called Meadowridge, which her father-in-law had given her husband.

Weeks after winning the Sun Valley tournament, as a mem-ber of the Bush Lake club, Carter won the NSA's downhill title, be-coming the first Central Division skier to win a national title in an

Fashionable Sun Valley emerged in the late 1930s as first and foremost a ski resort of the mountain west.

Al and Grace Lindley visit with Austrian ski racer Friedl Pfeifer at the 1939 National Ski Championships in Mount Hood, Oregon.

alpine event. The Central Division had had a phenomenal season with Grace Carter Lindley's victory, Fosseide's national cross-country and Nor-dic combined titles, and Ishpeming jumpers' first-place honors in both Class B and Class C jumping.

In 1940, Grace Carter Lindley was at the pinnacle of her racing career. Aside from winning the national title, she made the 1940 Olympic team, but the games were canceled for war. Al Lindley joined the navy as an intelligence officer and served with distinction in his usual style. Grace gave birth to a son in 1943 and would never have another crack at the Olympics, though she remained involved with up-and-coming skiers. She mentored a young athlete named Gretchen Fraser, who became in 1948, in St. Moritz, Switzerland, the first American to win gold in any Olympic ski event. Grace was present for the St. Moritz games, as chaperone of the fifteen-year-old phenom Andrea Mead Lawrence. Four years later, Mead Lawrence won two Olympic gold medals in Oslo. Grace kept skiing, first from Sun Valley and later at a promising Colorado resort where she was an initial investor. She had a long life ahead, marked by a tragic accident, a family curse lurking in her genes, and an unexpected contribution to the cross-country revolution that was still decades away.

♠

By some measures, women's opportunities to ski had improved. Ladies' divisions were standard in alpine events. A ski jumper from Massachusetts named Dorothy Graves had even established herself in the competitive circuit as a Class B jumper. Messages in ski periodicals of the times, however, were at best mixed. When a woman did well, like Graves, she would be inevitably praised for her ability and attractiveness. Papers fawned over Graves as they had Natalie Bailey, though, Bailey, of course, was denied entry into competition. Support for aspiring girl skiers was utterly lacking.

In downhill and slalom, women had been competing in the Olympics as long as men. One of Grace Carter Lindley's teammates from the 1936 Olympic team, Helen Boughton-Leigh, wrote a piece for the 1936 NSA *American Ski Annual*, the publication formerly known as the *Ski Sport*. The *Ski Sport*, whose name was the English translation of *idraet*, had been published in the Midwest, but its newer incarnation was printed in New England. The *American Ski Annual* began with thirty full pages of advertisements and made readers long for its former producer, Aksel Holter, who never would have let filthy advertising dominate the testament of his *idraet* gospel.

Boughton-Leigh discoursed on ladies' skiing: "Racing may endanger health and it may endanger bones, but unquestionably the greatest risk

Members of the U.S. Women's Ski Team during Winter Olympic Games at Garmisch-Partenkirchen, Germany, February 1936. *From left:* Clarita Heath, Grace Carter, Helen Boughton-Leigh, Elizabeth Woolsey, Alice Blaine Wolfe, Marian McKean, and Mary E. Bird.

of all will be to one's femininity." She went on to recall how she and a male friend had been sitting together looking at photographs of her fellow skiers. Her friend snarkily remarked what a bunch of "hard-bitten janes" these lady skiers were. Boughton-Leigh studied the women and concluded, "I was bound to confess that for the most part we were. The drawn, strained expression of the over-trained athlete was only too observable in most faces. No, we were far from being a bevy of beauty. So, if one attaches any great value to her feminine charm, she should drop all idea of earning fame in the field of international skiing. The two qualities are apparently incompatible." Boughton-Leigh went on to recommend that women ski casually for fun but avoid racing.

Germany's Christl Cranz, who won the 1936 Olympic gold medal in combined downhill and slalom, further pigeonholed her gender's place, saying, "Cross-country skiing and ski jumping are athletic performances for which a lot of strength and endurance is necessary, more than women can give without harming themselves. . . . Certainly no reasonable sporting girl would think about participating in a marathon or boxing, and that is how it is with us women skiers; there is no interest in running or jumping competitions."

In the early 1940s, derogatory comics began to appear regularly in ski periodicals. The *Ski Bulletin: The National Skiing Weekly* published a comic titled "Low I.Q." Featuring a drawing of a woman wearing skis and sitting on the ground with a dumbfounded stare, it read:

> Many a girl who looks well on the ski train
> Proves herself soon to be quite without ski brain.
> Bonwits, and staid Abercrombie and Fitches
> Daily outfit lots of ignorant ladies.

This arrogant verse becomes even more unpleasant upon recognizing that the obvious rhyme for the last line was not *ladies.*

Discouragingly, the Central Division's *Central Ski Sport* newspaper soon came up with its own comic character to mock women skiers. Her name was Central Sue. Central Sue was drawn by none other than Doris Maurin, who was married to Joe Maurin, the ski instructor and Arrowhead Derby racer. Central Sue was introduced by the paper as "a most intriguing angular imp of the ski." She would be better described as a vulnerable adult with Barbie doll proportions. "My form, he says," Sue states, "is perfect." Of course, he is referring to her body and not to the awful ski technique with which she was depicted.

In 1949, Sue's creator, Doris Maurin, would watch her husband die in

This highly gendered Swedish postcard expresses typical midcentury sentiments around the ski sport. *Vi valla!* roughly translates as "we wallow."

Skiers from the University of Wisconsin–La Crosse await the departure of their train, circa 1940s.

a sudden accident. Joe Maurin was in the Peoria, Illinois, armory, setting up an indoor ski jump for a sports show exhibition. Maurin was high on the jump when a cable that anchored it to the ceiling snapped, sending Maurin careening thirty-five feet to the floor and to his death. He was thirty-nine years old. That prewar cadre of dedicated cross-country racers had broken up by then, eroded by war, age, and changing values. Instead of blossoming into a more popular pursuit after the war, cross-country, and even jumping, would fade into the shadow of the hot new sport of downhill skiing.

Skiers on the slopes above
La Crosse, Wisconsin, 1940s.

5

Nordic Decline

1940s–1950s

In the early 1940s, Bob Hagstrom was a preteen living on the East Side of St. Paul. Both his parents had been born in the United States, though his grandparents came from Sweden. Hagstrom's parents gave him a pair of pine Strand skis for Christmas when he was eleven or twelve. The skis came with a simple leather toe strap for a binding, which Hagstrom improved by using popped inner tubes from his bicycle. The rubber, wrapped around the front of the toe strap and heel of Hagstrom's boot, kept his foot in the binding by providing tension from the heel. Sturdier leather bindings with transverse straps had been common for decades, though Hagstrom's first skis were evidently the budget-minded type that kept Strand flourishing through the Depression.

Hagstrom relished the lightness of his cheap Strands. Hickory skis were much heavier. He waxed them with paraffin left over from his mother's preserves. He would ski a track in fresh snow through the vacant lots around his house and follow the track again the next day. On weekends or after classes at Phalen Park School, Hagstrom and his buddy Roy Nordwall skied from their houses on Jessie Street to places like Devil's Hill, which ran under the old railroad viaduct on the east side of Lake Phalen, or Bunker Hill, which was crowded with young skiers and tobogganers on weekend afternoons. A grassland the boys knew as Smith's Field spread scant blocks north of Hagstrom's house. He liked to ski through it en route to another sliding hill called Idaho Hill, on Wheelock Parkway. Smith's Field would soon be covered in a tight matrix of postwar homes, but Hagstrom remembered flushing pheasants from it and skiing past the solitary man-sion that rose from the snow-crushed grass. He and Nordwall gave the home wide berth and were never bothered by its occupants. They'd ski north past Brainerd Avenue, where another large, lonely home stood, and cross the Grand–Mississippi streetcar line that ran downtown. It was a memorable time for Hagstrom: he was old enough to wander independent-ly yet free from major responsibility.

Hagstrom's entire family skied on the Phalen–Keller Golf Course, where today the city of St. Paul maintains a groomed trail. His father was a casual skier at best yet took his son to watch the annual St. Paul Winter Carnival jumping competition at Battle Creek. Hagstrom recalled large crowds and, in addition to some of the nation's best jumpers, talented athletes from Norway and Sweden.

Hagstrom attended Johnson High School in St. Paul, where he joined the basketball team instead of the ski team. He and Nordwall downhill skied at Barker's Alps in Bayport along the St. Croix River—a small hill with a tow rope powered by an old tractor. The tractor sat on blocks with its engine running, and the tow rope stretched around one of its bare rims, the spinning wheel pulling skiers up the hill.

Hagstrom met his wife, Diane, in high school. They married in 1951, when he was twenty-one and she was eighteen. Early in their marriage, the young couple skied to access a cabin Diane's parents had on the Sunrise River. Once they had children, though, and as Hagstrom's home building business took off, skiing fell by the wayside. He and Diane would not take

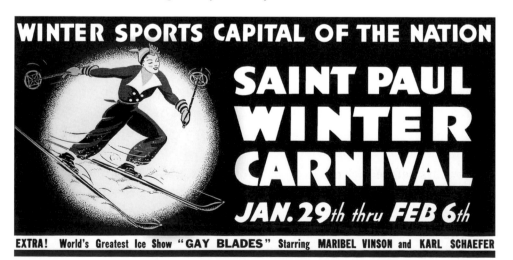

Skiing was often an important part of St. Paul Winter Carnival advertising. This 1936 placard adorned many streetcars that shuttled people around the Twin Cities.

At a ski meet in the 1950s, Len Soler of the St. Paul Ski Club leaps from the Battle Creek jump.

up cross-country skiing again until they were in their fifties, inspired by the sport's new popularity and their kids' participation on the Stillwater High School ski team. Hagstrom would find his interest in the sport un-wavering, even as he surpassed ninety years of age.

In the years before World War II, a new name was at the top of the national jumping scene. Five-and-half-foot-tall Torger Tokle had emigrated from Norway in 1939. He settled in Brooklyn and had a brief but dazzling career that captivated the nation in a way that American jumping never would again. The day after he arrived in the United States, he set a new hill record at the Bear Mountain jump in New York. He remained a Class B jumper his first season, but then, in 1940, he won every Class A tournament until losing the national to Alf Engen.

Tokle was untouchable the following season, not just winning almost every meet but setting a distance record on nearly every hill he jumped, winning the national Class A title in Seattle. In two seasons, Tokle set the American ski jumping distance record three times, first besting Engen's record of 267 feet with a jump of 273 feet, a record he soon broke with distances of 288 feet and 289 feet. Tokle's record would stand for seven years. His picture was featured regularly on the front page of Midwestern news-

papers, with Tokle always flashing an impish grin and often bending to grab a handful of snow as if to throw it at the photographer. Images of no other jumper had been or would ever be featured so frequently and largely as Tokle. The press called him "The Mighty Mite," "The King of Them All," and "The King of Ski Jumpers."

Tokle soon enlisted in the U.S. Army and left for Europe. He was the War Department's dream; his ever-beaming smile proved as unyielding to the pressure of pending combat as it had to the stress of running off the nation's largest jumps. Naturally, Tokle was placed in the Tenth Mountain Division, that famed cadre of troops trained and battle-tested in mountain warfare, often on skis. On March 3, 1945, in Italy, Tokle led his platoon up the steep side of a mountain in a sneak attack on a Nazi garrison dug into the ridgetop. A German 88-millimeter shell,

Torger Tokle had a short, spectacular ski jumping career in the United States before World War II.

With help from the Works Progress Administration, the Duluth Ski Club built a new sixty-meter jump on the west side of town next to Mission Creek, called Fond du Lac. Club members drew straws to see who would be first to run the slide; Erik Judeen won the honors. During the inaugural tournament in early 1941, Torger Tokle jumped farthest, though Eugene Wilson from Coleraine won the tournament. Erosion from Mission Creek eventually forced the jump to be removed in 1975.

an antiaircraft-caliber weapon, annihilated young Tokle, recalled Lyle Munson, a fellow ski jumper from Iron Mountain, Michigan, who was in combat that day with Tokle. "He died in much the same fashion he lived," Munson told a newspaper, "engaged in action up to the hilt." In his American career, Tokle had competed in forty-eight meets and won forty-three. His body was returned home to Norway, south of Trondheim, for burial. Tokle's brother Art continued to jump competitively in the United States.

During World War II, Duluth hosted the National Ski Jumping Championships in February 1942. The national tournament would be canceled the next three years and resume in 1946.

Tragedy also struck the Minnesota skiing community. Gale Cotton Burton, Al Lindley's nephew and a promising cross-country racer who had placed third in the 1940 national meet, enlisted in the Coast Guard. In a bitter twist of irony, what must have seemed like a much safer posting than, say, combat in France proved otherwise when Burton collapsed from pneumonia while patrolling Manhattan Island in a rowboat. Penicillin was still fairly new, and all supplies went to the troops in battle. Without the medication, Burton soon died. In 1947, his family established the Gale C. Burton Memorial Trophy, an engraved silver cup to be awarded each year to the winner of the national cross-country meet. The cup is still awarded annually to the national men's champion.

The war years disrupted the marginal upward trajectory of cross-country and hastened the development of downhill skiing. For three years during the war, the national ski meet was suspended. In 1946, when it commenced again, the American ski scene had changed. Americans had imported and were wholeheartedly embracing mainland European downhill culture as the country's dominant form of skiing.

Wealthy Americans who liked to travel were already familiar with this type of skiing before the war. Skiers like Al and Grace Lindley were involved in establishing Sun Valley and Aspen as ski resorts and began spending more time skiing out west than back home. American GIs serving in Europe

THE VIKING DIVISION

During World War II, the Strand and Northland companies churned out thousands of white-painted wooden skis for use in combat by the Tenth Mountain Division and other military units. The famed Tenth Mountain Division, clad in white snow camouflage and including some of the country's best skiers, suffered heavy casualties in the Italian Alps. These soldiers had trained at Camp Hale, high in the Colorado mountains, like another lesser-known ski troop. In July 1942, orders from army headquarters formed the Ninety-Ninth Infantry Division to fight a guerrilla resistance on skis in Nazi-occupied Norway. Also called the Viking Battalion, the Ninety-Ninth was to open a route of transportation through Norway to Russia and draw German troops into Norway and away from other fronts. The Ninety-Ninth's first commander was Harold Hanson, who was authorized to enlist up to 884 men.

Officers urged Norwegian-speaking soldiers to join the Ninety-Ninth. Recruits were required to be U.S. citizens, or at least have applied for U.S. citizenship, but native Norwegian speakers were preferred. No surprise—much of the division was made up of Minnesotans and Dakotans. The Ninety-Ninth first mustered in at Camp Ripley, Minnesota; then moved to Fort Snelling in the Twin Cities; and finally ended up at Camp Hale, where the soldiers trained on skis while carrying heavy packs through deep mountain snow.

Ultimately, the Viking Division's mission changed in the spring of 1943, for various reasons, including doubts that the Norway plan would succeed and concerns from the Norwegian government-in-exile that guerrilla warfare would lead to civilian deaths. About one hundred members of the Ninety-Ninth were recruited for what today would be called special forces operations in Norway; the rest of the division was sent to Omaha Beach, arriving two weeks after D-Day. The Ninety-Ninth began a long campaign through France, Holland, and Germany, experiencing heavy combat. After the war, the Ninety-Ninth was sent to Oslo to disarm one hundred thousand surrendered Nazi soldiers and personnel. After the division's arduous march across Europe, the aftermath in Norway was a joyful time for the Ninety-Ninth, who stood by at attention as Norway's King Haakon returned. Haakon designated the American division his personal honor guard. Many soldiers of the Ninety-Ninth took leave to travel to visit Norwegian relatives. Romances sprung up, some fleeting, others resulting in marriages. 🌲

Soldiers from the Ninety-Ninth Infantry Division at Camp Hale in Colorado, 1943.

COMMITTEE

DULUTH SKI CLUB

NATIONAL SKI JUMPING TOURNAMENT
1942 FOND DU LAC FEB-7-8

I AM A
SKI
BOOSTER
DULUTH SKI CLUB
DULUTH, MINN.

SKIERS-- Torger Tokle (left) and Art Devlin, one of his greatest rivals, look over the skis Tokle hopes will carry him to a repeat championship in the national jumping tournament at Fond du Lac Saturday and Sunday.

When Duluth hosted the 1942 national jumping tournament at its Fond du Lac jump, a twelve-year-old named Joe Nowak got signatures from the defending Class A champ, Torger Tokle, and Torger's brother Kyrre. In 1954, Nowak set a hill record on Fond du Lac that would remain for several years.

during the war were introduced to the continent's ski culture. When they returned, some with an entrepreneurial bent began opening ski hills in America that aimed to re-create the European downhill experience. One of these entrepreneurs was Tony Wise, who opened Mount Telemark, near Hayward, Wisconsin, at the end of 1947. Wise had skied in the Bavarian Alps a couple of years earlier and was inspired to bring that enjoyable experience home to the Midwest. He was a local Hayward boy made good, having earned his master's degree from Harvard and received the Bronze and Silver Stars as a first lieutenant in the army.

Casual downhill skiing provided ready thrills, was less strenuous, and proved more fashionable than cross-country or jumping. Downhill safety bindings were becoming more common, which drastically reduced injuries. With the old beartrap cable bindings, historian Roland Huntford noted, on any given day at a large ski resort, several skiers would break a leg. Often these were nasty spiral fractures. Unlike earlier cable bindings, the safety binding would release a ski when undue strain was placed on it (the inventor of the safety binding had thought of the idea while in the hospital with a broken leg from skiing). Improved safety made downhill skiing more approachable and popular. Cross-country went from being a niche activity to a niche within a niche. Forgotten was the Central Division's committee to advance cross-country.

In the National Ski Association's 1947 *American Ski Annual,* all of its fifty

Tony Wise began Mount Telemark near Hayward, Wisconsin, with a small warming hut. By the 1960s, the resort featured a sprawling, well-appointed chalet adorned with a Norwegian rosemaling design.

pages of advertisements are for downhill—clothes, hills, skis, and even portable chairlifts. Buried deep in its pages is an account of how Erling Strom, now settled in Stowe, Vermont, was trying to revive cross-country skiing by putting on a race called the Mount Mansfield–Stowe Derby. Strom put this ten-mile race on for years, with about twenty-five entrants per contest. He eventually quit after running the event alone one year—skiing the first four miles with the racers from the start on Mount Mansfield and then hopping in his car and driving to Stowe, where he manned the finish line with a stopwatch. The Stowe Derby has since been revived and is regarded as one of the nation's oldest cross-country races, with hundreds of entrants annually. To further illustrate cross-country's limited appeal compared to downhill in the 1950s, Strom lived two miles from the village of Stowe. He had a hill and tow rope behind his popular ski lodge and offered free downhill lessons to any kid who skied to his hill cross-country from town. No one ever took him up on the offer.

In the 1949 *American Ski Annual*, cross-country skiing resurfaced when Oscar Haug wrote about how to lay out a cross-country course. Haug noted,

Originally a swimwear company in Portland, Oregon, Jantzen added a fashionable line of sweaters and winter sportswear to its brand in the 1940s, as more Americans became interested in downhill skiing.

"A cross-country race should not be an obstacle race," explaining that, contrary to the prior decade's recommendation, a cross-country ski course should *not* involve fence crossings.

The Midwestern presence in the *Ski Annual* had waned dramatically since the publication's early days. After having led the movement to develop skiing in the United States, Midwesterners took on a self-effacing regional attitude. In the 1949 *Ski Annual*, the secretary for the Central Division meekly wrote, "We don't have ski resorts like Alta, Sun Valley, Aspen, or Yosemite, but we do ski in the Central." Two years later in the 1951 *Ski Annual*, Julie Bosshardt listed the ski hills in the area in an article called "Sun Valleys of the Upper Midwest." All the places she listed were downhill, starting with the big daddy of the time, Mount Telemark. Then there was Mont du Lac, south of Duluth; Tyrol, by St. Cloud; and Moon Valley and Norski, both in the Twin Cities; plus a promising new place called Lutsen. "Ten years ago," the author proclaimed, "the ordinary Upper Midwest sportsman didn't give a second thought to skiing." This was ludicrous. Less than thirty years before, the very same publication had called Minneapolis the "Ski Capital of America." The Nordic-centered era seemed completely forgotten.

The spirit of the country was no longer geared toward silent sports like cross-country. The war had been taxing; now there was no need to hold back. The gas shortages were over. Why walk when one could drive?

Relaxing at a West Michigan fireside, in one of Michigan's many fully developed winter sports areas.

SKIING

GUARANTEED TO MAKE YOU WONDERFULLY WEARY

What better proof of perfect skiing than the happy tired feeling that follows at night? Michigan is famous for it. From December to March, every breath is spiked with winter. Every daylight hour is frosted giddy white. And every night and every corner of the state is equipped with its own particular simmering fire. Ever since skiing first began, people have come to Michigan for the gentle slopes and twisting slaloms and the feel of skis biting into a fresh coat of powder snow . . . and for that rare state of exhilaration with tiredness. Try it yourself.

FOR FREE LITERATURE on Michigan in winter, write Michigan Tourist Council, Room 4712, Mason Bldg., Lansing 26, Michigan.

MICHIGAN
WINTER WONDERLAND

By the early 1960s, Michigan's Tourist Council developed advertising campaigns that celebrated the state's recently acquired status as a premier destination for downhill skiing.

Why ski up a hill when you could let a cable pull you up and let gravity do the work coming down? Ski hills were popping up all over the place. The *Minnesota–Wisconsin Ski News* ran a sarcastic poem titled "Conservation" that did much to sum up the ethos of the times:

> I think that I
> > Shall never ski—
> I'd hate to wreck
> > A lovely tree!

♠

Despite the shift away from Nordic forms of skiing toward downhill, the Midwest maintained strongholds of both dedicated langlaufers and jumpers. These stronghold communities kept up the Nordic ski culture through their youth. In Minnesota high school skiing, Duluth and Cloquet dominated the state meets in the early 1950s. Competition was still a combination of cross-country, slalom, and jumping.

In the late 1940s, Michigan's governing high school sporting body, the Michigan High School Athletic Association, forayed into skiing with a sanctioned meet at Caberfae ski area, between Cadillac and Traverse City. Youth skiers from Traverse City, Manistee, Leelanau, and Cadillac, including both girls and boys, competed in cross-country, downhill, and slalom. The ski teams were clubs, not official high school teams.

By 1952, enough schools in Michigan's Upper Peninsula had petitioned the MHSAA to sponsor high school skiing that a meet was held in Iron Mountain in February. The boys competed in

During the 1940s, Norman Kragseth of Duluth won a staggering twenty-one state high school championships in seven different sports, including consecutive titles in cross-country, jumping, and slalom. Kragseth eventually became an official in the National Football League.

downhill, slalom, cross-country, and jumping. Girls were limited to the downhill events, even though "skiing was the only opportunity for a girl to win a major sports award," noted the *Petoskey Evening News* in 1953. Girl skiers in neighboring Minnesota and Wisconsin had no similar opportunities to ski on a high school team, nor would they for decades. The MHSAA gave Michigan's Lower Peninsula its own regional league in 1954. The league was downhill only, had a girls' division, and was dominated by Traverse City. As elsewhere in the country, downhill skiing was growing in popularity in Michigan: thirty-three ski hills had been established around the Lower Peninsula. The Wisconsin Interscholastic Athletic Association began sponsoring ski competition in 1958, but the teams were exclusively downhill and continued only until 1975.

Conrad Mangseth, a grandson of Ole Mangseth, skied for Coleraine's Greenway High School in the 1951 Minnesota state meet. He recalled that the Coleraine ski team didn't practice cross-country. When the tournament came, the coach asked

Chester Park Junior Ski Club - 1941-Duluth-

Before and after World War II, a winter day at Chester Bowl brought kids of all ages to the famous jump and its surrounding ski trails.

for volunteers to do the cross-country race, and those who did went off and raced. This was standard practice for many teams: jumping was the main event, with cross-country as the traditional throwback.

By the late 1950s, young Charlie Banks was coaching the Duluth Central ski team with cross-country training methods that would be recognizable

Darryl Kurki marvels at the size of the trophy he holds at a Chester Bowl awards ceremony. Kurki is flanked by Charlie Banks *(left)* and Ray Wick.

today. Banks had built a ski trail system on his property north of Duluth on Korkki Road in Clover Valley, a rural area populated predominately by Finns. Banks was a Finn, as was his wife, Dorothy, whose maiden name was Korkki. Banks groomed his trails by snowshoeing the course, then skiing in tracks. He taught shop at Central High School, and after school during the ski season, he would drive his team twenty-five minutes to his home trail system where they trained. His ski team was typically small in numbers for the era and comfortably fit into his station wagon. Banks strung electric cable and lightbulbs in the trees so the boys could ski at night. Dorothy often made the team hot cocoa after practice, and then Banks would drive them back to Central.

Charlie Banks had been Minnesota's high school cross-country champ in 1942. Before settling in as Central's coach, Banks served on a naval ship during the war, where he'd started smoking cigarettes to deal with stress and loneliness. He resolved that once his tour was over he would quit smoking and get serious about training so he could make the 1952 Olympic cross-country squad, but he was sidelined by injury.

The 1952 U.S. Olympic Jumping Team was unusual for having no Midwesterners. Four years before in St. Moritz, Switzerland, in the first Winter Olympics since World War II, Walter Bietila and Joe Perrault, both from Ishpeming, and Sverre Fredheim, who had moved back to St. Paul, made up three-fourths of the squad. In 1956, in Italy, Willis Olson, from Eau Claire, and Dick Rahoi, from Iron Mountain, Michigan, made up half of the team.

The only time the Midwest had dominated the cross-country team, like they often did the jumping team, was in the first games in 1924, but the 1952 Winter Olympics featured a strong cross-country representation from Minnesota. Banks's friend and competitor George Hovland from Duluth traveled to Oslo to represent the United States as a member of the cross-country team. Banks and Hovland were an odd couple on par with Fosseide and Judeen. They'd known each other since they were boys skiing in Chester Park and had gone to high school together. Hovland had won the cross-country state meet in 1943, the year after Banks took the title. While Banks was an introverted Finn who lived contentedly and quietly in the woods, Norwegian Hovland was a tall, dashing extrovert who hobnobbed with the Duluth elite in pursuit of his numerous ski

George Hovland (right) with Ed McKeever in 1943 after winning the Class A title in slalom in the Minnesota state high school tournament.

business forays. Hovland was always interested in the ski business. When he was a young man, his father, also named George, asked Peter Fosseide whether there was any money to be made in cross-country skiing. "Well, I tell you, George," Fosseide said, "there's not too much money, but it's a healthy sport." Yet Hovland would try, starting in the 1950s, by building Duluth's first downhill destination, Ski Kenwood, near Chester's jumps, and by opening The Ski Shop on London Road in Duluth in 1955. In the 1952 Olympics, Hovland was joined on the cross-country squad by fellow Minnesotan John Burton. They would be the last Minnesotans to make the team for twenty-four years and the last Midwesterners for twenty.

In the years after World War II, John Burton and George Hovland both attended the University of Minnesota, where they helped revive the university's ski team, which had disbanded during the war. Hovland had spent two years in the Pacific on a navy geodetic survey ship, which surveyed harbors in advance of large destroyers and battleships. During college, he worked as a bellhop in a Twin Cities hotel. To train, he would take the elevator up with guests' baggage and then run down the stairs trying to beat the elevator. After college, he married, divorced, and became a ski bum at Lutsen. In 1950, the coach of the U.S. Alpine Ski Team invited Hovland to try out for the upcoming Winter Olympics in Norway. Hovland told the coach he would rather try out for cross-country and Nordic combined and promptly headed west to Sun Valley to train.

Norway's national pastime was on full display in this official poster for the 1952 Winter Olympic Games in Oslo.

John Burton at age eleven.

John Burton finished his undergraduate degree at Harvard and then returned to the University of Minnesota for law school. In 1950, he traveled east to Maine to compete in the World Championships, an international tournament put on by the International Ski Federation. In cross-country, the United States was not a contender. The top American finisher was a forty-five-year-old Finnish immigrant named Olavi Alakulppi, who took forty-sixth place. Burton finished fifty-ninth.

John Burton was athletic and dedicated to training. It didn't hurt to have grown up in a prosperous family that emphasized sports competition, though Burton was of a milder nature than his baron-esque forebearers. Still, he'd been named the most valuable player on the Harvard hockey team in 1940. He was also a skilled yachtsman, well in keeping with his family's legendary status in the upper-class world of competitive sailing. But cross-country skiing was always his favorite sport.

As a child in Deephaven, on the family's acreage at Lake Minnetonka, Burton and his brothers honed their cross-country skills in the Bush Lake

John Burton *(left)* and George Hovland at the 1952 Olympics in Oslo.

club's Sunday races held on a trail system that ran a few miles south to Christmas and Lotus Lakes. The old national champ Carl Sundquist laid out those trails, recruited to the Bush Lake club by the Burtons' uncle Al Lindley. By the 1950s, John was the last of his brothers still ski racing; Lindley Burton was pursuing an academic career, and Gale had died. The family was struck by another tragedy in 1951 as John Burton and George Hovland prepared to travel east for the Olympic tryouts.

On February 22, Al Lindley left Minneapolis by plane for Aspen. As chairman of the NSA's 1952 Olympic Ski Games Committee, Lindley was off to judge tryouts for the downhill team. He had recently run for Congress and suffered a stinging defeat; he was not accustomed to losing. Piloting the plane was Lindley's cousin, Eddie Pillsbury, the successor and vice president of Pillsbury Mills. Joining them was a friend, Dexter Andrews. The single-engine, four-seater plane was crammed with skiing and tennis equipment. The men flew through a freezing rain as they crossed Nebraska. Trying to get out of the dangerous weather, Pillsbury brought the plane low to attempt an emergency landing in a field near the train depot in the town of Paxton. He crashed into a tree. All three men died. Lindley was forty-seven years old, leaving Grace Carter Lindley a widow at age thirty-four.

Al Lindley was the one who had encouraged John and Gale Burton to try out for the Olympic cross-country team. The three had traveled to ski races in Duluth together. Now John was the lone survivor of the trio, and he wasn't even thirty. He finished in seventh place in the Olympic cross-country tryouts, twelve seconds behind his friend George Hovland in sixth. The skiers didn't find out right away whether they'd made the team. Later in March, the third-place finisher, Don Johnson, died in a plane crash in Colorado. Half a century later, in an interview, John Burton claimed he may not have made the team if not for the death of Johnson. His teammates disagreed, citing his strong showing in the nationals, but no doubt Burton was haunted by another plane crash death. It seemed an especially cruel turn of fate, not just for Johnson, of course, that a second crash fatality should influence the trajectory of Burton's young life, one month to the day after his uncle died.

After learning in May they'd made the team, Hovland and Burton returned to Sun Valley to train with famed coach Leif Odmark. Burton would not have needed financial support, but he recalled in 2002 that he and

In a promotional photograph taken at Sun Valley, members of the 1952 U.S. Olympic Cross-Country Team race a trio of pronghorn antelope. Coach Leif Odmark leads the group; behind him (left to right) are John Burton, John Caldwell, Si Dunklee, and George Hovland.

some teammates were employed in a sort of sponsorship by Averell Harriman's Union Pacific Railroad (Harriman, a skilled skier, had founded Sun Valley along his railroad to boost ticket sales). They did track maintenance for a few hours each day and received enough money to live on while they trained. Their training regime wasn't particularly organized, at least not from the top down. In November 1951, with the games scant months away, a member of the U.S. Olympic Committee advised Hovland to "start taking long walks" to get in shape.

The American skiers arrived in Oslo for the games. At least some of the cross-country squad had not brought their skis, so they had to buy new ones in a department store. Signs of Olympic success were not promising for the Americans. One day when they were training on the Nordmarka trails north of Oslo, a middle-aged Norwegian banker was on the course. He skied the young Yankees into the ground. Hovland had qualified to compete in both Nordic combined and cross-country. Watching him take practice jumps on a slide smaller than the famed Holmenkollen, where the Olympic competition would take place, the coaches had second thoughts. "We've never had a fatality on the ski team yet," one of the coaches told Hovland, "and we aren't going to start now." Hovland was dropped from the combined squad.

Being in Norway, the skiers made use of a sauna after a training session. Burton, as his teammates teased him at a reunion fifty years later, was the only one who showed up wearing a swimsuit.

Two other Minnesotans had traveled to Oslo for the Olympics, Pete Fosseide and Erik Judeen. The pair volunteered to help during the jumping competition and were in fan heaven as they strapped on skis and tamped down the snow of

Pete Fosseide and Erik Judeen in Oslo when they traveled to Norway to watch and volunteer in the 1952 Olympics.

The flame from the hearth in Sondre Norheim's cottage, seen here in 1964, has lit the ceremonial torch for the Olympic Games three times.

the Holmenkollen's outrun between jumps. Judeen's mother was still alive in Norway; he hadn't seen her for twenty-five years. Nor had he seen his sister since then, and they went skiing in the mountains during his visit. In her midfifties, his sister Ella was several years older than he was. She and Judeen skied to a mountain cabin and back. When Judeen returned home to Duluth, he told his wife and daughters that he hadn't been able to keep up with his older sister—"she skied my pants off."

The 1952 games kicked off with the first Winter Olympics torch relay. Sondre Norheim was long dead and forgotten in the United States, yet his name lived on in Norway. The torch lighting commenced on February 13 from the fireplace inside Norheim's cottage in Morgedal. Mikkel

A massive crowd watches the ski jumping competition at the 1952 Winter Olympics at Holmenkollen.

Hemmestveit was still alive at the age of eighty-eight, having returned to Morgedal from Red Wing almost sixty years earlier. Perhaps he was present for the ceremony honoring his mentor. Mikkel's nephew, Olav Hemmestveit, carried the lit torch on skis down the same slopes on which Norheim had taught the Hemmestveit children to shred like proper Telemarkings. Torch in hand, Hemmestveit schussed down the hill to a memorial for Norheim at its base, where a ceremony was held before a 225-kilometer relay began toward Oslo, during which ninety-four skiers carried the torch. The Olympic torch was lit again at Norheim's hearth for the 1960 Squaw Valley games (the relay involved an airplane) and once more in advance of the

1994 Lillehammer games. A broader recognition of Norheim in America would have to wait a while longer.

The American cross-country skiers were indeed not contenders. Of the eighty entrants who started the eighteen-kilometer race, the only American in the top fifty was Teddy Farwell from Massachusetts in forty-third place. John Burton finished in sixty-seventh place and George Hovland in seventy-first. The U.S. jumping squad fared better, with Willis Olson from Eau Claire finishing twenty-second.

The 1952 Olympic Games were the first to have a women's cross-country contest. Twenty skiers from eight countries competed in a ten-kilometer race. Three Finns took gold, silver, and bronze. The United States did not field a team, nor would they for another twenty years.

After Lydia Wideman, Mirja Hietamies, and Siiri Rantanen swept the podium, the women were ridiculed back home in Finland for being unladylike. An article written much later in *Cross-Country Skier* magazine, titled "Track! to the Male Chauvinists," described how the women were mocked in the Finnish media. One comic depicted Wideman battling her way along the track, her faced strained in exertion. The sight of a woman undergoing such physical strain prompted the spectators along the course to shield their eyes from the horror. Another comic expressed dismay over women snot-rocketing—that tried-and-true method of blowing cold-inspired snot from one's nose without having to let go of a ski pole and bother with a tissue. To stop her from snot-rocketing, a male race officiant held a handkerchief and wiped Rantanen's nose as she raced. As the author of "Track!" concluded, "For men to look like that was accepted. But for women? Disgusting! Simply, disgusting!" Nonetheless, by the 1956

John Burton racing in the 1952 Olympics.

Olympics, thirty-seven skiers from eleven countries raced in the women's ten-kilometer event, and a relay race was added.

After Oslo, John Burton wrote in a ski periodical, "There are probably many skiers and non-skiers alike who read the results of the 1952 Olympic Cross Country Races and wondered if any progress is being made. . . . The discrepancy in the cross country skiing ability of our skiers and theirs [Scandinavians] is considerable. The reasons for this were quite apparent to all of us after our first few weeks in Norway." In America, Burton noted, recreational skiing had developed largely around the tow rope and chairlift. But in Norway, ski touring was the great national pastime, and there were twenty tourers for every racer.

The Ishpeming Ski Club started having cross-country races again in 1951, after a quarter-century hiatus. The club's 1953 cross-country race was misleadingly called the North American Cross-Country Championships. The actual national championship was held the following month, with a much deeper pool of competition. A Minnesotan named Norm Oakvik won the Ishpeming race, ten seconds ahead of George Hovland, who finished seventeen seconds ahead of John Burton. Oakvik was a friend and competitor of Hovland and Burton, and no one would do more in building a Twin Cities cross-country scene in the next decade.

🌲

Al Lindley had left Grace Carter Lindley enough money to put their two kids through school and to pay taxes on and heat their large house, which, according to their daughter, sucked down fuel oil like a battleship. Lindley had stabled polo ponies at Fort Snelling. In the early mornings, Grace liked to ride one horse, while leading the other four across the Mendota Bridge over the Mississippi River and down to the undeveloped river flats where they were free to cavort. After Al's death, Grace reduced the string to two horses. She had to feed them, so she started working.

Well connected socially, Grace began writing a column called "Chanticleer" about sports and happenings around town for a Minneapolis newspaper, as well as hosting a radio interview show on WCCO, a popular Twin Cities station. In 1954, she wrote a column for the short-lived newspaper the *Minnesota–Wisconsin Ski News*. Some columns were recollections of her racing days, while others were flirty and more personal. In her most interesting piece, she took a gentle approach to promoting women's skiing.

The postwar era was proving to be more restrictive to women's skiing than earlier decades had been. By the 1950s, the ideas expressed jokingly in the crude comics of the 1940s had fully blossomed. Cross-country after the war fell to an even lower profile than before, mostly vanishing from skiing periodicals; therefore, to get an idea of women's skiing, one must look at the downhill-dominated literature. By the end of the 1940s and early 1950s, women were more often features of the ski hills than participants. Women skiers were wanted, but their role was to decorate the slopes and not ski in a way in which they might break a sweat and look gross or, heaven forbid, be competitors to men.

"Look at that Profile," states an advertisement in the 1949 *American Ski Annual* for Profile Ski Wear. Two dapper middle-aged gents grin lasciviously at the buxom profile of a young blond woman skier who grins obediently in return. The *Minnesota–Wisconsin Ski News* featured the Ski News Coupon

Even as technology improved, ski culture of the postwar era was known more for celebrating women's aesthetics rather than their athleticism. In this photograph from 1946, Lillian Stetler poses at Warner Hardware Company's downtown Minneapolis store with magnesium skis developed by Dow Chemical Company.

This suggestive advertisement for Profile Ski Wear appeared in the 1949 *American Ski Annual*.

Girl, who, as the paper noted, "may not be dressed for the skiing climate." The Coupon Girl was a beaming young woman who was topless and hid her breasts behind a sign reading "Ski News." In photographs, wearing short shorts and a tube top the size of a can cozy, the Coupon Girl demonstrated stretches that skiers could do to limber up before hitting the slopes.

After Al Lindley died, recalled Grace Carter Lindley's daughter, his powerful friends came along one by one to console and proposition his widow, to which Grace replied with characteristic spunk, "Sure, we can have an affair, right after you tell your wife." In her column, she discussed whether girls should race and picked up the thread discussed by her Olympic teammate Helen Boughton-Leigh in 1936. Carter, after all, was one of those "hard-bitten janes" that Boughton-Leigh warned skiing could turn a woman into. Carter began her column explaining that several times each year parents asked her if they should allow their daughters to race. "I usually tell the parent no," Grace started, "because that's what he wants to hear. . . . If a girl is really keen she'll race anyway. When the girl asks me, I say yes after delivering this free lecture. . . . The direst threats both to health and femininity have proven unfounded. Almost all of them [former women ski racers] have married—had children, and interestingly enough look pretty much as they did in their racing days."

🌲

In 1952, the International Ski Federation had tried to eliminate ladies' downhill competitions. The National Ski Association stood opposed to the idea, and the women's division remained. That same year, a girl named Linda Christianson was born in rural Barron, Wisconsin. In the fall, her father took apart a nail keg and made her a pair of skis from the staves. The little skis were just twenty-nine inches long and three inches wide. Her father, Glenn, added a block of wood to the center of the ski and a leather toe strap to serve as a binding. As soon as she could stand, Christianson was on her skis. As she and her older brother, Peter, improved on the snow, they traded in the barrel stave skis for Lund skis that Glenn bought from Boehmers Hardware in Rice Lake.

Living on a dead-end road by a creek, Linda and her brother could ski out their front door, following the creek and establishing trails as they went. They skied to the high school, which had a tobogganing hill they liked to run. Linda loved climbing the stairs to the top of the toboggan slide with her skis nonchalantly draped over her shoulder, imagining that she was climbing a ski jump. They'd schuss the slope, turn around, herringbone uphill until it grew too steep, and then take off their skis and climb the stairs again.

Starting on handmade barrel stave skis, siblings Peter and Linda Christianson eventually upgraded to Lund skis bought by their father from a hardware store in Rice Lake, Wisconsin.

Skis produced at C. A. Lund's factory in Hastings, Minnesota (advertised on this poster circa 1955), were sold wholesale to retailers like Boehmers Hardware in Rice Lake, Wisconsin.

Closer to home was a derelict creamery, and the kids would play in the milk can shed, where somebody had left a few pairs of handmade wooden skis. The skis were carved by hand and remarkably long and heavy.

Glenn convinced the snowplow driver to pile a massive snow mound at the end of his road. When the pile got big enough, he put up wooden stairs on the street side and then fashioned a ramp with a jump. The outrun for the ski slide ran through two neighbors' yards. Peter and Linda skied down the slide countless times. The neighborhood kids ran it on toboggans but didn't ski, which to Linda was preposterous. She skied with her father as he tended his trapline that caught beaver, muskrat, and mink. And when heavy snow made the roads impassable to vehicles, Glenn and Linda would ski to the drugstore. The pharmacist gave them the prescriptions that people needed, and father and daughter spent the day delivering medicine by ski.

Of Norwegian descent, Glenn Christianson had been a ski jumper in his youth. He'd grown up near Madison, in Stoughton, where many Norwegians had settled and formed one of the five original ski clubs in the NSA. On weekends, the Christianson family traveled to watch jumping tournaments in places like Viroqua, Westby, Eau Claire, and the Upper Peninsula of Michigan. Linda Christianson's girlhood heroes were ski jumpers, like

Linda Christianson's mother captioned this picture in her family photo album: "January, 1958, Iron Mountain, Michigan; –20 degrees Brrrr. Left home at 5 a.m., drove and drove for National Ski Jump Tourney. Called off on account of wind."

Gene Cutler, John Balfanz, and Lloyd "Snowball" Severud, from Chetek, whom she remembered as a "svelte little guy." "They were like gods to me," she said.

Linda wanted to be a ski jumper. At Eau Claire, she and the local boys would don skis and stamp down snow on the outrun beneath the jump to prep it for landings, the same task Fosseide and Judeen had done at Holmenkollen. But when she asked adults with the Eau Claire club if she could ski the slide, they always said no. Sometimes she tried to walk up the jump, but someone would stand in her way and block her passage.

The toboggan slide in Viroqua prohibited girls as well. Twenty-five years earlier, Wisconsin had held girls' jumping contests, but times had changed.

"That was one of my first hard lessons about that kind of thing," Christianson said, wondering what would have happened had she pulled down her cap to hide that she was a girl. She used to go with Glenn to sell his furs in Rice Lake. Every spring a buyer from the Hudson's Bay Company would hole up in a room at the Starlite Motel filled with trappers and their furs. The men smoked and drank. Linda was always the only girl. Glenn would tell her to pull her stocking cap down as far as it would go. When she was about twelve, she understood this was because she was a girl, and she stopped going. Eventually, she gave up her dreams of becoming a ski jumper. The prevailing attitudes on what was appropriate for girls were enough to keep most of them from developing an interest in ski jumping. Yet for the outliers like Linda, roadblocks, more tangible than expectations, prevented her from pursuing her desired sport. Had things happened differently, an infusion of girl jumpers may have propped up a sport on the wane.

♠

Hastened by the popularity of downhill skiing, jumping was entering its own period of decline. Downhill delivered thrills more readily than jumping and with less commitment. A popular jumper and 1936 Olympian from the Eau Claire club named Jimmy Hendrickson died after a crash at the Norge club's jump in Chicago in 1948. Hendrickson had survived Omaha Beach and the Battle of the Bulge only to die from his favorite sport at the age of thirty-five. That kind of tragedy could turn off many an aspiring jumper.

Aside from the risk inherent to ski jumping, simply maintaining a jump required regular work from its club. A wooden structure that rose above the surrounding landscape was subjected to high winds and routine damage. And unlike the slopes at a ski hill, a ski jump required preparation prior to use. The outrun had to be prepped so that it was even. Sometimes, if there wasn't enough snow, it would have to be painstakingly hauled up onto the jump in buckets.

At the Itasca Ski and Outing Club's annual tournament in Coleraine, spectator attendance began to drop in 1950. Previous years' crowds num-

Cloquet jumpers (*from left:* coach Joe Nowak, Tom Hanson, Ed Burman, and Lonnie Hvara) gather snow for the Pine Valley jump in December 1961. One reason ski jumping dropped in popularity as downhill caught on was the labor required to maintain a jump.

bered in the several thousands. Six thousand fans came to watch in 1949, followed by twenty-five hundred in 1950. By the next year, fewer than two thousand bought tickets. The competing jumpers in the annual tournament were still among the best in the country, but public interest had faded. One factor was the television. America's great sedentary revolution coincided with the Itasca club's decline in ticket sales. Television ownership went from uncommon in the late 1940s to usual in half of all homes by 1955. Additionally, ice hockey was becoming more popular on the Iron Range. The Itasca club lost members in 1952 when a youth hockey team

Hill captain Werner Schorr smooths out the snow near the base of the jump during the Blackhawk Ski Club's annual tournament at Tomahawk Ridge, west of Middleton, Wisconsin, 1956.

formed in town. The club dwindled to a dozen skiers, becoming disproportionately reliant on the progeny of Ole Mangseth. Five of Mangseth's grandchildren and one son made up the backbone of the Itasca club.

As club jumpers disappeared, the remaining members put more work into an adjacent downhill ski area that would soon be called Mount Itasca. "Jumpers learned early on if they wanted to ski they had to put in a lot of their own physical labor to ready the jump and landing," surmised Cavour Johnson, who made a documentary about the club in 2017. "This wasn't necessarily so with new skiers attracted to downhill skiing. Instead of becoming members of the club with all the work involved, they could just pay 25 cents for the tow and ride the slopes." The Itasca club was not alone in its struggle.

By 1954, the Central Division treasurer's report listed thirty-four clubs as late in paying dues and seven more as owing additional funds to the division.

One of the country's most venerable clubs was in its death throes. Red Wing's Aurora club had been limping along since the 1936 national championships, competing at a lower level than it had traditionally. By 1950, the club was struggling to reimburse its jumpers for gas money as they traveled to tournaments. It hadn't made enough money to host even a minor tournament for four years. Then a windstorm blew down the club's jump on Burns Hill. The Aurora club had to sell half ownership of Burns Hill to a motorcycle club that wanted to use it for hill climbing during the summer. By 1952, the Aurora club had only four competing jumpers, two in Class B and two in Class C. The club was so broke in 1955 that its secretary-treasurer paid the Burns Hill property taxes out of his own pocket. He entreated the city of Red Wing to donate to the club some discarded light towers from a municipal athletic field, hoping to somehow build a new jump from the towers and attract a new crop of jumpers. The city declined, and the secretary-treasurer kept on paying the club's taxes with personal funds.

🌲

The Northland, Lund, and Gregg companies continued to churn out skis after the demise of the Strand Ski Company. By 1945, C. A. Lund had three factories—the original in Hampden Park; one in Laconia, New Hampshire, which had opened in 1938; and one in Hastings, which made cheaper skis and contracted jobs for other brands, such as Macy's (the department store paid Lund to make skis affixed with the store's label).

Less than a week into 1945, the Hastings plant burned to the ground. The fire was blamed on an overheated motor. Mounds of wood shavings and lumber coupled with hot-running equipment made ski factories prone to combustion. Lund relocated the plant to a new location in North St. Paul, but that October his original Hampden Park factory burned. Nearing defeat, Lund moved all Minnesota operations to the new North St. Paul factory. His domination of America's ski market was a thing of the past. Laminate skis were growing in popularity, and new companies had risen in other parts of the country.

Lund's son Carl ran the New Hampshire factory. His other son, Ambrose, worked for him in North St. Paul. Ambrose envied his brother's distance and

As the exhilarating rush of downhill skiing took hold in America, advertising followed suit, as seen in this poster from Gregg Ski Manufacturing Company from 1948.

independence from their father. "Father didn't let Ambrose too far out from the leash," recalled a former employee in a 2014 interview by historian Greg Fangel. "He was a hard task-master. When C.A. walked in the office, it was kind of like a green eyeshade office, you could see them all tighten up. It was that kind of place."

The employee, Robert Hanson, was Lund's materials buyer in the early 1950s. As a young newlywed, Hanson had applied to Northland because the factory was near his home in North St. Paul, and he liked the idea of being able to walk home to have lunch with his wife. His wife joined him on lumber-buying trips to the east. They'd drive from Minnesota as far as the Catskills of New York to seek out ash and elm that would be made into skis and hockey sticks, which Northland also produced. Northland also bought rough hickory boards from southern states and still made some cheap skis from pine. All the lumber was kiln dried in a separate building outside the factory. Inside, workers lathed and bent the boards and then used a router to make a groove along the edges of the skis. Steel edges were put into the groove and mounted with tiny screws. By the 1950s, Northland no longer made cross-country skis.

Lund's unethical tendencies made lumber companies hesitant to work with him and Hanson's job more difficult. When raw boards arrived at the North St. Paul plant, in order to cheat the lumber companies out of full payment, C. A. Lund would falsely claim that part of the shipment was substandard and then refuse to pay the agreed-upon full price. Eventually the lumber companies refused to ship to Lund until he'd hired a third-party inspector to certify shipments upon arrival.

Lund had lost a court case in 1939 against the National Labor Relations Board. He permitted his workers to join a labor organization called the Independent Order of Ski Workers, which he himself controlled. When employees at the Hastings factory voted to instead join the Woodenware Workers Union, over which Lund had no sway, he fired the two employees responsible for organizing the switch. The Woodenware Workers took Lund to court, where he was ordered to bargain with the elected union and not only reinstate the two fired employees but pay them the wages they would have earned during the two years between their firing and the finding of the court. Perhaps irritation over those lost funds kept Lund up at night in his expensive home on Mississippi Boulevard in St. Paul.

Walter Spidahl, who in the 1920s watched in suspense as his father

Walter Spidahl glides down a hill at Theodore Wirth Park in Minneapolis, 1947. Spidahl began selling skis for Christian Lund in the early 1950s.

made him a pair of skis from a salvaged oak board, began selling skis for C. A. Lund in the early 1950s. Spidahl owned a ski shop in Fergus Falls and one day drove to North St. Paul to buy more stock. Although Spidahl had grown up Nordic skiing, he followed the wave of the times and catered his shop to downhill skiers. Spidahl sat down in C.A. Lund's office for a meeting with Lund and Ambrose. Walter impressed Lund with his knowledge of the several new models of downhill safety bindings that had come on the market.

"Valter, I think you should be working for us," Lund said to Spidahl, his accent recorded by Spidahl in a skiing autobiography written in 2007. Lund, who apparently never lost his Norwegian brogue, offered Spidahl a job as a Northland salesman for Michigan's Upper Peninsula, Minnesota, Wisconsin, and the Dakotas. Spidahl would earn a percentage from the

At its factory in Laconia, New Hampshire, Christian Lund's Northland company tried producing metal skis in the late 1950s but soon lost out to popular brands like Hart.

skis he sold. He loaded the skis he'd bought for his shop into his red pickup and drove home to Fergus Falls before accepting the offer.

In 1952 on his sales route, Walter Spidahl brought along his wife, Liz, young son, and infant daughter. The family toured Michigan and Wisconsin while Walter sold skis. The following year the North St. Paul Northland factory burned. A newspaper described the scene: "The pleasant piney smell of wood being molded into skis for the nation's skiers dissolved into the sickening pungent odor of charred wood." The night watchman, George Banks, accidently started the blaze while shoveling wood shavings into the boiler. He died in the conflagration. Robert Hanson lived nearby and was one of the first on the scene. He instructed the firefighters to drench a corner of the building where a big safe sat, which they did, saving many of the company documents. Most everything else was destroyed. A newspaper listed the loss at "over $500,000 in potential skiing thrills."

Within two days of the fire, Lund had rented office space in North St. Paul. Next, he took over the factory of the Gregg Ski Manufacturing Company, back in Hampden Park, at 2326 Endicott. Unable to keep up with its competitors in the production of new, laminated skis, the Gregg company had fallen deeply in debt. Lund purchased Gregg's debt from the bank and took over the factory. So ended Gregg skis, which had never been as big a manufacturer as Strand or Northland but had churned out many a pair of split boards since the 1930s for clients ranging from the Tenth Mountain Division to Sears. Two weeks after buying the Gregg company, C. A. Lund was making Northlands in its former factory. He continued making Northland and Lund skis until his death in 1965, when he had a stroke in May and died two weeks later at the age of eighty-two.

Lund's sons, Karl and Ambrose, wasted no time in selling the company to Larson Industries, a Minnesota boat maker. Walter Spidahl continued as sales manager under the new ownership. Northland tried modernizing its line by making fiberglass skis, but they flopped. Spidahl was offered a job in Seattle with Krystal Skis and headed west. Just as the Strand Ski

The Gregg Ski Manufacturing Company's headquarters in St. Paul, 1950.

always close to my
HART
Metal
SKIS

THERE'S A HART FOR EVERY SKIER !
STANDARD · PROFESSIONAL · COMPETITION · HART J/R.
FROM $79.50 TO $99.50.
TAKING LESSONS? BE SURE TO TAKE THEM FROM A CERTIFIED SKI INSTRUCTOR.
MORE AND MORE CERTIFIED INSTRUCTORS ARE USING AND RECOMMENDING HARTS!
THE HART METAL SKI, 2400 ENDICOTT STREET, ST. PAUL 14, MINN.
Canada: Harvey E. Dodds Company, 2274 Moreau Street, Montreal, P.Q.

Known for their "Cadillac ride," the metal skis produced by St. Paul's Hart Manufacturing Company were top-of-the-line quality. The Hart company evidently sponsored the Minnesota high school state meet, as young skiers raced in bibs bearing the company name into the 1970s.

Company had floundered after losing its founder, Northland and Lund skis soon disappeared.

The last of the Midwest's big ski companies was founded by Harry Holmberg, a ski engineer who had worked for both Gregg and Strand. Holmberg's brother and father shared the first name Hartvig and the nickname Hart. Hart Sr. was a Swedish immigrant; Hart Jr. was a carpenter with a custom wood shop that he ran with a tool-and-die operator named Ed Bjork. When the Holmberg brothers and Bjork teamed up to make skis, they named the company after Hart Sr.

Hart skis were highly innovative, with surfaces made from continuous pieces of metal: the edges were long strips and not little screwed-on segments; the tops and bottoms were metal, too, alleviating the need for a laminated hickory core, as all other skis at the time featured. Harts were strictly downhill skis, yet the Holmbergs were Swedes, and Harry had learned the craft at the tail end of the arc of Midwestern ski making that had begun with Norwegian peasant knowledge and Aksel Holter's seven imported Hagens. Harry's knowledge, gleaned from working at Strand and Gregg, was essential: he was the only one of the three founders who had ever skied, and only casually at that. This was an indication of how much skiing had changed in the past half century—it had become engrained deeply enough in American culture that even nonskiers would choose to pick it up for a business venture. The engineer had supplanted the craftsman, and Hart skis would prove to be excellent.

In 1954, a fire obliterated the Hart shop, but the men bounced back and by early 1955 were up and running again. Hart Jr. took sample skis to a gear show and sold orders. He took out a loan from First National Bank of St. Paul, and he and Bjork mortgaged their homes. The Holmbergs received a patent in 1958 for a "ski with steel and/or aluminum structural layers top and bottom with a light particle-board core." The founders' sons got involved in the business. Bjork's boy had started skiing on a Twin Cities golf course when he was twelve. When he began sweeping the factory floor at age sixteen, he became the most experienced skier on staff. They hired a star Swiss skier, who did much to promote the brand.

The Hart company thrived in the late 1950s and into the 1960s. The skis were expensive but had a lifetime warranty. They weren't racing skis but were nonetheless regarded for their "Cadillac ride." Harts were favored by the burgeoning freestyle ski movement. In 1966, the St. Paul factory produced 144,000 pairs of skis and employed two hundred people. Two years later, Beatrice Foods, a Chicago consortium, purchased Hart, and so began the company's decline. A series of businessmen gradually ran Hart Manufacturing Company into the ground. The era of commercial Midwestern ski making, which had begun with Mikkel Hemmestveit in St. Croix Falls in the late 1880s, had come to an end.

♠

In October 1961, Erik Judeen fell ill and was diagnosed with cancer. The decades of drinking, tobacco use, and asbestos work had caught up with him. In February, Erik Wilhelm Judeen died at the age of fifty-nine. He'd kept racing at least until the late 1940s, winning a race in Thunder Bay in 1947 and taking eighth place in the 1948 national cross-country championships at Fond du Lac. By that time, his protégés George Hovland and Charlie Banks, along with John Burton, had become faster skiers. Judeen had come to America with little and made a life and family. He left behind a wife and three daughters, two of them adults and the youngest seventeen. His widow, Doris, no stranger to grief after the early deaths of her father and brother, was lonely without him. At least his union job left her financially solvent. Her grandson, who would become a bush pilot and move deep into the Ontario wilderness, often visited her in the house at the foot of Enger Hill.

Judeen's death hit Charlie Banks hard. Without Judeen, who had so viscerally loved skiing, the relatively vibrant Duluth cross-country world seemed fragile. That passion for cross-country was like joy in a bottle, which Judeen and Fosseide had entrusted to Banks; Banks would always treasure that gift and carry it carefully in the hope that he might

Erik Judeen out for a ski.

continue its passage through the generations. On January 23, 1963, Banks held the first Erik Judeen Memorial Invitational Ski Race on his Clover Valley trails on Korkki Road. The winner of the Judeen Memorial would receive a trophy presented by the Judeen family; Doris and her daughter Joan presented the trophy to the winner during the race's formative years.

The Judeen Memorial is the longest-running cross-country race in the Midwest. In the early years, it was a sanctioned Central Division race, making it somewhat different from the citizens' races that would begin popping up in the early 1970s. In a Central Division competition, racers' scores would give them points for which young skiers could earn a spot on the U.S. Junior National Ski Team. Older skiers earned points for rankings, which didn't necessarily lead to anything other than high standing in the skiing community and bragging rights.

♠

In 1965, a great-granddaughter of Sondre Norheim began looking for her forebearer's grave. She lived in Atlanta. Her curiosity was piqued when she found her great-grandfather listed in the *Encyclopedia Britannica* for his contributions to skiing. She knew he'd died in McHenry County, North Dakota, so she wrote a letter explaining her search and sent it to the county courthouse. The letter found its way into the hands of the county judge, who after work simply walked it over to the house of his neighbor, Richard Wanberg. If anyone would know where the bones of the old Norwegian lay, it would be the 100 percent Norwegian, raised-on-a-homesteader-farm Wanberg. Wanberg had served as the pastor at Norway Lutheran Church since he'd graduated from St. Paul's Luther Seminary in 1919. The church was the center of social life for the area's Norwegians and stood some miles outside town. Surrounded on three sides by crop fields, its cemetery faced the old brick church, beyond which lay the modest relief of the Mouse River valley.

Pastor Wanberg took on the search for Norheim's grave, enlisting the help of the elderly church groundskeeper, Olaf Nelson—the boy Norheim had given ski lessons to so many years before. Nelson's parents had given Norheim's wife, Rannei, the nickname Lena Claypipe. The old man knew of two graves in the cemetery that contained unknown remains. Nelson and Wanberg concluded that Norheim, who had died in 1897, was buried

Towering over the North Dakota prairie, the Norway Lutheran Church near Denbigh stands as a monument to generations of Norwegian immigrants. Its cemetery is the resting place of the great Sondre Norheim.

in a wooden casket, whereas the other unknown burial had occurred later and would contain a metal casket. The untreated wood would have decayed in the ensuing six decades. If one of the graves contained a metal casket, they could rule that one out. Wanberg told Nelson he'd meet him at the cemetery to settle the question after the next long rain. Later that summer, following a three-day deluge, Wanberg stopped by the town maintenance building, grabbed a ten-foot length of rebar, and joined Nelson at the cemetery. They carried the rebar to the first unknown plot, placed their four hands on the length of it, and began pounding into the rain-softened earth. Nelson was elderly but strong from a life working the prairie. Down the rebar went. The men were kneeling now, ramming it down, until, finally, the rebar hit something hard. They knocked against the buried object. No doubt about it; they'd hit a metal casket. They moved on to the next site, working the rod deep into the ground. They kept pounding until there was little rebar remaining aboveground. They concluded this was Norheim's resting place.

Larrie Wanberg, the pastor's son, recounted this story about identifying the grave. Larrie was born in 1930 and grew up on the prairie. As a teen, he did some skiing, but it was "cowboy skiing," as he called it, skijoring behind a horse. Sometimes he and his friends would tie a rope to a car while one kid strapped on skis (the old wooden kind with leather toe straps for bindings), held onto the rope, and skied the ditches. They would go up to fifty miles per hour. "You had to know the territory," Wanberg said, mentioning the elevated grade of crossroads, which served as jumps.

The younger Wanberg traveled to Oslo in 1957 as a Fulbright Scholar. He was eager to learn how to ski by his own power, so he began by practicing with someone at his level—a five-year-old Norwegian boy. Wanberg and a group of five other Fulbright Scholars trained on weekends for a mountain ski tour they planned for the Easter holiday, when throngs of Norwegians often headed out on long jaunts through the mountains. Wanberg and his crew skied and hiked the two highest peaks in Norway, Galdhøpiggen and Glittertind. Sixty years later, he remembered his long, high ski with pride, recollecting the 360-degree view from the summit.

In the summer of 1966, in a joint effort between Norwegians and North Dakotans, a concrete pad was poured over Norheim's grave, upon which a large stone was placed. An iron foundry in Telemark made and donated a plaque that was affixed to the stone. Hundreds of people attended the dedication at the old Lutheran church, at which the state's leading historian called Norheim "the fastest man in the world at the time."

In Minot, North Dakota, near a replica of the Gol Stave Church, a handsome statue commemorates the legacy of the father of modern skiing, Sondre Norheim.

An annual wreath-laying ceremony is now held at Norheim's grave as part of Minot's Norsk Høstfest (Norwegian Fall Festival). When visiting Norheim's grave in the late 1990s, former Norwegian ambassador to the United States Tom Vraalsen gave a speech in which he said, "Without Sondre Norheim, no Aspen, no Vail, no Holmenkollen. I even doubt that there would be any Olympic Winter Games had it not been for this great man. He is the father of modern skiing."

Students traverse the trails at Bagley Nature Area on the Duluth campus of the University of Minnesota, circa 1973.

6

Cross-Country Revolution

1960s–1970s

After a promising start, state-sanctioned high school Nordic skiing in Michigan was drying up. Ishpeming and Ironwood were the dominant cross-country teams in the Upper Peninsula division, which began in 1952. In 1961, ten high schools competed in the Upper Peninsula championship, with fifty-two boys and thirty-six girls skiing downhill, twenty-seven boys racing cross-country, and eighteen boys jumping. By 1963, only three schools sent jumpers and two schools sent cross-country skiers; as a result, the Michigan High School Athletic Association dropped Nordic events. The MHSAA sponsored its first statewide meet in 1975, which featured only downhill events. The same year in Wisconsin, which had never sanctioned Nordic contests, high school downhill skiing came to an end for a lack of participating schools. In Michigan and Wisconsin, a limited number of youth Nordic skiing clubs would form to offer opportunities for competition. In the late 1960s in Minnesota, on the other hand, interest in high school skiing was about to explode.

Winning fourteen state titles and producing a number of Olympians, Cloquet was the dominant Minnesota high school team of the 1960s and 1970s. A small northern town with a large Scandinavian population, Cloquet had fielded a skiing squad since the first Arrowhead High School Meet in 1932, but the team didn't become a powerhouse until a star Duluth jumper named Joe Nowak moved there to take a teaching job in 1958. As a boy, Nowak idolized George Kotlarek, who had reclaimed jumping glory for Duluth by winning the national title in Red Wing when Nowak was just seven. Nowak started jumping in his backyard on pine skis with bindings made from bicycle inner tubes. Before settling down and taking the teaching gig, he competed for the U.S. Olympic team and was ranked among the top ten jumpers in the country.

Nowak's life was skiing; he never married or had children. At the time, Cloquet didn't have much in the way of skiing facilities, so Nowak found a good hill on forty acres owned by Northwest Paper, which ran the papermill in town. Nowak persuaded the company to donate the land and spearheaded developing what would become Pine Valley Ski Area.

Joe Nowak (*far left*) is excited to stand next to his hero, George Kotlarek, in Chicago at a competition hosted by the Norge club in 1946. Also pictured are Elwood Ramfjord, Mitch Ronning, and Les Pelander.

Rick Nelson, who won the state jumping championship for Cloquet in 1966 and 1967, remembered going for a hike with Nowak in eighth grade. Walking through untracked forest, when they reached the edge of a swamp, Nowak picked Rick up and carried him across to dry ground. "Here's where we're going to have the ski hill," Nowak said, gesturing excitedly at the thickly wooded rise ahead of them. By the end of 1962, the community had built a temporary jump, which was replaced the next year with a larger, permanent slide. Pine Valley soon grew to include cross-country trails and a couple of slalom runs with rope tows. "He was pretty special to

Cloquet's Pine Valley Ski Area was a fixture on the Minnesota high school ski scene for decades.

all of us," Nelson said of Nowak, who, some years when the school district lacked money to pay coaches, coached for free and paid assistants from his own pocket.

While Nowak coached jumping, he recruited a local man named Mike Marciniak to instruct cross-country. Marciniak was a recent Cloquet graduate who had taken third place in the state meet, gone on to compete internationally, and won a spot as an alternate on the 1960 Olympic team. With vibrant young coaches who were great skiers, Cloquet became the team to beat. The state meet moved from Chester Park to Pine Valley, where the home course advantage aided Cloquet's domination. Pine Valley

Pictured midflight during the 1967 state tournament at Chester Bowl, Cloquet jumper Rick Nelson won the Minnesota jumping title in 1966 and 1967.

Joe Nowak in 1963 with his skiers Dave Quinn, Gene Shotley, and Don Quinn. Shotley won the state cross-country title that year. In 1974, during the second American Birkebeiner, twin brothers Dave and Don Quinn took first and second place.

featured a big downhill called Gap Hill, which was followed by a sharp left turn. The corner was particularly arduous in the era of narrow classic trails and fragile wooden skis. Coaches knew to stick spare skis in the snow at the base of the hill. Cloquet skiers were ready to lay into the turn while out-of-towners were often unprepared and would crash. Those who snapped skis grabbed new ones from the snowbank and raced on.

By the mid-1960s, Americans were tired of the high cost of alpine skiing. Skiing periodicals frequently ran letters voicing concerns about how families had been priced out of the sport. Frank Elkins, perhaps the greatest ski journalist of the twentieth century, who covered all aspects of the sport for twenty-eight years with the *New York Times*, wrote an article about this concern in *Ski News*, the publication of the U.S. Ski Association (which in 1962 became the new name for the old National Ski Association). Elkins railed against the era of downhill-dominated skiing. The gear was too expensive, the clothes too fussy, the experience too manicured, and the resorts often high on price and low on good skiing.

Shifts in the American mindset also spurred interest in different forms of skiing. Ten years after the poem "Conservation" ("I think that I shall never ski—I'd hate to wreck a lovely tree!") mocked anyone opposed to denuding wooded slopes for ski resorts, a similar skiing periodical ran an article called "What Kind of Bug Are You?" Are you a ski bug or a litterbug? the article asked, urging the former. In 1966, instead of featuring a cover photo of a downhill skier, as it had done in virtually every other issue, the USSA's *Ski News* ran a photograph of a cross-country skier touring up a frozen river. The association began pushing cross-country ski touring in every issue. One article praised the retro-hip activity ("It is difficult to describe the exhilaration to be experienced in skiing up a logging road through dark timber") and listed five salesmen from around the country who sold cross-country gear. The only source east of the Rocky Mountains was Norm Oakvik in Minnesota. Ski touring was, of course,

An early member of the popular North Star Ski Touring Club, Dana Siskind skis at Murphy-Hanrehan Park Reserve in Savage, Minnesota.

cross-country skiing for fun, fitness, and connection to nature, in other words, a modern iteration of the *idraet*. The region's burgeoning interest in cross-country needed the changing manufacturing market in Norway to expand the availability of this type of ski.

As ski touring caught on in the United States, the competitive spirit of Norway's most famous export remained strong. Norwegian Gjermund Eggen won three gold medals at the FIS Nordic World Championships at Holmenkollen in 1966. For the first time in Norway, the ski races were televised. Norwegians tuned in and watched the skiers of their little nation trounce the all-powerful Soviets. Eggen became a star—as one translation of a Norwegian history book awkwardly put it, he was a "lady charm and role model to boys." In the mold of Sondre Norheim, Eggen "was a country boy who wanted to ski fast." Norwegians were buying more skis than ever before, and the country's factories expanded to keep up. A nation with fewer than four million citizens provided only so much market before manufactures began to look abroad.

Norwegian skier Gjermund Eggen speaks with reporters after a race in 1966. Eggen won three gold medals at the FIS Nordic World Championships that year.

Young Americans disillusioned with downhill skiing—and, more broadly, with America's indefatigable postwar glut of consumer materialism and suburban expansion—sought new priorities. Reconnecting with nature fit the bill. It was an era for the *idraet*, not as a formal approach to Nordic skiing but as a means of embracing the natural world while improving one's own self and chosen community. Ironically, Norwegian ski companies would assist by creating a product specifically for the American market. In 1971, four Norwegian ski makers banded together to form Skilom, a label that produced cross-country starter kits consisting of skis, poles, bindings, and boots. Madshus made the skis for Skilom, including the popular Birkebeiner ski first produced in 1970. The Birkebeiner was a beautiful dark-stained wooden ski with the model name written in runic-style letters sandwiched in an arabesque design. It was a ski that wouldn't look out of place on the foot of a hippie.

♣

The era also brought with it a reevaluation of gender roles. Sponsored by the U.S. Olympic Development Committee, the third annual National Institute of Girls' Sports convened in early 1966. Its goal was to get more girls and women involved in sports in order to build stronger Olympic teams. The USSA, still without women's cross-country or jumping teams, participated in the conference.

Gloria Chadwick, a former downhill racer and the executive secretary of the USSA, argued that American girls needed more physical education and sports opportunities in school in order for the country to excel in women's sports. The conference's keynote speaker, Dr. Phoebe M. Scott, said, "Until fairly recently, many persons viewed the few women who participated in sports as side show entertainers rather than serious performers." This statement perfectly described the role of lady jumpers like Natalie Bailey, who badly wanted to compete but had been relegated to separate exhibitioner status for the novelty of spectators.

Dr. Scott then broached the topic of the ages: the effect competitive sports had on "femininity," which seems as ridiculous today as the concern of nineteenth-century Norwegian doctors that an eleven-kilometer ski race would kill its participants from overexertion. "There is nothing in sports to say it causes the loss of femininity," Scott said. "Sports for women must

Jane Whitmore from Alaska competes in the 1967 girls' junior national at Charlie Banks's trail north of Duluth.

be based on their own interest, needs, and values." Dishearteningly, this was, in fact, a bold statement for the times, inferring that women should act in their own interests for their own sake rather than for men's approval. "It must help retain their feminine identity, not destroy it. Women will become full partners in this sports world," Scott predicted.

Later in 1966, preparing to field an Olympic cross-country team, the USSA declared that it would for the first time hold two girls' junior national cross-country events. Qualifying for the junior national team established rank and was part of the process of making the Olympic team. Charlie Banks hosted one of the junior national races at his Clover Valley trail on March 10. Several weeks earlier at the Judeen Memorial, Banks had instituted for the first time a girls' division. The lone contestant was his daughter Kathy, a seventh grader, though in future years the roster of girl skiers would grow.

The USSA soon invited Sweden's top two women racers to tour the country, stating, "It is our strong feeling that any psychological stigma that may be attached to girls racing will very rapidly be broken down upon contact with these two top international racers." Barbro Martinsson and Toini Gustafsson toured the United States for three weeks in early 1967, traveling through New England, Colorado, the Pacific Northwest, and Alaska.

"In America," one of the Swedes said, "everything seems to be geared to the easiest way of doing things. Hard physical work is to be avoided as much as possible." The technique of American skiers was adequate, the ladies observed, but conditioning was lacking. Gustafsson would go on to win gold medals in the five- and ten-kilometer races in Grenoble, France, the following year. The international skiing ambassadorship continued

A riveted crowd watches as a determined Toini Gustafsson sprints to victory in the 1963 Swedish Ski Championships in Luleå.

when two Olympic-caliber male Italian racers visited the Midwest. The Italians led ski seminars in Traverse City, Pine Valley in Cloquet, and Minneapolis, where they were hosted by Norm Oakvik.

♠

For most of the sixties, Norm Oakvik's house was the only place in the Twin Cities where a person could buy cross-country skis. He often stored his wares in his basement. "It was not a brightly lighted retail operation," recalled John Hollister, one of the many Minnesotans whom Oakvik turned on to cross-country. "I always thought of it as a dungeon." Prospective buyers made their way down a rickety staircase, navigating around Oakvik's weightlifting equipment and homemade chin-up bar. But the skis Oakvik imported—wooden Finnish Jarvinens and Norwegian Madshus—were top-notch.

Norm Oakvik was the son of Norwegian immigrants to North Minneapolis, where he was born in 1920. Oakvik's father, a carpenter, had been a jumper in Norway and taught his son to ski in Glenwood Park on homemade boards. Glenwood Park (called Theodore Wirth Park after 1938) in the 1920s was the heart of skiing in the Ski Capital of America, as Minneapolis was called for a time, and Oakvik would ski there all his long life. He jumped for Minneapolis North High School, which practiced on the Theodore Wirth Park jump, but didn't concentrate on cross-country until his late twenties. He won the Central Division's slalom title in 1947 and was the U.S. national Nordic combined champion in 1954. Oakvik was five foot three, lean, and muscular. He was the quintessential Norwegian bachelor ("He could have been a farmer, but he wasn't," one friend quipped), highly reserved and at times infuriatingly frugal. He would visit friends and bring them gifts such as a mostly full jar of mustard taken from his cupboard. On his way to Mora to ski the Vasaloppet trails, he relished stopping at a bakery in Cambridge to load up on discounted day-old doughnuts. When it came to spending time on the promotion of cross-country skiing, however, no one would give more in building up the Twin Cities cross-country culture.

Beginning in the 1950s, often with his friend John Burton, Oakvik coached skiers through the Minneapolis and Bush Lake clubs. Oakvik was a sheet metal worker, installing and repairing HVAC systems, or, as he put it, a "tin-knocker." From 1960 onward, he would take a leave of absence from his job every winter to teach cross-country skiing as a volunteer. Oakvik's association with the Bush Lake club was presumably through Burton. The club, of course, had been founded by Burton's uncle Al Lindley. Oakvik and Burton were yet another odd couple—the blue-collar immigrant's son with a high school degree and the monied descendant of Cotton Mather who'd gone to prep school and then Harvard—united by a mostly friendly sporting rivalry. They would squabble at times, like once after a race up north in which Oakvik led most of the way, with Burton trailing close behind. The trail they were on, as was typical for those primitive days of ski racing, was poorly groomed, and Oakvik essentially broke trail as he led, until the last quarter mile when Burton sprinted ahead and won. Oakvik was furious.

Jinny McWethy was one of Oakvik's closest friends. McWethy's husband had died in a sporting accident in the early 1950s, leaving her a widow with a young son. In the ensuing years, McWethy joined outdoor organizations to socialize with people of similar interests, like the Sierra Club and the Bush Lake Ski Club, through which she met Oakvik.

In 1965, the USSA formed a committee to encourage Midwestern interest in ski touring, reminiscent of the 1930s Central Ski Association committee with Peter Fosseide and H. C. Bradley. This time, though, unlike the unfulfilled promise of cross-country before the war, the stars aligned and the cross-country boom would actually happen. Oakvik and McWethy both joined the committee, helping to produce a forty-page booklet on ski touring, establishing a two-mile ski trail near the Bush Lake ski

In the 1960s and 1970s, few people were more recognizable in the burgeoning cross-country ski scene of the Upper Midwest than Norm Oakvik.

North Star Ski Touring Club founder Jinny McWethy at the Victoria Jonathan Chaska race in 1974.

jump, and making inroads with a state senator named Henry McKnight.

In 1967, Oakvik and McWethy cofounded the North Star Ski Touring Club. With nineteen members during its first winter, the club scheduled several ski trips and grew quickly. Once the club picked up steam, its members nicknamed McWethy "Mother North Star," embracing the earthy whimsy of the times. One of the club's earliest recruits was Solveig Olson. Olson had immigrated to the United States in 1965 from Norway, where she'd skied to school as a girl. She married an American and moved to Minnesota in 1968. Wanting something to do during the long Minnesota winters, Olson visited local ski shops looking for a pair of cross-country skis. Some of the clerks didn't understand what kind of ski she was asking for. If it wasn't downhill, what was it? None of the shops in town sold cross-country skis. She happened to see a small ad in a newspaper for the North Star Ski Touring Club. She and her husband went to the meeting, where they met Oakvik.

The Olsons soon made their way to Oakvik's house in Robbinsdale, where she recalled skis stacked up in his minimally adorned living room. The smell of pine tar was unmistakable. Olson and her husband each bought a pair. Later that same year, Hoigaard's, the venerable outfitter in St. Louis Park, Minnesota, started selling cross-country skis after buying out Oakvik's full inventory of one hundred pairs.

A North Stars trip to Steamboat Springs, Colorado, in the late 1960s or early 1970s.

One of Oakvik's protégés was Bonnie Fuller-Kask, who started skiing in the late 1960s when her younger brother became interested in ski jumping from a school friend and started taking weekend jumping lessons at Theodore Wirth Park from Minneapolis Ski Club coach Selmer Swanson. "My dad assumed I wanted to go too," Fuller-Kask said. "I don't remember being too interested either way." Fuller-Kask was older and learned more quickly than her brother. She was the only girl in the jumping lessons, but neither Swanson nor the other boys made an issue of it. After her brother biffed a landing and broke his leg, the Fuller kids' ski jumping equipment mysteriously vanished from their house. The Fullers switched from jumping lessons to cross-country with Norm Oakvik.

"Norm was pretty much the man who taught anybody," Fuller-Kask said. Boys' and girls' lessons were held separately. The girls' lessons didn't have as many skiers as the boys, but she recalled other girls skiing, and the Minneapolis club held separate boys' and girls' races Sundays on the trails by the Eloise Butler Wildflower Garden. Fuller-Kask got into the grind and

In 1960, outdoor retailer Hoigaard's moved their headquarters to a three-acre property in St. Louis Park off Highway 100. The company announced a specialty ski shop in 1963, which began selling cross-country gear in 1968.

After learning to ski from Norm Oakvik, Bonnie Fuller-Kask moved to Duluth and took over as head coach of the Duluth East Nordic team. Her boys' team held the title going into the 2005 state meet and is pictured here after finishing second. *From left:* Fuller-Kask, Joe Tofte, Max Jeronius, Jason Kask, Will Mitchell, Ted LaFrance, Karis Jones, and assistant coach Dave Kask.

trained hard. Her brother joined the Robbinsdale boys' ski team, but she had no competitive outlet aside from the Theodore Wirth races. "Everything was set wonderfully for the boys," she said. "There was nothing for the girls. You could be a cheerleader, which I wasn't interested in. They [the Minnesota State High School League] had the Girls Athletic Association. It was nothing. I wanted more than that. I skied on my own." The Girls Athletic Association was the MSHSL's powder-puff league, with a highly limited offering of casual girls' sports.

While Fuller-Kask's brother took the ski team bus to Theodore Wirth Park after school, she had to go home and get a ride from a parent to the park so she could train. Occasionally and arbitrarily, the Robbinsdale coach permitted Fuller-Kask to ride the bus with the boys. Sometimes at meets, the coaches let her ski the course before the race, for which she would receive a time, though it wouldn't be official. Occasionally a coach or two would get mad that she was skiing on the *boys'* course, sometimes yelling at her to get off the trail—it wasn't a place for girls.

♣

John and Leslie Hollister were early recruits to the North Star club. In the winter of 1970, they were walking on a sidewalk in Theodore Wirth Park when they saw a lone woman cross-country skiing. They'd never even seen someone cross-country ski, let alone tried it themselves. They'd been downhill skiing but were turned off by the chairlift lines. The solitary skier was obviously having a great time. Her face beamed as steam rose from her sweater. It made an impression John remembered fifty years later. At the time, he was forty years old and Leslie thirty-eight. They wanted a new hobby.

The Hollisters found cross-country skis at Paul Geyer's Tatra Ski Shop on Wayzata Boulevard, west of Minneapolis. Geyer told them about a new ski club they should check out, the North Stars. The first time John Hollister met Norm Oakvik, Hollister was skiing on the wildflower garden trail in Theodore Wirth Park. Hollister was chugging along with his dog on his new skis when he encountered the most graceful skier he had ever witnessed. Oakvik stopped and plainly told him two things: first, that this was a one-way trail and Hollister was going the wrong direction, and, second, that dogs weren't allowed. The Hollisters became regular members of

Leslie and John Hollister at the 1979 Torger Tokle Tour.

the club and never brought their dog skiing there again. The North Stars soon named John chairman of a ski race they were planning, the Victoria Jonathan Chaska, or VJC, race.

The Erik Judeen Memorial had been going on for years, but it was a USSA Central Division race and geared toward competitive skiers keeping points for their status in the division. Although the region offered high school races and Central Division circuit races that changed location year to year, the Midwest hadn't ever had much in the way of citizens' races, other than little club competitions like the ones Fuller-Kask competed in. The North Stars had convinced state senator Henry McKnight to allow the club to build a course for the VJC race through the experimental community he was developing southwest of the Twin Cities.

McKnight despised the postwar suburbanization that had been metastasizing through the countryside. He wanted to build a carefully planned town that would be aesthetically pleasing and would protect the environment. He thought he could build the perfect community, called Jonathan, on eight thousand acres within Chaska city limits. As a boy growing up in a wealthy family on the shores of Lake Minnetonka, and later as a student at Yale University, McKnight had idolized the exploits of an older boy named Al Lindley. After Lindley died in 1951, McKnight courted Lindley's widow, Grace Carter Lindley. They wed in 1958, and McKnight became stepfather to her two children. He named a lake after Grace in Jonathan, and the family split their time between Deephaven and McKnight's farm in Victoria. Under Grace's influence, McKnight learned to ski. He wasn't a natural at it, but he trained year-round to keep up with his athletic wife. They cross-country skied on his farm in Victoria, which grew to one thousand acres. Grace convinced Henry to invest ten thousand dollars in a new ski resort in Colorado, a little place called Vail. She'd skied the back bowls with the resort's founder, Pete Seibert, and knew it was a good bet. McKnight wrote the check and received an undeveloped lot in exchange on Vail Mountain, on which he and Grace built a chalet in 1963.

Grace skied with the Bush Lake club, as did Norm Oakvik and her nephew John Burton. How exactly Norm Oakvik connected with Henry McKnight is unclear, though Grace was obviously involved in facilitating the introduction and perhaps in convincing McKnight of the benefits of permitting a ski trail to be built through his property.

Paul Geyer's Tatra Ski Shop was one of several retailers in the Twin Cities that had begun offering cross-country ski equipment by 1970.

The North Stars pitched to McKnight the idea that a ski trail system would add a salubrious aspect to Jonathan. He agreed and gave them an old farmhouse to use for club activities. The North Stars went to work building trails and remodeling the farmhouse, which was dubbed the Oakvik House, in honor of Norm's ski boosterism, which was finally seeing results. Oakvik

The first citizens' race of the era, starting in 1971, the Victoria Jonathan Chaska race was often plagued by less than ideal snow conditions, as seen here during 1974.

recruited the high school skiers he coached on the weekends at Theodore Wirth Park to help build the trails.

At the North Star club's first meeting of the 1970–71 ski season, more than nine hundred people interested in cross-country skiing showed up to learn more about the new old sport. That kind of turnout for cross-country skiing would have been unthinkable in any previous decade. In February, the club held its first VJC race with nearly three hundred skiers. By the next year, turnout had tripled to almost nine hundred. McKnight donated a silver cup for first prize, which was won by a young skier named Tim Heisel.

Tim Heisel won the first three VJC races and got to keep the cup, per tradition. Heisel had never even heard of cross-country skiing until scant years earlier, when his older brother, Steve, a gifted cross-country runner, was recruited for Hopkins's ski team. The team's coach was Norman Kragseth, the extraordinary all-around athlete from Duluth Central who was a state

champion in cross-country, jumping, and slalom and would become
in 1974 the first official from Minnesota in the National Football
League. One weekend in 1967,
Steve brought home a borrowed
pair of skis, and Tim, an eighth
grader, tried them in their backyard. Steve, in only his second season of skiing, won the high school
state meet. Tim would win the
state meet twice, in his junior and
senior years. The Heisels were natural endurance athletes, yet their
quick rise to top youth ski status
in the state spoke to the limited
pool of competition. When Tim's
younger Hopkins teammate Don
Lee won the state meet in 1974, the
second-place finisher, Sten Fjeldheim, from Minneapolis, came
in three minutes later (Fjeldheim
became a legendary coach for the
powerhouse Northern Michigan

Star skiers of the 1969 Hopkins High School cross-country
team. *From left*: Dan Moll, Russ Perlich, Kevin Schoenfelder,
and Tim Heisel, who just two years later would go on to win
the first three Victoria Jonathan Chaska ski races.

University ski team). Finishing that far out from first in the 2020 boys'
state freestyle championship would have landed a skier in 138th place.

Tim and Steve Heisel both trained with Norm Oakvik at Theodore Wirth
Park. Echoing Bonnie Fuller-Kask, Tim Heisel said, "Oakvik taught the vast
majority of kids in Minneapolis how to ski." The kids loved Oakvik and
were inspired by his dedication to the sport. They helped him with his ski
importing business, which for a time grew big enough to rent a "crappy old
warehouse." They helped Oakvik maintain the Theodore Wirth Park and
VJC trails. In 1973, during a poor snow year, when Roosevelt High School
coach Lars Kindem won the bid to host the U.S. national cross-country
meet at Hyland Park under the Bush Lake jump, Oakvik enlisted the
Heisels to shovel snow all day onto the course. They obliged when Oakvik
told them unexpectedly that he wanted them to race the next day.

Steve Heisel (*front row, far right*) was a standout on the newly formed Hopkins High School ski team in 1966. The team was coached by former Duluth star skier Norman Kragseth (*top row, far left*).

    The general public was still oblivious to cross-country. With the boys' skinny wooden skis strapped to the top of Oakvik's car, Norm would drive the Heisels to weekend Central Division races at places like Pine Valley and Charlie Banks's trail. "Whenever you'd pass somebody," Tim recalled, "they'd all be pointing and laughing at the funny skis on top of the car." "People thought it was weird," said Kathy Pierson, Charlie Banks's daughter. Most just didn't understand why anyone would embrace such a grueling sport.

    Young families were flocking to the Minneapolis suburb of Hopkins. As a result, the overpopulated high school split into Hopkins Lindbergh and Hopkins Eisenhower, with Norman Kragseth going to Lindbergh. Eisenhower needed a coach. The school's athletic director approached a young cross-country running coach named Pat Lanin. "All cross-country skiing is is cross-country running with skis on," the athletic director coaxed Lanin.

ED PAULS'S NORDICTRACK

In the mid-1970s, a mechanical engineer named Ed Pauls struggled to find time to train for the VJC race. By the time Pauls returned home to Victoria after a day of work, night had already fallen, and he begrudgingly resorted to jogging on the icy suburban streets. Pauls worked at Rosemount Engineering, where he had invented a downhill boot and binding system. He'd met his wife, Florence Melhuse, at the Ullr Ski Club, a Twin Cities downhill club. He didn't get into cross-country until a trip to Norway, where Florence's relatives gifted the couple each a pair of cross-country skis.

Pauls fashioned an exercise device to help him train for the VJC, making the prototype from a pair of wooden skis and a pillow from his family's sofa. Norm Oakvik convinced Pauls to market the contraption, and Pauls patented the NordicTrack in 1976, starting the company from his garage. With Florence taking over as business manager and their two kids working the phones, they soon moved to a larger space in Jonathan. "Early on," Pauls's daughter, Terri, told the *Chicago Tribune* for her father's obituary, "when we would sell one, my father would gather the family in a circle in the dining room to sing and dance in celebration." By the mid-1980s— fueled by cross-country's growing popularity, an endorsement from Bill Koch, America's first Olympic medalist in cross-country, and Americans' growing focus on fitness—the Pauls company had sold a half million NordicTracks, making the device a household name. The company employed about four hundred people in 1986, when the Pauls family sold NordicTrack to a consortium for a reported $24 million. ▲

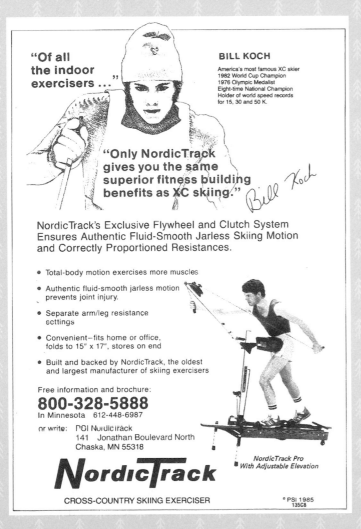

By the mid-1980s, NordicTrack had become a household name of at-home fitness, even securing endorsements from Olympic sensation Bill Koch.

Pat Lanin was an icon in the Twin Cities running community before being recruited to coach skiing at Hopkins Eisenhower High School.

Lanin had skied as a kid growing up north of Virginia, Minnesota. In the late 1940s and into the 1950s, he'd watched his Finnish immigrant grandparents glide on eight-foot homemade birch skis between farms to socialize with neighbors. Lanin was an avid distance runner, but he hadn't skied for twenty years. He started coaching the ski team in 1972, the year after Tim Heisel graduated. Heisel came back to his alma mater and trained with his old team, effectively acting as the coach while Lanin relearned how to ski. Sometimes the kids and the almost-kid de facto coach took advantage of Lanin's greenness. One day at practice, team members asked Lanin to set a track through fresh snow down a steep hill. The team knew, but Lanin did not, that a drift of snow obscured by the flat winter light bisected the hill. His team howled with laughter as Lanin started down the hill on his wooden skis, hit the drift, and wiped out in a glorious cartwheel. "Good tough humor," as Lanin remembered it.

While Lanin was getting his bearings at Hopkins Eisenhower, Henry McKnight died unexpectedly in 1972. Without his vision, Jonathan would never become utopia. The VJC race had to be canceled numerous times for poor snow until, coupled with hasty development in Jonathan, the race was moved. McKnight's will was settled acrimoniously enough that Grace dropped McKnight from her name and went back to being Grace Carter Lindley. She continued to ride horses and to ski but struggled with her family curse of alcoholism. Her mother, an alcoholic who had survived tuberculosis on the houseboat, came to live with her, and Carter's drinking worsened. After her mother died in 1976, Grace sought treatment at the Hazelden facility and remained sober for the rest of her life. She moved to Duluth to be near her daughter, an equine veterinarian living in the woods of northwestern Wisconsin; Grace skied around a pond next to her daughter's house when she visited in winter. Grace died in 2002 in Duluth, watching ships in the harbor from her bed, a view not unlike the one she had experienced as a young woman in Seattle.

♠

As a cross-country scene coalesced under the aegis of Oakvik and the North Star Ski Touring Club, another hot spot was kindled on the eastern edge of the Twin Cities, in the hamlet of Marine on St. Croix. The trajectory of the nation's most successful Nordic skier of all time would intersect with the legacy that sparked in Marine. One of the oldest towns in Minnesota, Marine on St. Croix was founded in 1839 by lumbermen from New England seeking their fortunes in the nearby pineries. A local boy from nearby Taylors Falls started working as a logger and eventually established his own profitable logging companies. His name was William O'Brien. The eponymous state park that later formed from the land that his adventurous daughter Alice donated to the state of Minnesota would be key in cultivating the Marine ski culture.

The first Swedes to immigrate to Minnesota settled around Marine, founding the neighboring township of Scandia. They farmed the cutover (the ghostly stumpland of erstwhile forest) and worked in the lumbermills. Surely the Swedes skied in the winter months as they tended their livestock, gathered firewood, and recreated, but this introduction of skiing to the area did not last in any significant way. Bertha and Myrtle Holmstrom had been girls in Marine in the 1920s, and in their old age watched with amusement as skiing became popular. They recalled to a young neighbor how they had once skied down the valley wall into town on homemade wooden skis. Back home, the girls would carefully prop their skis with the tips wedged under the base of their house's siding strips to maintain the curved ends.

Whatever ski culture Marine possessed had faded away by midcentury, only to be revived by the fad of cross-country and a crop of idealistic new residents beguiled by the charming village in the 1960s and early 1970s.

The history of skiing runs deep in the St. Croix River Valley, all the way back to the Norwegian Ski Club of Stillwater, seen here in their festive uniforms in 1888.

Jack Warren arrived with his family at Marine in 1963. He had come from the East Coast several years earlier and had recently married a Minnesotan. Marine seemed an ideal place to start a family. It fit that sweet spot of being situated in natural splendor along the St. Croix River while still near the Twin Cities so Warren could commute to his job at the 3M company. Warren recalled that when he was new in town, skiing was a "fringe activity." Several years later, like many residents, he and his young family took up cross-country.

Another person captivated by Marine on St. Croix in the early 1960s was a traveling salesman named Ralph Malmberg. In his twenties, Malmberg sold S&H Green Stamps to grocery stores. The stamps were a customer reward gimmick in which consumers could amass stamps and trade them in for products. One of the grocery stores on Malmberg's route was the Marine General Store, an old store in an old building smack-dab in the middle of town. Malmberg learned that the store was for sale. He consulted his wife and parents back home in North Minneapolis, and they pooled their money and bought the place, taking over in 1962.

Malmberg had skied as a boy in Minneapolis, and later in the decade, as people started picking up skiing, he decided he was going to start again. But there was a problem—he couldn't find a pair of skis to buy, which gave him an idea. In 1970, Malmberg opened the Village Ski Shop above his general store. He purchased his inventory from Norm Oakvik.

That same year a graduate student named Bill Simpson moved to town. Short in stature with a big black beard, Simpson had wanted to move to Marine since he was a kid. In high school, he had downhill skied on a hill called Engelwood, just across the St. Croix River from Marine on the four-hundred-foot-high river valley wall. It wasn't far from the Twin Cities but felt like wilderness. Simpson initially roomed in Marine in the farmhouse of a young landscape painter named James Wilcox Dimmers. Dimmers's artist friends would visit, and locals, fearing the counterculture was invading Marine, began to call their farm residence the hippie house. When Simpson tried to rent a cabin, its owner complained about

In 1970, Ralph Malmberg started selling skis above the general store he owned in downtown Marine on St. Croix.

Stillwater coach Bill Simpson at a race in Pine Point Park, circa 1982.

him to another townsperson: "He sure is a nice guy, but why he has all this hair I don't understand." Simpson, though, hadn't moved to town only to party. The sixties' ideal of community appealed greatly to him and would direct the course of his life, and he in turn would catalyze the state's youth ski world into what it is today.

He wasn't a skier at first. That high school trip to Engelwood notwithstanding, Simpson hated the sport after cross-country skiing on a trip to Colorado in college. He had the wrong type of kick wax on his skis, and the snow balled to their bases, which made for a wretched slog. "What kind of miserable sport is this?" he thought. In the hills and woods surrounding Marine, however, Simpson slid through untracked snow on wooden skis under the bare branches of oak and maple trees and found himself very much in love with the sport.

Ralph Malmberg was an affable kind of businessman, genuinely enthusiastic about his product. At his house in the woods just outside the village, he liked to ski from his front door over to the state park. In 1971, he decided that an organized event would galvanize the local interest in skiing that was starting to percolate. Plus, it would help him sell more skis. Thus the Marine O'Brien ski race was born. The Marine O'Brien and VJC races both commenced that winter and set the mold for many other citizens' races. Its first year, the Marine O'Brien race ran north through the woods to William O'Brien State Park, did a lap, and came back to town. In later years, organizers began grooming the trail by dragging a mattress behind an old yellow Ski-Doo snowmobile.

Malmberg donated a set of several old skis to the Marine Elementary School, where a teacher took kids on annual ski adventures and the

Bob Hagstrom *(left)* and Bill Simpson cross the finish line at the fortieth-anniversary Marine O'Brien ski race in 2011. The event features a wooden ski tour named in Hagstrom's honor.

kids skied during recess. Skiing had become so popular in town by this time that most kids had their own skis and brought them to school. Malmberg also started manufacturing his own binding. "I pretty much took the design from a Norwegian one, but they never came after me," he said. Malmberg contracted a metal shop in North Branch to make the bindings, and he was forever driving back and forth in his station wagon with parts sliding around in the back. Malmberg had his brother ("He was a hippie," Malmberg noted) draw the design for the box that his bindings sold in. The drawing, of a bearded man on skis resting on a log while off-trail in a thick and wild wood, encapsulated skiing at the time, often a solitary adventure to connect with nature.

Bill Simpson started teaching special education in 1972 in the nearby Stillwater public schools. After Peg Arnason moved with her young family into Marine, Simpson gave her and her husband ski lessons. Eventually, Simpson would coach both Arnason's daughter and granddaughter. Arnason's new neighbors in Marine were the elderly and never-married sisters Bertha and Myrtle Holmstrom, who recalled their early skiing adventures to her. For the Holmstrom sisters and others of their generation, it must

The box for a pair of Malmberg bindings.

have been a curious delight to see the younger generation enthusiastically diving into what had been an old-world activity.

About the same time, up on Minnesota's North Shore of Lake Superior, the daughter-in-law of Harold Moe—the Arrowhead Derby racer and skiing romancer—drove down to Duluth to buy a pair of skis. Although she was vaguely aware of Moe's own skiing history, her prime motivation came from cross-country's rising popularity; she thought it sounded like a good thing to get into. She and Moe's son lived in a cabin on Lake Superior. Moe's home-building career had taken over his life, and he hadn't skied for decades. But when his daughter-in-law returned from the ski shop in Duluth, Moe was waiting outside to see what she'd come home with. They were a pair of hickory Normark skis with three-pin bindings. Moe picked the skis up and fondly studied their design. His eyes twinkled as he said in his Norwegian accent, "Yoo got some goot skis. Day are from Norvay!" Then he recommended to his daughter-in-law how she might wax them.

🌲

Coach Pat Lanin and the Hopkins High School community had a profusion of talented young endurance athletes. Between 1967 and 1976, Hopkins skiers won the individual state cross-country skiing championship race eight times. For the 1969–70 season, a promising underclass student runner named Toni St. Pierre joined the Hopkins Eisenhower ski team. St. Pierre picked up cross-country skiing from the influence of her running friends. Then as now, the running and skiing crowds overlapped. One of her friends was the two-time state skiing champion Tim Heisel, who lived nearby. Eventually, she and Heisel would marry and have three children.

At the time, girls' cross-country ski teams did not exist; encouraged by Lanin, St. Pierre unofficially joined the boys' team as the only girl. Section 8 of the MSHSL rules expressly prohibited girls from participating on boys' teams and vice versa. At meets, most coaches consented when Lanin asked whether they minded if St. Pierre participated in the junior varsity race. Yet St. Pierre wasn't officially racing, and her times didn't count.

St. Pierre, who died of cancer in 2013, was a talented endurance athlete and fierce competitor. Her younger brother, Sam, recalled: "She wanted to

In 1973 the Hopkins Eisenhower cross-country team took over an abandoned farmhouse for a photograph. Toni St. Pierre, sitting in the top left window, sought and won a federal court ruling the year before that permitted her to compete on the Hopkins cross-country running and skiing teams.

race, and she talked to my mom about it and the adults discussed options. My mom was always like, 'let's go get those guys.'" As a junior, in 1972, St. Pierre contacted the Minnesota Civil Liberties Union, which coincidently had just taken up the cause of another female high school athlete. At St. Cloud Tech, high school senior Peggy Brenden wanted more than what the school's intramural girls' tennis team offered, which was court space once a week for the duration of one month. Once weekly practice wasn't enough for Brenden, who had been one of only four Minnesotans selected for a junior nationals training program. Tech's tennis coach refused Brenden's request to play on the boys' team. She accepted his underwhelming offer of practicing as a stand-in when one of the boys was absent.

The Minnesota Civil Liberties Union thought that joining the two girls' cases would improve their odds at winning. "I didn't want to make it a class action," MCLU attorney Thomas Wexler said. "I had a nice clean case." Brenden's sister, Sheri, published an article about the proceedings in 2020 after interviewing many of the parties involved. She surmised, "Wexler's strategy was straightforward: build the case as a violation of the Fourteenth Amendment, which provided all citizens equal protection under the law. Forbidding these two girls, who could compete effectively, from playing on their schools' sports team was arbitrary and unreasonable." Wexler ran his approach past a staffer with the national American Civil Liberties Union, who approved the strategy. The staffer's name was Ruth Bader Ginsburg.

The MSHSL had only begun managing girls' sports in 1968. The league's plan was to gradually build up girls' sports through intramural and extramural teams, the latter of which would provide an "occasional, sometimes spontaneously arranged, contest with girls from another school." This plan—the Girls Athletic Association—was the one that had irked Bonnie Fuller-Kask. Intramural girls' sports were intended to offer teams more on par with the boys' level of immersion, but in the early 1970s most Minnesota high schools had yet to provide this option. In the year of the girls' lawsuit, 171,509 boys participated in MSHSL activities, contrasted with 46,000 girls. At St. Cloud Tech, boys' sports had a budget of twenty-six thousand dollars, while the money for girls' sports had to be siphoned from physical education funding. The MSHSL hired a popular Twin Cities gym teacher in 1970 to develop girls' sports, but the league was in no hurry to make changes. A MSHSL publication stated of their new hire: "We believe she

The Hopkins Eisenhower cross-country ski team *(left to right)*: Gary Lee, Toni St. Pierre, Mark Saufferer, Don Lee, Dave Lorenzen, Rod Chelberg, Mark Larson, and Sue Schaefer.

will be patient and understanding in our attempt to find the proper place for girls in the competitive sports programs." For athletes like Brenden and St. Pierre, this measured approach was far too slow.

The MCLU filed the lawsuit in U.S. Federal Court, and the case was assigned to Judge Miles Lord in early 1972. Representing the MSHSL was Bernhard LeVander, whose brother, Harold, had lost reelection as Minnesota's governor the year before. LeVander himself had lost the race for Minnesota attorney general to Lord back in 1954 and evidently nursed a grudge, stating in his memoir, "I have never had any respect for Miles Lord." Loved by many and hated by some, Miles Lord was a flamboyant and controversial judge. The following year he would famously shut down the Reserve Mining Company on Lake Superior. In the Brenden and St. Pierre case, he took an active role, stating in an unpublished book: "I did considerable cross-examination of the witnesses myself. . . . Since there was no jury there to be prejudiced, I thought it appropriate that I could ask questions as they occurred to me. Plaintiffs' counsel did not object, but the heat emanating from the defendant's table was almost palpable."

Lord intervened when LeVander's line of questioning irritated him, like when LeVander grilled the athletic director at St. Pierre's school about the possibility of a girl athlete suffering injury to her private parts.

"And she could get hurt anyplace on her body, isn't that true!" LeVander cried.

George Reynolds, the athletic director, the same person who had told Pat Lanin that cross-country skiing was just "running with skis on," conceded this was possible.

"And do you think it is feasible for a male coach to give her first aid any point on her body, I mean, that this is perfectly acceptable?" pushed LeVander. Pat Lanin, who had also been subpoenaed and was in the courtroom, recalled watching Judge Lord's hand tighten around his gavel.

"Well, I have a couple of daughters," Lord interjected. "If they were hurt and somebody treats them, that's all there is to it. I wouldn't send for a nurse."

LeVander employed his own witnesses to pursue similar tacks, such as the assertion that girls would often lose, which would result in crying, and the claim that their performance would be impaired by hip development.

On May 1, Judge Lord ruled in favor of St. Pierre and Brenden. The plaintiffs had shown that they could "compete effectively" on the boys' teams and therefore were being excluded solely because they were girls, which was in violation of their Fourteenth Amendment rights. The MSHSL appealed Lord's ruling, but for the time being Brenden and St. Pierre could join the tennis and cross-country teams. Though the ruling only applied to the two of them, the tide had shifted. In January 1973, another federal judge issued a restraining order barring the MSHSL from keeping an Edina girl off that school's slalom team. In April, the Eighth Circuit court upheld Lord's ruling. "Females," the court ruled, "have been barred from competition with males on the basis of an assumption about the qualifications of women as a class." This deprived girls of the "individual determination of their own ability" and was in violation of the Equal Protection Clause.

Later that month, the MSHSL held an emergency meeting to suspend

Sporting the latest ski fashions, students from the University of Minnesota Duluth take to the trails near campus in the early 1970s.

the rule restricting girls from playing on boys' teams and vice versa. Sports writers groused that mediocre boy athletes would now join girls' teams, but this didn't happen. By the next school year, the number of MSHSL schools with girls' athletic programs grew from 198 to 302. Between 1970 and 1974, the number of American girls on high school sports teams more than tripled to over one million.

A month after Lord's ruling, President Nixon signed into law Title IX of the Education Amendments Act of 1972, which restricted gender discrimination in tax-funded educational institutions. Implementation of Title IX wasn't immediate—specific regulations weren't released until 1975, and schools had until 1978 to comply. The MSHSL held the first girls' cross-country skiing state meet in 1976. Girls' sports developed so quickly that in 1980, when Bonnie Fuller-Kask had become a ski coach, one of her girl skiers asked her how she'd fared in the state meet. When Fuller-Kask replied that she hadn't been allowed to race in high school, the young skier, who only a few years earlier would have been banned, was shocked. Today, Fuller-Kask, who went on to become a coach at Duluth East High School and a member of the Minnesota Nordic Ski Coaches Association Hall of Fame, sometimes regrets the lack of historical knowledge of high school students. "I have girls come up to me and say, 'I'm going to do an article on Title IX,'" she said. "They usually think Title IX is bad, because, for example, the boys' golf team at UMD had to be cancelled. I try to enlighten these girls that without Title IX we wouldn't have this sport."

During Toni St. Pierre's senior year of 1972–73, she skied with the boys' team and placed as high as fourth in conference competition. In January 1973, she headed north to race in the Erik Judeen Memorial. St. Pierre had taken second the year before in the women's division, but this year, for the first of three consecutive years, she won it, almost five minutes ahead of Bonnie Fuller-Kask in second place. In third place was young Patrice Jankowski from Cloquet, who would go on to win the first three MSHSL individual girls' state cross-country skiing championships, from 1976 to 1978, and compete on the U.S. Olympic Biathlon Team in Albertville, France, in 1992.

♠

The same year St. Pierre won her first Judeen Memorial, two of the Midwest's premier ski races kicked off, both based on famous Scandinavian races. In Sweden, the Vasaloppet ski race had been running since 1922. The course ran ninety kilometers from Sälen to Mora, tracing in reverse the route of the young nobleman Gustav Ericcson Vasa. Norway began holding the Birkebeinerrennet in 1932, its participants racing fifty-nine kilometers between Lillehammer and Rena to commemorate the rescue of the young

Skiers take their marks at the starting line of the first Birkebeinerrennet in Lillehammer, Norway, 1932.

king Haakon IV. Birkebeinerrennet skiers carried a backpack filled with several pounds of ballast to simulate the weight of the toddler king.

At Telemark Resort in Hayward, Wisconsin, Tony Wise was transitioning away from downhill and into cross-country. It was a good move. Wise's friend George Hovland had led the push to build Spirit Mountain in Duluth, which would open the following year on a far bigger hill that was easily reachable off the interstate and would siphon downhill skiers away from Telemark. Mount Telemark had been described by Olympic alpine skier Billy Kidd as "the only ski area I've visited where the lodge is bigger than the hill."

Wise had built cross-country trails and wanted to draw attention to them. Carl Hanson lived in Hayward after having emigrated from Mora, Sweden. Even in Telemark's downhill era, Hanson used to bring Wise newspapers detailing the Swedish Vasaloppet, in hopes of prompting Wise

Tony Wise in front of the enormous soaring fireplace at Telemark Resort.

to do something similar. Wise's grandmother had been born in Rena, Norway, at the end of the original Birkebeinerrennet route. In collaboration with his resort—called Telemark after his own heritage and the Telemarkings' influence on modern skiing—Wise decided to hold a race called the American Birkebeiner.

The first American Birkebeiner in 1973 was forty-five kilometers, beginning in Hayward and ending at Wise's Telemark lodge. The massive building had been completed only the year before. Designed by an associate of Frank Lloyd Wright, the glass and wood lodge, which featured a fifty-five-foot-high fireplace, cost Wise five and a half million dollars. Wise was extravagant and called himself a "business adventurer." He kept the lodge's outdoor swimming pool heated all winter.

The first "Birkie" had only thirty-five skiers. With barely any registrants in the days leading up to the race, Wise personally called skiers and begged them to participate. Charlie Banks was a firm believer in the U.S. Ski Association, and since the Birkie was not a sanctioned race, he demurred that it was merely a tour and did not race; he would, however, start skiing it in later years. Wise called George Hovland, who regretfully couldn't participate because he was finalizing a divorce. Wise had better luck with Rick Scott, a distant cousin of Aksel Holter. Scott joined the small group of racers who would eventually be known as the Founders. The first Birkie followed forest roads until reaching Telemark's trail network. "The track setter had made only shallow grooves in the packed snow," one participant recalled. The course led "onto an open field in loose corn snow with occasional piles of horse turds."

A separate twenty-kilometer race was held for women and skiers under age twenty. One woman, Jacque Lindskoog, had come from the Twin Cities and did the full forty-five kilometers. "I thought if I'm going to drive this far I'm going to ski the longer race," she said in an interview. "I didn't do it for any reason of women's lib or protesting or anything like that. I just did it because I wanted to. And I didn't feel I was making a statement. I just like skiing."

The next year, the second American Birkebeiner increased to fifty kilometers, and the number of entrants doubled. A women's division was still not available in the full Birkie, so Jacque Lindskoog skied the full race again. The identical Quinn twins from Cloquet—Dave and Don—took first and second. Numbers grew quickly in the coming years, causing

The first American Birkebeiner in February 1973 was a small affair, as thirty-five skiers raced from Hayward, Wisconsin, to the finish line at Tony Wise's Telemark lodge.

George Hovland didn't ski the first American Birkebeiner but became one of the race's most ardent champions in later years.

growing pains. Before starting in waves as the race does today, with the faster skiers going out first, the early Birkies began with a mass start. Neophytes would come early and stand in front of the speedy racers, who would get stuck behind them.

"You'd swear you'd never come back," said Bob O'Hara, an early Birkie skier, member of the North Stars, and fixture in high school racing. "Then Tony would be at the finish line asking what we can do, then he'd send out a newsletter saying here's what we're doing differently, and there's a discount if you sign up early."

George Hovland said of Wise: "He could attract the right people with the right ideas and turn it into a premier ski event. Considering everything to develop an event like that is basically impossible, but Tony did it." Wise did manage to build the greatest ski race on the continent, but he would eventually find himself boxed out of his own creation.

The Mora Vasaloppet ski race also started in 1973. A conception of Glen Johnstone, the idea for the race stemmed from his meeting with the Mora Jaycees club. The Jaycees wanted to start a winter event, something fun to break up the season's drudgery. Of Norwegian descent, Johnstone was in his midforties, was an avid downhill skier, and ran a tire shop in town. He'd grown up in the area and since childhood had run a trapline on skis. Johnstone soon floated the idea of a ski race. Mora, Minnesota, was a sister city to Mora, Sweden, the town where the ninety-kilometer Swedish Vasaloppet ended. The Minnesota Mora didn't have much of a cross-country ski scene at the time, so Johnstone knew he'd have to tap into the growing pool of Twin Cities langlaufers. He drove to Minneapolis and pitched the chamber of commerce, whose members brushed him off. Like a good Norwegian, Johnstone was not defeated by this rejection from the urban elite; rather, it only piqued Johnstone's interest in making the race a success.

Like Tony Wise, Johnstone liked dreaming up something new and had the follow-through to execute the idea. Unlike Wise, Johnstone did everything as a volunteer and didn't like seeing his name on things. Johnstone did, however, like pomp and circumstance. He wanted to mimic the Swedish Vasaloppet by building scenes that skiers and onlookers would remember. He enlisted little boys and girls to ring bells while wearing colorful Swedish garb, arranged for traditional Swedish music to play all day on Main Street, and commenced the laying of a huge wreath over the winner's head. Ninety-six skiers gathered in a farm field in northern Kanabec County for the start of the first Mora Vasaloppet. Later, Johnstone traveled to Sweden to study the original Vasaloppet. In 1977, he convinced members of Sweden's national marathon team to come race in Minnesota,

Mora Vasaloppet founder Glenn Johnstone stands outside the iconic wooden bell tower on the route of the renowned Minnesota race in 1985.

According to tradition borrowed from the Swedish Vasaloppet, the winner of the annual race in Mora, Minnesota, is gifted a laurel wreath by a specially appointed *kranskulla* (wreath maiden). In 1976, Andy Desmond of St. Louis Park, Minnesota, received the ceremonial wreath from *kranskulla* Daisy Samuelson after winning the fifty-kilometer Vasaloppet with a time of 3:26:35.

and the Swedes began traveling annually to the Midwest to compete in the Vasaloppet and the Birkie.

Racing against these world-class Scandinavian skiers provided Midwesterners a glimpse into the elite echelons of the sport, which was beginning an era of rapid change. In Sweden, 1973, the same year as the inaugural American Birkebeiner and Vasaloppet, marked the last time anyone would win an international-level competition anywhere on wooden skis, when Norwegian Magne Myrmo won a fifteen-kilometer race. In an accompanying thirty-kilometer race, four of the top six finishers used synthetic skis. The Twin Cities wooden ski industry was already dead, so this development had little bearing there, but, as Roland Huntford wrote, "for the Scandinavian ski makers this was their day of doom."

In 1974, Ralph Malmberg invited the son of his Norwegian ski distributor to stay with him as a foreign exchange student in Marine on St. Croix. Malmberg had an ulterior motive. Oystein Loseth would join the Stillwater High School ski team, coached then by Greg Palm and with about ten skiers. At the time, Stillwater had jumpers who practiced at the Battle Creek jump but wouldn't get its girls' team until 1976. Loseth showed up at Still-water High School in November. He didn't come to ski practice, recalled a younger teammate named Kevin Brochman. Yet Loseth did participate in the races—and won every single one. At the time, there were no rules preventing such things.

"He was a hired gun," Brochman said. "I had only skied thirty or forty times in my life by my sophomore year. Oystein had probably been skiing 100 times; he had more technical finesse, was smoother; I was just a bear running through the woods. He wasn't all that fast in Norway. He opened up my eyes. I don't get passed by a lot of guys, but he's skiing circles around me."

Brochman didn't come from a skiing family ("My dad was a beer drinking and bowling kind of guy," he quipped), but he was a natural endurance athlete. Earlier, during his very first practice with the cross-country running team, Brochman easily won the time trial that day. As with Toni St. Pierre and the Heisel brothers, cross-country skiing was a natural extension. "When you got the motor you just turn it on," Brochman said.

Kevin Brochman ran cross-country before turning to skiing. A star athlete on Stillwater's Nordic team in the mid-1970s, he sported bib number 6 for the 1987 American Birkebeiner after taking sixth place the prior year.

Cloquet skier Brent Smith raced during the state meet at Pine Valley in 1973. Years later, in the era of large ski teams, Smith coached the cooperative Cloquet–Esko–Carlton Nordic team.

Loseth promptly returned home to Norway after winning the individual title at the state meet in February 1975, Stillwater's first such victory (Loseth also won the Mora Vasaloppet that same month). Getting beat by Loseth lit Brochman's competitive fire. Two years later, he took fourth in the state meet and the Stillwater boys' team won their first team state championship. Stillwater would overtake Cloquet as Minnesota's dominant high school ski team. Brochman credited Stillwater's new coach for this—the special education teacher Bill Simpson.

With young families flocking to the suburbs, teams like Stillwater were the future of the sport. In the northeast corner of the state, on and near the Iron Range, the population in ski towns like Cloquet and Coleraine was shrinking as residents moved to the suburbs.

Simpson's coaching method would form the paradigm for the modern Minnesota youth ski team. He embraced the fast skiers, like Brochman, but also encouraged younger skiers without a natural gift of speed. The Stillwater ski team began to grow in size, and other schools' programs followed suit.

In 1976, when Stillwater started a girls' team, girls didn't exactly flock to join. But all the Marine kids had learned how to ski in elementary school, and Simpson was able to cajole enough of them into forming a small team. One time, in advance of a relay race, Simpson realized he didn't have enough girls to compete. He hurriedly paced the hallways of Stillwater High School, looking for Marine girls to recruit. He found two. "It worked out fine," Simpson recalled, in typical understatement. The Stillwater girls were about to become arguably the strongest, of either gender, Nordic team in state history. The next year, 1977, the USSA formed the Bill Koch Ski League, named after the first American to medal in cross-country. Simpson soon got involved with the Koch club that Ralph Malmberg started in Marine, which trained at William O'Brien State Park. It quickly became the largest such club in the region and served as a feeder for the Stillwater High School team.

In 1978, the MSHSL broke apart the combination of jumping, cross-county, and downhill skiing. Ski jumping was eliminated completely from high school competition; cross-country and downhill became their own respective pursuits. The league also changed the format for racing: instead of a team racing three skiers and the team's score coming from the top two finishers, a team would now field six skiers and the top four would contribute to the team score. Schools from small towns like Cloquet could no longer compete with bigger teams from larger communities.

Jumping was fading, yet the Midwest still dominated the U.S. Olympic teams. In 1968, in Grenoble, France, the four-man team consisted of Adrian Watt, from Duluth; John Balfanz and Jay Martin, from Minneapolis; and Bill Bakke, from Menomonie, Wisconsin. Four years later, Jay Martin's brother, Jerry, and Greg Swor, from Minneapolis and Duluth respectively, made up half the team. Then, in 1976, Minnesotans made up the entire U.S. five-man jumping team, with Jerry Martin back again; Jim Denney and Terry Kern, both from Duluth; Kip Sundgaard, from St. Paul; Greg Windsperger, from Minneapolis; and Jim Maki, from the Itasca club in Coleraine.

Jumping was still solely a man's sport, with a few exceptions. The prior decade, during the 1960s, a couple of girl jumpers from Duluth competed, the twins Paula and Patti Grady. Olympian Jim Maki's younger brother, Doug, competed against the Grady twins and was quite taken by them. The

For decades, Duluth ski booster Guy Olson presented an annual trophy to a member of the Duluth Ski Club. Here he presents the award to Adrian Watt in 1969. Watt is holding the skis with which he had set the U.S. distance jumping record the prior year.

Skiers from the St. Paul Ski Club take part in a Christmas training camp in 1975.

Grady girls had bright red hair and usually beat him. The Gradys also raced most years at the Judeen Memorial.

The loss of jumping from high school was emblematic of the sport's decline. While girl langlaufers and girl downhill skiers started to face better prospects, the smaller world of jumping continued on much as before. In Iron Mountain, Michigan, Therese Altobelli started jumping as a four-year-old in 1964. Altobelli was a pioneering athlete in the modern era leading up to gender-equitable jumping. Yet for Altobelli, her experience was anything but equitable, and the sexism she endured led to an early and bitter retirement. She grew up jumping with her two brothers in her backyard, part of a neighborhood with nineteen boys. "My mom and dad tried really hard to make a girl out

Therese Altobelli on the slopes at Iron Mountain, Michigan, in 1979.

of me, but I didn't care about that," she said in a newspaper interview. Early on, Altobelli decided she was going to run the Olympic-sized, ninety-meter Pine Mountain jump. Coaches refused to work with her, brushing her off with comments such as "Go play with your dolls" and "Go bake cookies." So Altobelli coached herself by emulating the boy jumpers. Through the mid-1970s, as the only girl, she competed with the local Kiwanis Ski Club and won numerous junior-level contests. Still, her gender upset members of the old guard. When Altobelli was seventeen, in 1978, she jumped Pine Mountain, becoming the first female to do so during competition. For the next three years, she jumped in Central Division tournaments around the Midwest, doing well but always alienated. She retired in 1981, at the age of twenty-one.

Skiers flood the countryside near
Cable, Wisconsin, at the annual
American Birkebeiner, 1979.

7

Modern Nordic

1980s–1990s

One would be hard-pressed to find a better excoriation of the downsides of the alpine culture that had taken hold after World War II than Charles Bradley's 1979 polemic "Waxing Nostalgic" in *Nordic Skiing* magazine, in which he surmises what the legendary Dartmouth ski coach Otto Schniebs (a German native with an *idraet*-like philosophy) would have thought of mainstream American skiing. Charles was of the venerable Bradley family, son of H.C., of the 1930s Central Ski Association's cross-country committee, and brother to David, the 1937 national cross-country champion. Charles was also no slouch, having served in World War II in the Tenth Mountain Division and as a dean at Montana State University. After his wife died in 1969, Charles married his childhood friend Nina Leopold, a daughter of the brilliant conservationist Aldo Leopold. Charles and Nina moved to Leopold's Sand County farm and continued Aldo's pioneering habitat restoration work.

Charles lived in Bozeman, Montana, as it transitioned from a ruggedly authentic mountain town to an often irritating tourist town, and in the article he channeled the old Dartmouth coach in what was more accurately his own view of the ski world: "If Otto should rise from his grave today and take a look around, he would probably never recognize the sport he once referred to as 'not choose a shport but a vay uff life.'" Bradley continued:

> Instead of his vision of well-rounded skiers who could compete in all four
> events [cross-country, jumping, downhill, and slalom] or ski up into the

mountains and enjoy the freedom of the high country, he would see those long lines of what might look to him like automated, plastic people, programmed to ski from the upper terminal of a chair lift to the lower terminal of a chair lift located in the middle of a real estate killing carrying the euphemistic title of "Ski Area." One glance would suggest to Otto that the purpose of skiing is no longer the freedom of the hills in winter but is rather a specialized downhill technique for finding the quickest chairlift uphill. Having solved the riddle of modern skiing and noting what had become of his "vay uff life" Otto would probably hurry back to his grave, close the lid and throw the key away.

What an excellent distillation of the corruption of the *idraet*, the pure sport that had been taken in by America's corporate influence and turned into a cash machine. The downsides of the alpine ski culture were permanent. Great skiing notwithstanding, in the eyes of Schniebs, Bradley, and others sympathetic to the *idraet*, towns like Vail and Aspen were vulgar nexuses of wealth and tackiness. At Vail, Grace Carter Lindley's modest chalet receded into the shadows cast by the ever larger mansions built around it. The upside for cross-country skiers was that this discontent fueled the rise of the sport throughout America's snowy reaches. Plenty of trails were now available, and the culture had flowered into more than a niche—well, it may have still been a niche, but it was a sizable niche with enough practitioners to support specialized gear and dedicated periodicals.

Cross-country skiing would never be the cash cow that downhill was. Inherent to cross-country was an aversion to the consumerism that surrounded downhill. "There's no money in Nordic skiing," said Mark Helmer, on running a ski area, "because the season is short and the season is iffy. You can pay the bills and have enough money for a beer on the weekend and maybe even a hamburger." Helmer would unexpectedly find himself caretaker of the most tangible artifact of a particularly rich cross-country legacy, a path prompted one day in 1982 when he stopped by Charlie Banks's house on Korkki Road to ask if he could train on Banks's trails. Despite being a Finn and growing up in Duluth in the early 1960s, Helmer never skied as a kid. He remembered riding the bus to school in Duluth and seeing a sign for the Korkki Travel Agency (run by a brother-in-law of Banks). Helmer liked the sound the name made when he ran it through

Downhill skiing flourished nationwide after World War II. Throughout the Midwest, ski areas like Buck Hill in Burnsville, Minnesota, catered to Americans' newfound attraction to the sport.

his brain. "Little did I know how my life would be intertwined with that name," Helmer said sixty years later.

Helmer went to college in Alaska on a hockey scholarship, and he had a campus job with the school's recreational sports department loaning out cross-country skis. He would stand at his workstation during the dim Alaskan days and watch as his peers scooted about the university commons under the lights. Naturally, he wanted to try it, too, so he borrowed a pair of skis and set out. He taught himself classic stride by emulating an image of a skier featured on maps affixed to light posts along the trail.

Helmer finished college, moved to rural Duluth in 1974, and started working for the railroad in Two Harbors. In the coming years he would get married and have a baby daughter. He'd bought a pair of skis in Jackson, Wyoming, on his way back to Minnesota, and figured he better use them. He often skied around the woods but didn't get serious about racing until after

Charlie Banks skis his home trail. This photograph is in the Korkki warming house in memory of Charlie.

1980, when a friend got sick before the Birkebeiner and gave Helmer her bib for the race. Helmer skied the twenty-nine-kilometer Korteloppet in blue jeans and a down vest. He enjoyed the experience so much that he decided to get serious about skiing. He'd heard of a coach who maintained a trail system on private property not far from where he lived; he drove to Charlie Banks's house, knocked on his door, and asked if he could use the trail. Banks asked if he was a skinny skis racer, and, after Helmer said yes, Banks told him he could use the trails anytime he wanted. Banks kept the trails opened and groomed as a service to the ski community, but he didn't allow just anybody to use them. "Dad was kind of picky about his trails," his daughter Kathy Pierson said. "He worked real hard on them and didn't want anybody to make a mess of them."

Most days when Helmer trained there, Banks would stick his head out of his back-porch door and say, "How you doing, young feller?" Banks was not particularly social, though he kept an eye on people skiing his trails to make sure they made it out of the woods. The trail featured a large hill that injured its share of skiers. One day Helmer suggested to Banks they go fishing, and thereafter the men began taking annual fishing trips to the Boundary Waters every May. A deep friendship was forged. "He was my best friend and he still is my best friend; there isn't a day that goes by that I don't think about that man," Helmer said.

Banks was older now but still an avid skier. He teased his four daughters that if any of them got married on the opening day of either skiing or deer hunting season he wouldn't attend the wedding. Early in the day of his daughter Carole's wedding, Banks skied fifty kilometers. Preparing for the wedding, he showered and put on his suit but was stricken with leg cramps. He lay on the floor of his house trying to shake the cramps. His family was rushing around in their finest, getting ready for the wedding, stepping over prone Charlie. Dorothy, his normally equanimous wife, abandoned her Finnish reserve and ordered him off the floor. Years later, to celebrate his seventieth year and his daughter Kathy's fortieth, father and daughter skied the American Birkebeiner together.

The ski world was changing. When Mark Helmer showed up at the starting line of the Birkie in the mid-1980s, all the skiers in the elite wave knew one other. The region's diehard skiers were still a small group. During the next decade, the Midwestern ski world would become a much bigger place.

♠

Minneapolis came one warm spell away from having its first City of Lakes Loppet in 1981. The City of Lakes Loppet would eventually kick off in 2003 and remains one of the region's premier cross-country events. In the early 1980s, Steve Sponsel, a wealthy financial planner, watched the growing success of the American Birkebeiner and thought the Twin Cities should have a similar event. Sponsel wasn't even a skier. He roped in David Paulson, a high school ski coach who groomed the Theodore Wirth Park trails. Paulson and Sponsel did radio interviews, found a major sponsor with First Bank of Minneapolis, and hired local photographer Gerald Brimacombe to take pictures for a poster, which featured Paulson in a ski suit in midstride. The

In the late 1970s, an enthusiastic group from Minneapolis skied to promote awareness of world hunger. By the time the group ran the 1985 American Birkebeiner, the Ski to End World Hunger was a nationally recognized program raising tens of thousands of dollars each year.

The twelve-kilometer Lotvola Cup began in 1977 at the Maplelag Resort in Callaway, Minnesota. The race was named in honor of Elias Lotvola, a local Finnish pioneer known for crafting handmade classic wooden skis.

race was to be thirty kilometers "through the magnificent Minneapolis City Park System." "Join tradition in the making," the poster teased. Less than two weeks before race day, on January 24, the temperatures soared, and, as Paulson put it, "every flake of snow melted. We could have had a running race, or biking race, or marbles competition, but we didn't do anything." The race's sponsors disappeared, putting an end to the City of Lakes Loppet until it resurfaced twenty-two years later.

The North Stars' VJC race continued intermittently through the 1980s in Carver Park but was canceled more times than not until it disappeared within the decade. The North Star club continued to grow, and the numerous citizens' races that popped up around the Midwest spoke to the sport's growing popularity. In Bemidji, Minnesota, the Snowjourn race had begun

THE TORGER TOKLE TOUR

Among the first crop of popular citizens' races that sprang up in the 1970s was the Torger Tokle Tour in Avon, Minnesota, near St. Cloud. The race's organizer was Al Waverek, a Tenth Mountain Division veteran who had fought alongside Tokle. Waverek told the *St. Cloud Times*, "If ever a man deserves to have a memorial skiing event named after him Torger Tokle does." Waverek further dedicated the race to the 972 Tenth Mountain Division skiers who had died in the war. He had come close himself, after lying about his age of fifteen years and enlisting in the army.

In 2007, Waverek recalled to National Public Radio how on the night of February 19, 1945, in Italy, the Tenth had climbed Mount Belvedere under heavy fire from the Germans on top of the mountain. As the Americans climbed the steepening slopes in the dark, the Nazis tried to get a bead on them by lighting bright phosphorous flares. Nearing the top, Waverek was hit in his arm with mortar shrapnel. He looked down to see his wrist bones exposed and gleam-

ing in the light of the flares. The Tenth climbed on and took the mountain. Tokle was killed less than three weeks later.

The first TTT was held on Sunday, February 6, 1977. Waverek plotted out a sixteen-kilometer course that started on a lake before winding through the hills and woods of Avon. By its second year, 350 skiers participated. The number eventually grew to over 700, including many from the Twin Cities. The last TTT was run in 1991 with only 98 skiers. Poor snowfall and issues with landowners led to the race's demise. The Nordic Ski Club of Central Minnesota, which Waverek cofounded in the mid-1970s, lives on to this day. ♦

Al Waverek pauses for a drink while training with the Tenth Mountain Division on Mount Rainier, 1941.

in 1976 and the Minnesota Finlandia in 1979. In its first years, the Finlandia was a hundred-kilometer race run over two days. Both the Snowjourn and Finlandia continue today. In the Upper Peninsula, the Great Bear Chase fifty-kilometer marathon commenced in 1981 on the enviably snowy Keweenaw Peninsula.

The North Stars joined with cross-country boosters from other ski clubs in greater Minnesota, like Bemidji and St. Cloud, to advocate for a ski pass that would fund trail construction and maintenance. North Star Tim Knopp had been working with the state government on trail development since the 1970s and observed how snowmobilers had created a vast network of trails by initiating a snowmobile registration program and reaping a portion of gasoline sales tax funds. Knopp and skiers from other clubs approached a newly elected member of the Minnesota House of Representatives named Darby Nelson, who was a skier. He lived in Champlain within sight of Elm Creek Park and maintained his own trails by snowshoeing them in and then skiing in tracks. In consultation with the skiers, Nelson wrote and introduced the resolution creating the Great Minnesota Ski Pass as his first piece of legislation in his three-term political career.

The legislation mandated that skiers buy a pass to use participant trails. European ski trails had long required such a pass. The Minnesota trail pass money would be split between ski clubs, local governments, and the Department of Natural Resources for trail creation, equipment purchases, and grooming. The legislation squeaked through and became law after Governor Rudy Perpich signed it on June 14, 1983. With a shared source of funding

North Star club member Tim Knopp at the 1974 VJC race. He was instrumental in creating the Great Minnesota Ski Pass program.

for trails around the state, the ski pass fueled rapid growth in the state's trail network, which today covers about eleven hundred miles over ninety state, regional, and local properties. In Bemidji, eight trail systems make up a combined one hundred kilometers of groomed trails. Volunteers keep track of hours spent grooming and report them to the state, which provides reimbursement to the clubs up to a capped amount based on the length of the trails. The money comes from ski pass sales proceeds.

The DNR currently sells anywhere from fewer than five thousand to nearly twenty thousand passes per year, depending on conditions. In recent years, the trend of regional parks to invest in snowmaking equipment, unenroll from the state ski pass program, and institute their own trail pass has led to decreased sales. Mem-

Money raised by the Great Minnesota Ski Pass program helps fund trail creation and maintenance of the state's extensive ski and snowmobile trail network.

bership in the North Star Ski Touring Club peaked in 1992 at sixteen hundred. The club would be strong for some time, though its relevance as a force in attracting skiers and directing the course of the local culture would be overshadowed by a growing roster of youth programs.

🌲

Maintaining ninety kilometers of separate trails for the Mora Vasaloppet's fifty-eight- and thirty-two-kilometer races, which cross through the properties of about one hundred disparate landowners, took the daunting sort of diplomacy only Glen Johnstone could have pulled off. Johnstone lived his entire life in the remote country around Warman, north of Mora, and possessed a detailed mental map of the obscure logging roads the course could be routed onto. He knew and was trusted by the landowners and had the personality to smooth over the occasional inevitable misunderstandings.

Keeping the trails open was always a herculean effort. At first the Vasaloppet volunteers didn't even have chainsaws, though their maintenance arsenal widened and evolved through the years. Swampy ground often sucked in tractors. Sometimes a landowner would shoot a deer on his property in the fall and then drive in with a truck or four-wheeler and tear ruts into the ski trail. Race organizers couldn't exactly reprimand property owners for using their own land, so they had to deal with the ruts themselves. The rougher the trail, the more snow required to make a good skiing surface, and, unfortunately for organizers, the windy plains of Kanabec County were not known for abundant or lasting snowfall.

Still, race participation continued to grow, surpassing one thousand for the first time in 1980 and climbing to double that number later in the decade. Numbers would peak at the millennium, with twenty-nine hundred skiers. Around 1980, organizers added a half-marathon and a canoe race to the suite of Vasaloppet events. Darby Nelson skied the first Vasaloppet on a whim. He'd never done a ski race before and raced on heavy, white-painted (snow camouflage) World War II surplus skis. Nelson relished the experience and kept doing Vasaloppets, using the long race looming in his legislative and teaching schedule as motivation to stay in shape through the year.

The Vasaloppet trail was initially groomed by dragging old-fashioned, bare-metal bedsprings with a snowmobile. The springs did a good job of flattening the snow to make it suitable for classic skiing, but sometimes an obstruction, like a stump, would snag a spring, causing it to quickly tear apart. The snowmobile driver would occasionally turn around to check his groomer only to find a few strands of trailing wire. Devoured by the trail and no longer used on beds, the springs became harder to find. Volunteers switched to hog panels, which were rigid fencing squares made of thick wiring welded together at right angles. Later, they began using a tracked garden tractor with a homemade roller made from a thirty-six-inch-diameter length of steel culvert with big caps welded over the openings. They eventually purchased a groomer meant for snowmobile trails, which worked fine until people began skate skiing, at which point

Early organizers of the Mora Vasaloppet race recruited locals from the community to help with maintenance as the organization worked tirelessly to keep the trails clear for skiers.

the roller-compacted snow was too soft. Many of the Vasaloppet boosters weren't actually skiers, and on occasion there was a disconnect between them and the racers. Skiers of early races sometimes navigated through livestock manure, and one year, when the race was routed along a road, a scattering of discarded beer cans emerged from the rolled snow.

In the early 1980s, Mora had a small high school team coached by the athletic director. He didn't know anything about skiing, but the town lacked an experienced ski coach, so he did what he could. "He'd come out and look at us at least four times a year," joked Jon Larson, a member of the team at the time. A Swede named Sven Broberg had come to Mora, racing for the Swedish marathon team and selling skis for manufacturers back home. Broberg struck up a romance with a local lady, married her, and settled down in town. He opened a ski shop in Mora and began coaching the high school team. Because he didn't have a coaching license, he wasn't officially the coach, but Broberg introduced the young Mora skiers to a much more sophisticated approach to the sport. "If he'd been around longer, I think I'd have been competitive," said Larson, who graduated after one season with Broberg. "He brought the Euro model of train hard and perform harder." Broberg scoffed at habits like warm-up stretches and the same weightlifting regime as the basketball team and instead introduced concepts like interval training alongside distance workouts. As an unofficial coach, Broberg got away with things like joining his skiers during races, running on foot behind them and shouting advice. When the finish line drew near, Broberg ran into the woods to avoid being seen.

Broberg tried to convince Jan Haug, the president of U.S. sales for the Swedish ski maker Edsbyn, to open a factory in Mora. Edsbyn had been a major ski producer in the 1970s, but as fiberglass skis caught on and people began to skate ski, Edsbyns fell out of fashion. The Twin Cities (as well as American) ski industry was dead, so it's unclear how close the factory came to becoming a reality; announcements were made that a Mora factory would open, but this never happened. Broberg's ski shop in Mora failed, as did his marriage; he returned to Sweden.

After having been fairly stable for decades, cross-country ski technology was changing quickly. Ever since the 1920s, Rottefella-type three- and four-pin bindings had been the standard. Adidas introduced the Norm

Art Cassell sits on a Ski-Doo Skandic owned by the Bemidji Area Cross Country Ski Club. The Skandic, a popular model for trail grooming, is a wide-tracked snowmobile built for pulling loads.

Sporting bibs marked with Swedish ski manufacturer Edsbyn, skiers begin the annual Mora Vasaloppet in Warman, Minnesota. By the mid-1980s, the thirty-six-mile race had attracted around twenty-five hundred skiers to the quaint Swedish-looking town of Mora north of the Twin Cities.

38 binding in 1976, with matching shoes. The shoes featured a plastic tab that clipped into the binding and rose no higher than the ankle, making them decidedly shoes and not boots. The U.S. Ski Team used Adidas in the 1980 Olympics. In the 1980s, Rottefella unveiled its New Nordic Norm (NNN) and a French company popularized the Salomon Nordic System (SNS). Both of these bindings featured a horizontal bar under the boot's toe that hooked securely into the binding's clasp. The two types make up the majority of bindings today, evolving to include a maddening array of incompatible variations.

Synthetic skis made of fiberglass supplanted wooden skis as standard, and wooden ski manufacturers went out of business, like Edsbyn did in 1984. After the company's demise, thousands of tubes of Edsbyn kick wax found their way to Ax-Man surplus store in St. Paul. One day, Stillwater coach Bill Simpson received an excited call from a parent of one of his skiers. The dad asked Simpson what he wanted to hear first, the good news or the bad news. Simpson opted for the good. The dad exclaimed that he knew

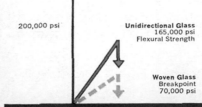
Northland advertised its attempt at a fiberglass ski in an issue of *Sports Illustrated* in 1966. The skis were a massive flop, and the company soon became another casualty of changing technology and the industry's demand for sharp innovation.

where Simpson could buy kick wax for ten cents a tube. The bad news was that he'd have to buy all twelve thousand tubes and all were Edsbyn.

Simpson was all too familiar with Edsbyn wax. At the time, kick wax was more important than glide wax, and Edsbyn wax was terrible, coming in only two temperature ranges, red or blue. "It was nasty wax," Simpson said. "It chipped off and came off in clumps." Simpson declined to make the purchase, but somehow—he doesn't remember how—the team still wound up with a significant quantity of it. With Stillwater as the dominant team in the state, at meets other schools paid attention to how it operated. As a prank, Simpson wrapped white athletic tape around the outside of the Edsbyn tubes and pretended to apply it to his skiers' skis before races. The team called it Ax-Man wax. Other teams looked on, wondering what secret formula Stillwater was using. Again, disguising the wax with tape, Stillwater coaches presented tubes of Ax-Man wax to skiers as awards. At first the skiers would try the wax and find it to be terrible, but before long it became an inside joke and a rite of passage. More than thirty years later, a few tubes of Ax-Man wax can still be found in Stillwater's waxing shed on the property of Bob Hagstrom.

The Stillwater team become so big in the 1980s that it required two buses to transport its skiers. One day an athletic department official sat Simpson down and explained that his team's transportation costs were

Bob Hagstrom has been a longtime supporter of the Stillwater High School ski team and frequently provides skiers with advice (and cookies) at his home wax shed.

too high: he needed to cut some of his skiers so the team could fit into a single bus. Simpson saw his team as a home not just for a growing roster of state champions but for unathletic kids who had been cut from other sports and wanted an activity. Cross-country's greatest virtue was not in claiming championship glory but in being a salubrious, lifelong outdoor activity. Simpson told the administrator he would never cut anyone from his team. The administrator saw his seriousness and never brought it up again. Simpson had brought acclaim to the school by building arguably the best cross-country team in state history, though winning was only part of the equation. His focus remained on the individual growth of his skiers. In the youth ski league he coached at William O'Brien State Park, the coaches conducted races and handed out purple ribbons to all the finishers. "You're out there to have fun and everyone wins a ribbon," Simpson said. "I still have people come up to me and say how important it was to them as a kid to come across and get the ribbon, even if they finished last."

🌲

Tony Wise congratulates Berit Lammedal *(left),* winner of the 1977 American Birkebeiner women's division. Alison Owen-Spencer *(right)* was the first American finisher and went on to win the five-kilometer race during what was arguably the first women's Nordic World Cup in December the following year.

One person who tried to instill the lux resort experience of downhill onto the ethos of cross-country was Tony Wise of Telemark. Telemark Resort near Cable, Wisconsin, was a happening place in the late 1970s and early 1980s; the U.S. Ski Team trained regularly on its trails. In December 1978, the best skiers in the world, including the Norwegian national team and Swedish stars Thomas Wassberg and Thomas Magnuson, gathered at Telemark for what was initially billed as a Nordic World Cup event. Of more interest, the race was the first Nordic World Cup event for women and was won by American Alison Owen-Spencer (later Alison Kiesel). Years later she was disheartened to learn that the FIS and USSA had determined that the race was a "test" World Cup.

A related but independent venture was the Telemark Academy, founded by Peter Davis, a prominent New England coach. Beginning in 1977 and lasting for three years, the academy was modeled on New England ski academies, private schools that focused on cross-country ski racing. Telemark Academy was an ambitious training program in which kids and young adults lived near the lodge while pursuing their education. Col-

Martha Rockwell trains at Telemark in 1976 during the Olympic tryouts for the U.S. Ski Team.

lege kids took classes at nearby Northland College in Ashland. A small contingent of high schoolers as young as thirteen received their schooling at Telemark Academy from tutors.

In 1977, the summer after Kevin Brochman graduated from Stillwater High School, he received a call from Davis. Brochman considered himself a mediocre student and, prior to Davis's call, had no plans of attending college. By fall, Brochman was living at Telemark and taking classes at Northland. Following the model set by New England ski academies, Telemark Academy's scholastic schedule was built around the ski season: skiers had a heavier academic load in the fall, followed by a lighter class schedule during the racing season, and then an increased workload again in the spring. The academy was small, with a smattering of athletes each in high school, college, and out of school. The academy skiers did well in junior national meets, sometimes taking the top five slots. Brochman would go on to ski in two Olympics, as would Telemark alum Dan Simoneau from Maine. Hopkins skier Todd Kempainen became an Olympic alternate.

**SNOW AND FUN:
GRADE A
IN DAIRYLAND**

February as usual found the world
full of skiing. There was a jam in the
Austrian Tyrol to watch the world ski
championships (*see page 40*), seemingly unending processions on the
slopes of the Sierras and the Rockies,
not to mention the venerable ski
slopes of New England. In the Lau-
rentians, 40,000 skiers' cars clogged
the Montreal road for six hours. But
perhaps the most interesting pictorial
evidence of skiing's fascination came
from the dairy and lake country of
Wisconsin—a land with hardly a top-
ographical lump worth mentioning.
Here, too, skiers were finding slopes.
The run at Mt. Telemark, Wis. (*left*),
a half mile from top to bottom, last
week logged in its 20,000th skier—
he and all his predecessors apparently as happy as if the Tyrol and the
Rockies had never been invented.
Telemark skiers were but part of a
record tally of 300,000 skiers in the
Midwest this winter. One good reason for all the activity: the 300 ski-
tow areas in the Midwest are having
some of the best snow conditions ever.

Photograph by Anthony Linck

SPORTS ILLUSTRATED *February 17, 1958*   29

As seen in a *Sports Illustrated* feature in 1958, the expansive property at Mount Telemark entertained thousands of visitors each weekend. At the height of its popularity, the resort employed four
hundred locals.

Tony Wise called himself a "business adventurer" and lived up to that
role. But his "if you build it they will come" philosophy of paying for ambitious projects with numerous loans eventually failed. Wise had created
separate corporations for various aspects of Telemark and for his other
enterprises, such as the Lumberjack World Championships. He had one
company for the lodge, another for the nearby airport, and so on. When
one company made money, he infused that cash into his other interests
to keep them afloat. In 1980, Wise built what he called the Colosseum, an
indoor stadium with tennis courts, bleachers, and large doors on each
end. His plan was for Birkie and World Cup participants to ski through

the building during races and
receive cheers from fans comfortable in their indoor seats.
But the onlookers did not fill
the seats as he envisioned.
In 1981, Wise was eight million dollars in debt and declared bankruptcy. By 1984, a
judge demanded that his thir-
teen-million-dollar resort be
liquidated. He was in hock to
a staggering 650 creditors. The
bankruptcy was acrimonious.
Ownership of the American
Birkebeiner was stripped from
Wise, and he was even banned
from setting foot on Telemark
property. Nobody was sur-
prised at Wise's demise, but
his friends were incensed by
how the bankruptcy unfold-
ed. The bank sold the debt-
strapped resort for a dollar to
a developer, who promptly unloaded Wise's golf course for a
big profit and walked away.

Skiers of the 1980 American Birkebeiner take advantage of a trailside wax
service as they advanced toward the finish line in downtown Hayward,
Wisconsin.

Wise was shattered and
alienated from the community. "I really resent these vul-
tures flying around trying to pick my bones when I'm not even dead yet,"
he said in a newspaper interview. He even threatened to move the Birkie
to Minnesota, but the Birkie wasn't his anymore. It was an ignominious
ending for someone as bright and industrious as Wise, who had forged
the unlikely path from northern Wisconsin to Harvard, had been a war
hero, and had hewn a thriving, top-level ski scene in an improbable setting
through the power of his own vision. When Wise died in 1995, a Hayward
cabinetmaker made and donated his pine coffin. In the following years,

despite numerous attempts at rebooting it, Telemark Lodge fell into ruin, and the building was finally torn down in the spring of 2021. Some of Wise's creations live on, like the World Loppet Ski Federation (a network of twenty ski marathons around the world) and the Lumberjack World Championships. Most notably, the American Birkebeiner has grown into the largest ski race in North America.

♠

As Telemark Resort fell apart, a new cross-country hub opened on Minnesota's Iron Range. Giants Ridge in Biwabik started as an alpine ski hill in the late 1950s and lasted into the 1970s before going bankrupt and transferring ownership to a bank. Towns on the Iron Range were suffering as mines shut down, and the mines that remained became increasingly automated. Between 1960 and 1990, Eveleth lost nearly 30 percent of its population and Biwabik over 40 percent. The Iron Range Resources and Rehabilitation Board, a state organization funded by money paid in lieu of property taxes by mining companies, bought Giants Ridge in 1984. Hoping to breathe life into the struggling Biwabik community, the IRRRB spent six million dollars developing thirty-five kilometers of cross-country ski trails and expanding the downhill runs. Esteemed Olympic and Dartmouth coach Al Merrill laid out the course. Organizers started a citizens' race for Giants Ridge. Modeled after the growing success of the Birkebeiner, the Pepsi Challenge was a fifty-kilometer marathon first run in 1985. The soft drink company was the initial sponsor, and the name stuck. At its peak, the race attracted over eight hundred skiers, and though numbers have since dropped to about three hundred, the Pepsi Challenge continues every March.

Minnesota hosted its first ever World Cup cross-country competition at Giants Ridge in December 1985. Hosting a World Cup event was (and remains) a large financial and organizational undertaking, though the state of Minnesota essentially underwrote the competition through the IRRRB. The favorite to win the men's contest was Gunde Svan, a twenty-three-year-old Swede who had won a gold medal the year before in the Winter Olympic Games. Vladimir Smirnov raced, too; he was only twenty at the time and would eventually win Olympic gold and two World Cup season titles for his native Russia. Bill Koch was there, along with Minnesotans

Giants Ridge began as an alpine hill in the 1950s. The ski patrol (seen here in 1971) provided emergency medical assistance and rescue services to stranded skiers.

from the national team like Kevin Brochman and Todd Boonstra. A number of other Minnesotans competed after qualifying in an earlier race at the Ridge. One of them was a young langlaufer from Stillwater High School named Kris Hansen, who was just a junior in high school. During the racers' dinner before the event, Hansen happened to be seated at a table next to the Swedish team. She watched, impressed, as Gunde Svan "filled his plate at least three times with what looked like half a chicken each time."

Competition was slated to begin Friday morning, but the weather was so frigid that the women's fifteen-kilometer race was delayed until temperatures warmed from twenty below zero to a mere four below. The men's race was postponed from Saturday to Sunday, when the air was still five degrees below zero. Instead of doing two runs on the longer and more difficult fifteen-kilometer loop, the men raced three laps on the easier ten-kilometer course. The women raced two laps.

Kris Hansen was so excited to be competing against the world's best that she didn't much notice the air's arctic sting. Still on her first lap, Hansen started getting passed by the older women at the top of the circuit

Pavel Benc, of Czechoslovakia, and Erik Ostland, of Sweden, vie for positions around a turn during the 1985 World Cup at Giants Ridge in Biwabik, Minnesota.

completing their second go-around. "Hup," the European skiers said when they wanted to pass, as opposed to "Track," which was standard in America. "I'd try and ski with them as long as I could and then basically stop on the course, exhausted until the next one came along for me to chase," Hansen remembered.

She had developed quickly as a skier. Just three years earlier, as an eighth grader, she'd been tepid on the whole idea of cross-country. At the beginning of her first season with the Stillwater team, she'd lost interest in dryland training spent running up and down the Stillwater streets, gloomy in November. The team was huge, 120 skiers, so she decided to quietly skip practice, thinking her absence would go unnoticed. The next day in school, Bill Simpson, as Hansen later wrote, "cornered me in the hallway and asked where I had been the day before, and then proceeded to reprimand me for not keeping my commitment to the team and working up to my potential." Hansen quit skipping practice. She was surprised again later in the season when after a race Simpson complimented her in front of the team, even though she was nowhere near the top of the standings.

Hansen trained hard and got gangbusters results, winning the state meet in 1985 as a sophomore.

On the narrow Biwabik trail made for classic skiing, the World Cup athletes raced using the new skate skiing technique. The snow was so cold that their skis squeaked noisily against it. Apparently fortified from his multi-chicken meal, Gunde Svan easily won the men's race. Vladimir Smirnov took eighth. Fans near the finish line backed up as Bill Koch free skated by, casting his poles wildly behind him as he pushed hard off his powerful legs. Koch finished twenty-first, followed by Todd Boonstra in thirty-sixth and Kevin Brochman in thirty-ninth. After sucking in that frigid air so ardently for the duration of the race, Brochman wouldn't get his lungs working again at full capacity for another month.

Giants Ridge hosted two Nordic combined World Cup competitions, in 1986 and 1987. The jumping portion of the events happened in Ely on a

Braving subzero temperatures, a skier warms up on the course of the 1985 World Cup at Giants Ridge in Biwabik, Minnesota.

seventy-meter jump that has since been demolished. In 1987, the Minnesota high school state meet was scheduled to take place at Sugar Hills in Grand Rapids. With poor snow, the state meet was moved to Giants Ridge, where it has remained since.

♠

Elements of skate skiing are ancient, as evidenced by an archaic style of Scandinavian ski called the *andor*, in which one ski was very short and used for pushing off, providing glide on the other, much longer ski. George Hovland remembered skating around corners in pursuit of Erik Judeen in 1930s Duluth. Vermonter Bill Koch elevated skating to a standard form of skiing. Koch had roused American skiers when he won a silver medal in the 1976 Olympics, the first medal in cross-country for the United States, but then suffered a disappointing showing in the 1980 Olympics. After watching a Swede skate across a frozen river during a race later that year, Koch decided he would try skating in competition and see where it got him. It was a bold move and paid off huge. Koch practiced technique and prepared his comeback, stunning the world at the outset of the 1982 World Cup season. He won the World Cup title that year, another first for an American, and skating rippled through the ski world. In a boon to manufacturers, skate skiing would further complicate the increasingly technical array of cross-country equipment. Even casual skiers would want separate pairs of boots, poles, and skis for both classic and skating, whose shorter and stiffer skis were coupled with firmer soled boots that had more ankle support.

The Mora Vasaloppet was soon won by a pair of Scandinavian brothers who finished first and second. In a postrace interview, the winning brother explained his technique: doing what today is called marathon skating, keeping one ski in the groomed track and skating with the other. He did five skates with one leg, switched over and did five with the other, and finished the set by double poling for five strokes. That he won a big-time race this way seems hilariously quaint, but at the time it was cutting edge. "All of a sudden you knew skating was here to stay," recalled Bill Simpson. Simpson wanted to learn the technique so he could pass it on to his team.

For three years in the mid-1980s, Ahvo Taipale, a Finnish immigrant and owner of the Finn Sisu ski shop in St. Paul, hosted members of Sweden's

Nine years after Bill Koch became the first American skier to win an Olympic cross-country medal, Mora Vasaloppet founder Glen Johnstone took this photograph of the famous skier competing at the 1985 World Cup ski race in Biwabik, Minnesota.

national marathon team to put on a ski clinic between Christmas and New Year's. Taipale had been a fixture in the Twin Cities ski world since the 1970s, teaching classes through the St. Paul parks department and opening his ski shop in 1978. Taipale paid the Swedes' airfare and put them up at his house. The team was named after its sponsor, Scania, a Swedish truck manufacturer, and coached by Kjell Kratz. This was the same team that Glen Johnstone had convinced to fly in for the Vasaloppet some years before, and sojourns to the Twin Cities for the Vasaloppet and Birkie had become annual events as the Scania members forged relationships with Midwesterners. Two of its members, Ola Hassis and Lars Frykberd, had won recent Mora Vasaloppets. Hassis won the Birkie in 1982.

Bill Simpson frequently teamed up his Stillwater skiers with a club from nearby Mahtomedi that was coached by a Swedish teacher named Barb

Rolling hills and ample open space make Phalen Park in St. Paul a popular site for cross-country skiers. The park hosts an annual ski race that coincides with the Winter Carnival.

Cartford. When Simpson and Cartford heard that the Scania team was in town, Cartford contacted them to set up a meeting. She and Simpson met the Swedes at Phalen Park in St. Paul on January 2, 1985. The Swedes told Cartford in Swedish that they had skied fifteen kilometers just to warm up. Simpson was impressed. He had trained his team through long and steady distance workouts, and here were these Swedes treating the distance workout as an appetizer before their interval training, something Simpson had never paid much mind. "We weren't doing anything at this level," he recalled.

On a little hill by the park's clubhouse, the Swedes demonstrated skating for the American coaches, showing the V1 skate, in which pole placements were timed to coincide with the planting of the skier's lead foot. Then the Swedes did what they called the Gunde skate. Named after the chicken-devouring gold medalist, the Gunde skate was their moniker for open field, when the skier's pole baskets were thrust into the snow before the skier's foot reached the ground. The V2 skate didn't exist yet.

"It really opened up a whole new world for me," Simpson said.

Kris Hansen was introduced to skating that same winter, at a camp in Isabella, Minnesota, on the edge of the Boundary Waters, put on by a top U.S. skier named Tammy Valentine, who was coaching a group of Minnesota's best youth skiers through the Minneapolis Ski Club. Hansen's earlier go with skating had proved challenging. After placing well in a classic race at a junior nationals event in Steamboat Springs, she and a friend had decided they'd forgo kick wax and try skating in the next race. Hansen dropped to the wrong end of the standings, and her friend had such a hard time with the new technique that she had to be carted off the course and given oxygen.

Hansen, along with everyone else, had classic skied the first year she won the state meet. But by the time she went to defend her title at Sugar Hills in 1986, the tide had shifted and virtually everyone skated. That year Hansen won her second consecutive individual state meet and the Stillwater girls their fifth team championship in a row. Being a part of that technique transition in the sport remains one of Hansen's proudest accomplishments on skis. Years later, Hansen would join Simpson in instructing the Stillwater team and eventually became head coach.

One of Barb Carford's Mahtomedi skiers, Everett Meyers, qualified for the state meet that year. Simpson invited Meyers to ride to Sugar Hills on the Stillwater bus.

Kris Hansen (right) was the defending girls' state cross-country champion in 1986. Among her tough competition at the February meet that year was fellow Stillwater skier Sonya Stoklosa.

Seen here in the 1960s, Sugar Hills in Grand Rapids hosted many of the cross-country ski meets sponsored by the Minnesota State High School League.

During the long trip, Meyers became acquainted with a Stillwater skier, Ann Arnason. Arnason was from Marine on St. Croix and the daughter of Peg Arnason, to whom Simpson had given ski lessons in the early 1970s. After the meet, Peg recalled her daughter mentioning a boy she had met on the bus. Eventually, Ann and Everett would marry and have a daughter named Liv, who skied for Stillwater in the 2010s. Marriages stemming from the Stillwater ski team are not that unusual, though this case is notable because Liv was the third generation of her family to be coached by Simpson. His deep involvement in the river valley ski community isn't something Simpson usually dwells on, but sometimes a kid will come up to him with a story from a parent or even a grandparent, and the memories flood back as Simpson and the kid share a laugh. "It's kind of cool," Simpson said.

Meanwhile, in neighboring Wisconsin, without the support of their state's athletic association, a cooperative of high school clubs organized and executed a cross-country state meet in 1982. This was the first cross-country state race in Wisconsin since the Rosholt meet of 1939. Eleven clubs from around the state gathered in Minocqua on a brutally cold day. The air temp was twenty-two degrees below zero, and the windchill was a staggering seventy degrees below zero, but, instead of canceling, the race was reduced to 3.8 kilometers. Twenty-seven skiers competed from clubs that had traveled from as far as Oregon, in the southwestern driftless area, and from around Madison. Clubs from Tomahawk and Lakeland, respectively, won the boys' and girls' divisions.

The state meet continued to be held in Minocqua for the next two years. Forty-one skiers—twenty-four boys and seventeen girls—raced in 1983; the number grew to seventy-seven in 1984. Two years later, the championship was switched to a skating race and won by a future Olympian named Luke Bodensteiner. Although the state's clubs wouldn't form the Wisconsin Nordic Ski League until 2004, interest in cross-country skiing in Wisconsin grew throughout the 1980s. The decade brought significant and lasting snow to Milwaukee, where weekly ski races drew up to three hundred skiers. The 1990s had a number of poor snow years that set back youth skiing in the state's most populated areas.

Ted Theyerl, who skied in some of the first state meets, served as president of the Wisconsin Nordic Ski League, and coaches in Eau Claire, noted that what set Minnesota apart from its Midwestern peers in terms of a massive youth ski scene was the better snow in the Twin Cities compared to Madison, Milwaukee, Chicago, or Detroit. "Take out all Minnesota's Minneapolis and St. Paul teams from their high school league, what does that leave you with?" Theyerl explained. In the 1980s and 1990s, the new crop of elite skiers coming out of Minnesota were indeed mostly from the Twin Cities.

By the 1980s, the Midwest was back as a producer of international-caliber skiers. No Midwesterner had skied on the cross-country Olympic team for twenty-four years—not since George Hovland and John Burton in 1952—until Doug Peterson from Minneapolis raced in the 1976 Olympic Games. Peterson made the squad again for the 1980 Olympics. Kevin Brochman and Todd Boonstra both competed in Sarajevo and Calgary in

Kevin Brochman skates around a corner in Oslo at the 1985 Holmenkollen World Cup race.

1984 and 1988. Boonstra, from Burnsville, had won the Minnesota state meet in 1980. Nine years later, he attained the national cross-country title, the first time a Midwesterner had won since Peter Fosseide in 1940, breaking a dry spell of nearly fifty years.

John Bauer, who is widely regarded as the best modern Midwestern langlaufer prior to Jessie Diggins, won the state meet in 1986 and 1987 for Anoka High School. Bauer claimed the national title in 1991 and again in 1996. Another state champ, Ben Husaby from Eden Prairie, won the national championship in 1993. Under the tutelage of Lee Borowski, an influential eastern Wisconsin coach, Luke Bodensteiner, from West Bend, won the Wisconsin state meet in 1986 and 1987. Bodensteiner claimed the national title in 1994. Bryan Fish, from Rhinelander, was runner-up in both the classic and skate races in the 1993 Wisconsin state meet. Both Fish and Bodensteiner went on to careers working with Olympians as part of the USSA.

Bauer, Husaby, and Bodensteiner were all on the 1992 Olympic team. The Winter Olympics happened again just two years later (to stop the winter and summer games from occurring the same year) in Lillehammer, Norway, where the ceremonial torch relay was again lit from the hearth in Sondre Norheim's cottage. Husaby, Bodensteiner, and Boonstra represented the United States. In 1998, John Bauer was the lone Midwestern cross-country skier to compete in Nagano, Japan.

These were heady times for Midwestern men's skiing. No women from the region had yet to make the Olympic cross-country team. In biathlon, Minnesotans Patrice (formerly Jankowski) Anderson and Joan Guetschow made the team in 1992. Guetschow was back in 1994, followed by Minnesotan Kara Salmela (sister-in-law to biathlete, coach, and Olympic announcer Chad Salmela) in 1998.

♠

In the 1990s, the Minnesota State High School League changed the name of cross-country skiing to Nordic skiing. The move was led by longtime coach Bob O'Hara to eliminate the confusion between cross-country skiing and cross-country running. The change spoke to the state of the sport at the end of the century. Jumping and Nordic combined were forms of Nordic skiing, yet both specialties had become so unknown to casual and young skiers that the new name caused little confusion. Jumping had supplanted cross-country as the esoteric specialty.

Skiing was becoming an athletic event more on par with swimming or track, as it tilted away geographically from areas of Scandinavian heritage and toward affluent suburbs. Trails snaking through golf courses like a can of worms didn't exactly make for *idraet*-like communion with nature. Skiing was a healthy lifetime sport, however, whose practitioners rarely suffered concussions or torn knee ligaments. Highly educated and well-compensated parents embraced the sport and expected their children to do the same. Teams were bigger than ever.

The Bill Koch Junior Ski League had sprung up after Koch's silver medal win back in 1976. In Marine on St. Croix, Ralph Malmberg started a Koch club in 1979. The silver medalist starred in a couple of fun videos that were distributed to clubs and showed Koch weaving wildly through trees on his skinny skis and jumping over hay bales. Kids watched and got excited. The Koch league was headquartered back east, and when Midwestern coaches sent their dues to New England, they often expected to receive more back

Steve Gaffney remembers meeting Bill Koch at the 1977 Koch League Championships in Williston, Vermont. Steve's father, James, snaps a picture of the famous langlaufer signing autographs for eager kids after the event.

than they did. Every kid paid fifteen dollars a season and in return received insurance, a newsletter, and a patch. Anne Rykken and John O'Connell started a Koch club in St. Paul in the mid-1980s and were blown away when fifty kids showed up at Como Park. "I just thought it was a glorious sight to see all those little creatures scattered across the golf course," Rykken said.

One rainy fall afternoon, a group of Twin Cities Koch club coaches met to share ideas at Finn Sisu, including Rykken, Ahvo Taipale, and Steve and Kathy Gaskill, who had a Koch club in Burnsville. Steve, who worked at Finn Sisu, had been the USSA's head Nordic combined coach. With world-class coaching available locally, the group decided to start their own league, eventually founding the Minnesota Youth Ski League in 1992. The league would grow to fifty-four clubs and over three thousand skiers.

New citizens' races that continue today popped up with Book Across

The singular Book Across the Bay ski race crosses the frozen surface of Lake Superior between Ashland and Washburn, Wisconsin.

the Bay in 1996 and the Noquemanon marathon in 1998. Book Across the Bay started as a fundraiser for a local library (note the pun) and followed a distinctive ten-kilometer course across Lake Superior's frozen Chequamegon Bay from Ashland to Washburn, Wisconsin. The race is held at night, with the course lit by thousands of candles. The Noquemanon is a fifty-kilometer marathon that starts in the highlands of Ishpeming and drops (peppered with climbs) about eight hundred vertical feet to Marquette on the shores of Lake Superior.

🌲

One of the country's most vibrant jumping scenes ground to a halt with the past century. Long gone were the days when scores of Chester Bowl boys gathered every weekend to jump. In the 1960s and 1970s, Duluthians had regularly won the national Class A title, with Dave Hicks, Gene Kotlarek (George's son), Adrian Watt, Greg Swor, and Jim Denney, who was the last from his city to win in 1977. But after that, jumping dried up quickly in the Zenith City.

The four jumps once in the city's vicinity came down one by one. By this time, Duluth offered plenty of other diversions. Kids took up downhill and cross-country skiing and they played hockey, but they didn't jump. A minor jumping competition was held at Chester Bowl in 2005; it would be the last. Big Chester, which had towered over the city for nearly a century, was finally torn down in 2014 (the jump's final straw came at a summer performance of musician Charlie Parr in Chester Park, when Duluth's mayor worriedly noted a number of concertgoers perched on the dilapidated structure), as eighty-

Some of Duluth's star jumpers gather at Fond du Lac in 1970: Adrian Watt *(back)* with Greg Swor *(center)* and Ken Harkins.

eight-year-old George Hovland watched. He summed up his feelings at the time to a reporter as outrage and sadness: "It's like losing an old friend." When asked about it again in 2019, Hovland didn't want to talk about it. "Thinking about it makes me want to cry," he said.

Ski jumping settled into its new role as a minor sport. Some clubs remained strong. Alana Maki-Foust started jumping in 1987 with the Itasca Ski and Outing Club when she was four. Her dad, Doug, was a passionate jumper and coach, and her uncle, Jim, had been an Olympian. A smattering of other girls were in the club, but Maki-Foust was the only one serious enough to work her way up onto the big slides. She competed with the Junior Olympic team all four years of high school and racked up jumps in Lake Placid, Steamboat Springs, and Alaska. She didn't feel ostracized

Big Chester, the jump that was the centerpiece of the Chester Bowl ski scene for almost a century, was torn town in 2014.

Alana Maki-Foust with her dad, Doug, at a jumping event in 2012 sponsored by the Itasca Ski and Outing Club in Coleraine, Minnesota.

for being a girl, though she was one of few. On the big ninety-meter jumps, she never competed against more than three other girls.

During Maki-Foust's best season, in 2001, she had a wipeout that effectively ended her competitive career. Her ski binding wasn't attached correctly on a practice jump off Itasca's seventy-meter ramp, and one of her skis fell off in midair. As she landed, she face-planted, badly scraped her face in the snow,

A young jumper with the St. Paul Ski Club eyes his approach before launching off the jump during a Christmas training camp in 1984.

and suffered internal bruising. She recovered from her injuries but never regained the fire to really push herself. "Ski jumping is all about what you're thinking," she said. "It's 90 percent your psych."

The year of Maki-Foust's big crash, a promising jumper from the Cloquet club was named the most improved junior male skier in the Central Division. His name was David Sobczak. Sobczak's father, Mike, had been a jumper, too. Jumping ran deep in their family, all the way back to David's great-great-grandfather, a Norwegian immigrant from Telemark by the name of Torjus Hemmestveit. Jumping no longer roused large public crowds, yet the sport had evolved and lived on in its own insular world.

🌲

Dorothy Korkki Banks died unexpectedly in 1992 at the age of sixty-five. In his nearly twenty years of close friendship with Charlie Banks, Mark Helmer saw him outwardly emotional only a handful of times. The only

Charlie Banks *(left)* and Mark Helmer ski north of Duluth.

time Banks ever was angry with him was while the men were working on
a project and Helmer started backing a tractor down a hill. Banks thought
the hill was too steep and the tractor might tip over. When Helmer continued anyway, Banks said, "If you don't stop, I'm going home." "He didn't
raise his voice, but his tone changed," Helmer recalled. That was the most
heated exchange between them. When, shortly after Dorothy died, as
friends and family sat in mourning in the Banks home, Charlie walked up
to hug Helmer, it was a highly emotive action for the stoic Banks and an
indication to Helmer of how devastated he was.

Helmer began thinking about opening the ski trails to the public and
mulled over the notion for some weeks before suggesting it to Charlie.
Banks was retired from teaching, and maintaining the trails under increased usage would keep him busy. Charlie liked the idea. He and Helmer
christened the trail system Korkki Nordic, named after the road on which

the trails were located and the surname of Dorothy's Finnish family. Banks and Helmer didn't charge anything to ski at Korkki. "It wasn't some altruistic act," Helmer said. "We just had so much fun together." During the first winter, the Korkki trails were busier than ever before. At the time, the trailhead was right behind Banks's house. Helmer asked Banks if he'd sell him a couple of acres nearby, at an old homestead site. Helmer wanted to build himself a house and a new trailhead with a small warming cabin for skiers. Banks said he wouldn't sell him a couple acres and instead offered twenty. Helmer bought the land, and he and Banks built the Korkki cabin in 1993. Now divorced, Helmer moved into a couple of rooms at the back of the cabin.

Banks and Helmer met in the cabin each morning for coffee. When skiers started showing up, Banks would head back to his house. "It's not that he didn't like people," Helmer said. "He was more comfortable alone." Every night Helmer would follow a footpath from the cabin to Charlie's house and check on him. Charlie would often be asleep in front of the TV. Sometimes Helmer would sit a while.

Peter Fosseide and Charlie Banks, approximately age ninety and age seventy, respectively, at the Erik Judeen Memorial in the mid-1990s.

Charlie Banks died suddenly on a gorgeous late April day in 1998. He was seventy-four years old. When the two men met for coffee on Banks's last morning, Helmer suggested they drive to the Boundary Waters to canoe and portage a big loop out of Wood Lake up to Basswood Lake. Banks told Helmer to go on, that he would stay behind and have the sauna hot for him when he returned. Helmer had noticed Charlie slowing down over the past year. "We'd go out to work on the trail, and I'd turn around and he wouldn't be there," he said. Helmer returned to his vehicle after a day of canoeing and decided to visit a friend on his drive home. When Helmer showed up at the friend's house, the man came out right away and told Helmer that he needed to go home, that Charlie had died. Banks had collapsed outside the door of the Korkki warming cabin, where a neighbor found him on his back, his eyes fixed on a clear sky.

Banks was buried in the township cemetery. George Hovland and ninety-one-year-old Peter Fosseide drove together to the interment. Fosseide leaned heavily on Hovland as the old-timer hobbled up a long grassy incline toward Banks's grave. Once they reached it, Fosseide placed his hand on Banks's coffin and said, "Charlie, I'm going to live to the year 2000, then I'm going to find you." Fosseide wanted to experience the millennium but would die a few months short in August 1999. The formerly arcane sport he had promoted for most of a century would continue to garner popular appeal.

A skier glides past the camera during the start of the 2020 City of Lakes Loppet Winter Festival in Minneapolis.

8

A Thriving Ski Scene

2000s

The bitter irony of Nordic skiing in the twenty-first century is that now that the sport has finally caught on as a popular pursuit, Midwestern winters have become too mild to reliably keep snow on the ground. Unusually warm winters have always periodically disrupted ski seasons, such as the winter of 1888–89, which flummoxed what was to have been a year of skiing glory for St. Croix Falls, or during the previous major pandemic, when the 1919 national jumping tournament was canceled for lack of snow. The frequency and intensity of mild winters continue to increase. The two ways of dealing with the problem are to head north and to make snow. Northern Minnesota, Michigan's Upper Peninsula, and the highest reaches of Wisconsin more often retain snow as above-freezing days become progressively common to the south. Yet south is where the region's population centers lie, so a growing list of ski sites have adjusted to the new normal of warmer winters.

In the Twin Cities, Elm Creek Regional Park, Hyland Lake Park Reserve (both in the Three Rivers Park District), and Theodore Wirth Park have established popular loops based on fake snow. Across the river, after years of prodding, boosters including Ahvo Taipale and Anne Rykken finally succeeded in prompting St. Paul parks to hop on the bandwagon by funding, in late 2020, a similar system for the outstanding Battle Creek

Park trails. The Vasaloppet and Birkie races both make snow, as do parks in Duluth, St. Cloud, Coleraine, Milwaukee, and Madison. Trails in Eau Claire, Wausau, and Green Bay are considering snowmaking.

"There're actually much better training opportunities in Minnesota in the winter now than there ever has been, with the three places with lit snow, that's seven more miles than back in my day," said Kevin Broch-man, speaking of the growing roster of ski areas with lit loops featuring manufactured snow. "It's not real fun skiing, which is detrimental, but it's still skiing. Now you go do four laps at Elm Creek and it's boring. But look at swimming. You somehow overcome the boredom and say, 'this is what it takes.'"

An equivalency between swimming laps in an artificial pool and Nordic skiing will strike traditionalists who tour to get out in nature as anathema. For others, particularly young and new skiers in the lower reaches of the Upper Midwest, short laps on fake snow will be the type of skiing they know best, a fact that will become increasingly true as the years slough away like kick wax skids left behind in the snow. Yet, without the oppor-tunity to revel in nature, this is not exactly the *idraet*. "Skiing with five hundred other kids doing the same loop versus going out to Lebanon Hills or Terrace Oaks, someplace in the woods, is such a different experience

A snow machine blasts fresh powder on the trails at Hyland Lake Park Reserve in Bloomington, Minnesota.

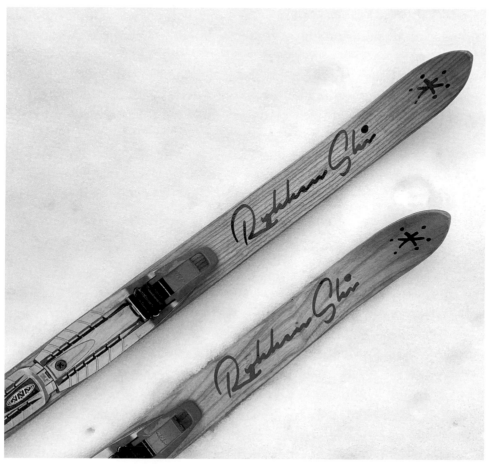

Minnesota Youth Ski League cofounder Anne Rykken is one of very few people today making wooden skis, which she soaks in her bathtub and bends on a rack in her basement. She started making skis for her grandkids and continues to sell her handmade wooden skis for children.

than what I grew up with," said Anne Rykken, longtime president of the Minnesota Youth Ski League. "I'm not sure I would have fallen for the sport going around Elm Creek as a kid." One veteran coach said, "Old skiers have all these incredible stories and experiences. These young kids, they call it Nordic skiing now because none of them have ever skied cross-country. With these kids I wonder why in the world, after the racing season, why they bother to keep skiing. To them all they see skiing as is racing."

For skiers who prioritize fitness and live near a snowmaking facility, the future of cross-country is bright. "You can put your finger on a map in the Twin Cities and nowhere in the world is there as many trails as maintained here," said Ahvo Taipale. Taipale noted that the three and a half million residents of the metropolitan area form a population not so much smaller than the entire national census of Norway or Finland, which each have a little more than five million citizens. Taipale's claim may be a bit of an exaggeration since the famed trails of Nordmarka contain hundreds of miles of trails within a twenty-minute train ride for the seven hundred thousand residents of Oslo. Yet no comparable population in the United States has such ready access to ski trails as the residents of the Twin Cities. With snowmaking and skiers on the upswing, warming winters will not eliminate skiing opportunities in the Twin Cities and in other systems using snow guns.

♠

Near Lake Superior in the Upper Peninsula of Michigan, lake-effect snow still usually plasters the region and lingers longer than residents would prefer. One evening in February 2020, the plow-excavated streets of Ishpeming lay buttressed between four-foot snowbanks. At the famed Suicide Hill—where the Flying Bietilas and about every other American jumping icon of the past one hundred years have jumped—the cross-country squad of the Ishpeming Ski Club was finishing practice and being debriefed by Coach Dick Ziegler. Ziegler has a lanky langlaufer's build and grew up skiing in New Hampshire, later moving to the Upper Peninsula when his wife took a professorship at Northern Michigan University. Their son Tim had just been named to the junior national Nordic combined team.

Many parents would balk at the idea of their kid ski jumping, yet Ziegler believes the sport to be surprisingly safe. He cited a 2012 study from the Consumer Product Safety Commission that found that kids who skied in general were injured at a rate of 1.7 per 100,000, while kids who played football were injured at a rate of 584 per 100,000. The FIS surveyed elite skiers in 2006–8 and found that ski jumping was statistically safer than snowboarding and all forms of downhill skiing. The newer designs of jumps and landing slopes have made the sport safer. While a top jumper will soar one hundred meters off a ninety-meter jump, that jumper won't be more than fifteen feet above the ground because the landing slope has been designed to parallel the trajectory of the jumper. Older jumps were not so carefully designed. Still, jumping careers often end in injury.

When it opened in 1926, Suicide Hill had a one-hundred-foot gap between the takeoff at the end of the jump and the angled landing slope: jumpers had to leap at least one hundred feet to avoid a nasty fall. Despite protests from the Ishpeming club, a local newspaperman dubbed the new slide Suicide Hill. The gap was fixed but the name remained.

The sport is kept alive by a combination of individual passionate coaches and the pull of clubs with rich histories. Both of these factors are in play for the Ishpeming club, one of only two jumping clubs left in Michigan. The other, the Kiwanis in Iron Mountain, no longer has any active jumpers and continues solely for the purpose of an annual tournament at the club's massive 120-meter slide, the only one of this size in the Midwest. Minnesota, which once had dozens of jumping clubs, today has only four, in Cloquet, Minneapolis, St. Paul, and Coleraine. Wisconsin has held on

On a blustery February day in 2020, a young jumper tries her luck on the small hills at Ishpeming's Suicide Hill Ski Bowl.

to six clubs, and Illinois has the Norge Ski Club, outside Chicago. These thirteen teams make up the Central Division. The Eastern Division is made up of a dozen clubs in New England, and to the west there's a single team in Steamboat Springs, Colorado; another in Park City, Utah; and one in Anchorage, Alaska. That's the entire roster of jumping clubs in the United States.

At Suicide Hill, Kim Larson showed up with her eleven-year-old son Isaac. This was Isaac's third season jumping. He started out running the landing slope and worked his way up to the twenty-five-meter jump. Isaac proudly showed off his new Slovenian Slatner skis. Nobody sells jumping gear in the United States anymore, so his mom special-ordered them from Europe. Kim shelled out eleven hundred dollars for skis, bindings, and boots, plus another two hundred dollars for the padded jumping suit. Isaac's seven-year-old brother just started jumping, so the skis should get additional mileage as hand-me-downs. Kim warmed the seven-year-old up on the outrun slope beneath the thirteen-meter jump and then lugged the boy halfway up the approach slope above the jump, held him under his armpits, and let go. The boy said "hup" and slid over the bump at the end of the jump. The thirteen-meter jump sounds larger than it is. The size assigned to a jump refers not to its height but to its critical line (or K-line, from the German word *kritisch*), which is deemed a reasonable distance to soar from the end of the ramp. Jumpers lose scoring points for every meter they are short of the K-line. The vertical height off Isaac's jump was only two or three feet.

The Larsons weren't previously a jumping family. They'd been recruited by the Ishpeming jumping coach, Gary Rasmussen, who had retired from a career as an investment adviser and started driving a school bus, where he handed out club fliers to his riders. Rasmussen had first jumped the ninety-meter Suicide Hill slide in 1972, at the age of thirteen, and had gone on to jump competitively through college. His father, Wilbert, had twice held the distance record on Suicide Hill, first setting it when he was just fifteen. Wilbert later won the 1957 national Class A title.

Unsurprisingly, jumping instruction is much more regimented today than it was in past decades. Stories of jumpers from previous generations are evocative of a Huck Finn-esque fairy tale, like in the 1930s when eleven-year-old George Hovland and four buddies decided they were ready to leap

With the legendary ninety-meter slide in the background, jumpers from the Itasca Ski and Outing Club test their skill on the slopes at Ishpeming's Suicide Hill, February 2020.

for the first time from Duluth's Big Chester. They had no parents or coaches around, no approval: they simply climbed the jump after a tournament and argued about who would go first. A boy named Fred Anderson took the first leap. "We almost carried him to the edge and pushed him over," Hovland said. "He survived. We figured the rest of us could probably make it."

Isaac Larson was the same age as Hovland had been but lived in a different world. As he queued up for another run down the twenty-five-meter slide, Rasmussen suggested he end his run with a Telemark turn, as proper form dictated. Isaac readied himself at the top, said "hup," and started down, giving a little hop at the bump. He soared several meters, caught his landing, and began to pull one foot back for a Telemark ending but chickened out and snowplowed instead. Rasmussen was only two years older than Isaac when he first ran the ninety-meter jump, which towered like a piece of industrial equipment in the darkening cobalt sky.

Six kids of the Ishpeming club's usual dozen practiced that night, all of them preteens. The waxing moon rose over a massive mound of iron mine tailings that had been sitting there long enough to grow trees. Given the crowded public spectacle that ski jumping had been decades prior, it was extraordinary and endearing to watch these kids soaring off jumps almost anonymously, witnessed by scant few parents, a couple of coaches, and a stranger with a notebook.

♣

Doug Maki, coach of the Itasca Ski and Outing Club, thinks maintaining a jumping team in a small, close-knit community like Coleraine–Bovey is easier than in a large city. Coleraine and Bovey sit snugged next to each other along Highway 169 in northern Minnesota. The route to Mount Itasca and its ski jumps is well signed from the highway. Flanked on one side by downhill runs and by smaller jumps on the other, the big seventy-meter jump standing on the top of Mount Itasca is named after Ole Mangseth, the club's first star. The view from the top is 360 degrees of woods interrupted by lakes, derelict iron mills, and mounds of red tailings.

Doug Maki finally quit jumping in 2020 at the age of sixty-five. He took his last leaps in Eau Claire and was happy with his first attempt of twenty-five meters but not so much with his second of twenty-one. Maki's last wipeout was four years earlier on the same hill, when he banged up his

A ski jumper soars over the rolling Iron Range during the qualifying events for the 2009 Junior Olympics at Mount Itasca in Coleraine, Minnesota.

elbow and shoulder. "That's one of the reasons I decided to hang up the boards," he said. "If I fall it's going to hurt. I don't heal that fast anymore." Maki has never been a cross-country skier; he's more into seeking thrills than quietly communing with nature (his other hobbies include driving race cars and flying powered parachutes).

The Itasca club keeps up its numbers by holding an annual learn-to-jump event, which is advertised in the newspapers and through the schools. "Some years we're lucky, we might fish seven or eight kids; some years we only fish in two or three," Maki said. "We've been able to keep the program that way. They come out and try it, we give them skis and boots, and they get to ride the pommel lift, they like that and they want to join. So we get some new kids all the time. Word gets around and they bring their friends."

Maki is also the club historian, so when a woman living in a house that once belonged to Bob Riley, a champion skier and nephew of Barney Riley,

Young jumpers practice their form at Mount Itasca in Coleraine, Minnesota, 2015.

found an old pair of skis in her house, she assumed they had belonged to Bob Riley and called Maki. Maki discerned from one glance, based on the lines engraved into their tops, that the skis were from an earlier era and more likely had belonged to the Wild Irish Rose. The brand label has worn off, but Maki thinks the skis are Strands. He cleaned the century-old wax from their bases and refurbished the hoary wood to a clean shine. He still wants to strap his boots into the worn leather bindings and run down the thirty-degree landing slope beneath the ski jump, but he's afraid the bases will grab the snow and send him careening on his nose. For now, the skis hang from an interior wall of the Itasca clubhouse as a commemoration of the team's most memorable alum.

The Itasca club, with twenty jumpers ranging in age from five to eighteen, is actually bigger now than when Maki was a kid on the team in the 1960s, when jumping was already past its peak in popularity. Despite Maki's Finnish ancestry (*maki* means "hill" in Finnish), he didn't come from a skiing family. He just happened to live near the Itasca jumps, and he and his brother fell into it, eventually maintaining their own ski trail from their yard to the jumps. Maki was never able to keep up with his older brother Jim, who went on to compete in the 1976 and 1980 Olympics. In the 2019–20 season, fifteen Itasca club members traveled the jumping circuit, heading to weekend tournaments around the Midwest.

Maki is optimistic that the sport will endure. To reduce jump maintenance, the painstaking labor that, in his view, attributed to the sport's decline relative to the rise of downhill, the Itasca club retrofitted their seventy-meter jump with plastic tracks. Ski tracks that run down jumps these days are set not through snow but through ice with a big machine. Ice tracks can be cut in early winter and, with a little refreshing, last all season. The plastic tracks obviate the need for cutting tracks altogether. The top of the jump has a water spigot for simply icing over the plastic.

Barney Riley holds a pair of skis at a tournament in which his bib denoted that he was the first-ranked jumper in Class A.

But even the optimistic Maki predicts more clubs will die out. In the 2019–20 season, the Kiwanis Ski Club in Iron Mountain had no active skiers; the venerable Snowflake Ski Club, of Westby, Wisconsin, was down to two. Wisconsin's Iola club has similarly dried up. Yet, as Maki said, "All it takes is one or two people to get in there and grab the bull by the horns and you can get a club going again." His daughter, Alana Maki-Foust, did just that, recently resurrecting

There are considerably fewer spectators at competitive jumping events today than there used to be. At this February 1965 tournament in Westby, Wisconsin, hosted by the Snowflake Ski Club, the crowd was estimated at twenty thousand.

the Cameron Ski Club in Wisconsin. Ruth Frankenberg had won a tournament in the short-lived ladies' jumping circuit of 1938 for the Cameron club, which disappeared soon thereafter. The rebooted Cameron club has a dozen jumpers ranging in age from five to thirteen.

"It wasn't that hard," Maki-Foust said. An elementary school music teacher, she handed out fliers to her students and recruited a few that way. Her own two children, a boy and a girl, joined. The club didn't have money to buy jumping skis, but Maki-Foust found a set of old downhill equipment for free that held them over for the first year. "In Cameron we have a tiny hill. We call it a ten meter but it's probably six." It's a good intro hill, and she soon found two donors who paid for a team set of proper free-heel jumping gear. In the 2019–20 season, Maki-Foust drove three of her skiers once a week to Eau Claire, where they used the Flying Eagles Ski Club's slides. For the coming 2021 season, she expects at least five skiers will make the weekly trip. "The families are encouraged to stay at practice—we're just one big team," Maki-Foust said. She still jumps and rode the thirty-meter slide with her dad in 2020, though with coaching, judging, and managing her own kids, she doesn't know if she'll have time keep it up. "My dad will probably convince me to," she said, sounding hopeful.

The Central Division's biggest club in the 2019–20 season was Cloquet, with a staggering fifty-six jumpers. The club has been growing since local physician Ken Ripp took over. Two of Ripp's kids, Aidan and Charlotte, were named the Central Division's top male and female Nordic combined athletes for the 2020 season. In March, twenty-year-old Aidan competed in an FIS junior world championship in Germany. The strongest club in the Central Division, and the nation, is Chicago's 115-year-old Norge club. With about fifty jumpers, the Norge was represented by three of the four jumpers on the U.S. men's Olympic squad in 2018.

As many girls as boys are jumping today. In addition to coaching, Alana Maki-Foust is a scoring judge for the Central Division. As she officiated a tournament in Eau Claire in 2020, she was struck by how jumping's demographics have changed since she was a teen. "There were so many girls up there it was unbelievable. . . . Even at a high level on the 90 meter there are

Alana Maki-Faust *(far left)* with young jumpers from the newly resurrected Cameron Ski Club.

Jumping skis lined up during the 2014 Junior and National Masters Tournament at the Tri-Norse Ski Club in Wisconsin.

a lot of girls." Girls are generally lighter weight than boys, which is an advantage for soaring farther. One school of thought about why women were discouraged for so long from jumping is that insecure men feared being outjumped and as a result barred women from competing. The same could be true of cross-country. In her recent autobiography, Minnesotan star skier Jessie Diggins mentioned that after she was allowed to race against boys and subsequently beat them all, she was no longer allowed to compete with them. Women's ski jumping finally became an Olympic sport in 2014. Several years before, Pat Lyons, a coach from an august jumping family with the St. Paul Ski Club, told a newspaper reporter, "I've watched several girls grow up in this sport with the same dreams and aspirations that the boys have. And they're denied that privilege. I think there's a couple old farts in charge out there that ought to be put in a barn."

At the local level, female jumping progressed quickly in the twenty-first century. The Central Division began annually awarding a title to its top girl skier in the late 1990s. In 2001, the award was named in honor of Therese Altobelli, who had been treated so poorly as she strove to compete. The FIS started the Women's World Championships for jumping in 2004, which Michigan native Lindsey Van won in 2009. The FIS urged the International Olympic Committee in 2006 to start a ladies' jumping division for the Winter Olympic Games, though just the year before the president of the FIS had said of women and ski jumping, "It's like jumping down from, let's say, about two meters on the ground about a thousand times a year, which seems not to be appropriate for ladies from a medical point of view."

The IOC declined to make jumping a women's sport, justifying the decision not with the president's implication that it would damage female reproductive organs but with the claim that there wasn't enough interest in the sport. By this time, many sports formerly thought of as residing soundly in the male domain, like boxing, hockey, and wrestling, had been opened to women. In 2009, the Wisconsin jumper and coach Karla Keck joined other top women skiers, including Lindsey Van, in suing the IOC in

Wisconsin jumper Nita Englund pictured midflight during the 2017 FIS Ski Jumping World Cup in Hinzenbach, Austria.

an attempt to get their sport included in the 2010 Vancouver games. Van didn't buy the IOC's rationale about lack of interest and put more weight in reasons stemming from the delicacy of the male ego, saying in an interview, "It was the original extreme sport. And so if you all of a sudden add women to it, is it as extreme?" Even though a Canadian judge ruled in the women's favor, the ruling didn't legally compel the IOC to include women's jumping.

The following season saw the first women's World Cup, after which the IOC finally decided to include women's jumping in the 2014 Olympic Games in Sochi, Russia. However, the women had only one competitive event versus three for the men. By the 2018 Olympics, a young Wisconsinite named Nita Englund, who jumped for the United States, said in a newspaper interview, "I don't really feel like I have to fight for women's rights. I'm just there as an athlete. That matters a lot." As a teenager jumping with the Kiwanis club of Iron Mountain, Englund had handed out flyers and circulated a petition to promote girls' jumping at the club's annual meet, yet she was in the first generation of women jumpers to progress without roadblocks to an international level.

🌲

The biggest ski happening of the 2018 Olympics was, unquestionably, the gold medal success of Minnesotan Jessie Diggins and Alaskan Kikkan Randall in the sprint relay. The United States had won only a single Olympic cross-country medal before (Bill Koch's silver in 1976) and Diggins's and Randall's golds were the first ever in any Nordic event, including jumping, biathlon, and Nordic combined. Diggins was the fully realized woman athlete Dr. Phoebe M. Scott predicted would exist back in 1966. "Women will become full partners in this sports world," Scott said. More than being a full partner, Diggins, a three-time winner of the Minnesota state meet, became the most famous U.S. cross-country skier in history, far more recognizable to younger generations than Bill Koch. Koch was the only American to have won the World Cup overall title, which he did in 1982 using skate skiing, until Diggins claimed the championship for the 2020–21 season, a first for an American woman.

The Midwest took its time in sending a female cross-country skier to the Olympics, followed by a flurry. The first was Barb Jones in 2002. Like

Its door gilded by a Jessie Diggins poster, the Lumberjack Hall of Fame, a rustic, replica logging-era building, is the center of events for the twelve-kilometer Snowjourn race in Bemidji, which had its fortieth running in 2020.

Diggins, Jones, skiing for St. Paul Central, was a three-time state meet winner. John Bauer made the U.S. men's squad again that year. Four years later, Abby Larson from St. Paul, Lindsey Weir from Mahtomedi, and Lindsay Williams from Hastings competed in Turin, Italy. Larson and Weir had both won the state meet. No local men competed that year. In 2010, Garrott Kuzzy from Hopkins was the lone Midwestern representative of either gender. Diggins first participated in the Olympics in 2014. Another east metro graduate, Leif Nordgren, competed that year on the biathlon team.

Kris Hansen, who developed a close relationship with Diggins that continues today, credits Diggins's success to a complex array of factors. "She

Stillwater coach Kris Hansen with the girls' cross-country ski team after winning the 2010 Minnesota state meet at Giants Ridge, including future Olympian Jessie Diggins *(bottom row, second from right)*.

likes to say that what differentiates her is her willingness to go into the pain cave. I accept that but think that's just a good answer for an interview," Hansen said. "Jessie is the most cerebral athlete I ever coached." Aside from her commitment to an assiduous physical training regime, Diggins studies and strategizes on how to practice and race, for example, calculating the most opportune moments for risk, such as when exactly to commit to a dead sprint to the finish, like she did in PyeongChang to claim Olympic gold. Hansen also cites the impetus that Diggins derives from being on a team, which she would have first learned from her tight-knit family and later the Stillwater Nordic squad. "She is always racing for something bigger than herself," Hansen said. At the heart of it all, though, "Jessie truly keeps the joy of skiing at the center of her focus. I think it's funny how often that gets dismissed as an irrelevant sentiment, but what else could keep you living out of a duffle bag for six months of every year except something you truly love to do?"

According to Bob O'Hara, who directs the Nordic skiing program of the MSHSL, in the 2019–20 season, Minnesota had ninety-six schools with both boys' and girls' teams, which comes out to 192 ski teams. The number is actually a little higher, with 110 schools providing skiers, though some schools are part of co-op teams that lump together skiers from separate schools, like Chaska–Chanhassen or the Mesabi East area teams. Winona is the only school in the south of the state with a team, and there are a few in western Minnesota. O'Hara estimates that Minnesota has about four thousand high school skiers.

Organized youth skiing in Wisconsin is managed by the Wisconsin Nordic Ski League, an independent organization. The WNSL has about four hundred skiers in twenty clubs and continues to hold its annual meet. The Wisconsin teams are a mix of club teams linked to schools to varying extents. Some clubs are sanctioned by their governing school to the point where athletes can earn a skiing letter. The situation in Michigan is similar, with three main Nordic centers for high school competition, the Superiorland Ski Club from Marquette, the Copper Country Tigers (a co-op club representing Houghton, Hancock, and Calumet), and Traverse City. In the 2020 Michigan state meet, seven club teams competed. Traverse City tied the Copper Country Tigers for first place, lengthening the Tigers' winning streak to eight years. The other Michigan clubs are from Roscommon, Petosky, and Grand Rapids, in the Lower Peninsula, and Ishpeming.

Alaska and New England still produce more elite skiers than the Midwest, yet Minnesota has far more high school skiers. According to Kevin Brochman, Minnesota coaches "are more focused on numbers and social

Jessie Diggins is welcomed home by Stillwater coach Bill Simpson *(left)* and Bob Hagstrom after her gold medal win at the 2018 Olympics.

SKI SHOOTING: BIATHLON

The only form of Nordic skiing that requires a firearm, biathlon is a combination of cross-country ski racing and target shooting. Athletes ski a course while stopping—with pouring sweat and racing hearts—to shoot at targets with a specialized rifle two or four times along the way, sometimes shooting while standing and other times while lying down on their stomachs. In its modern form, the sport was first featured in the Olympics in 1960, though an earlier iteration, called military patrol, was present in the earliest Winter Games. Military patrol started in the late eighteenth century when Scandinavian ski troops would challenge one another in contests of skiing and shooting. Biathlon is more vaguely derived from ancient hunting and skiing traditions, though today the sport is almost entirely based in competition, meaning people don't casually go out for a ski and a shoot.

Minnesota has a small but well-established and thriving biathlon scene, with courses in Alexandria, at Snowflake in Duluth (a ski area developed by George Hovland), in Elk River, at a new one in Red Wing, and at Mount Itasca, in Coleraine, which is home to the state's strongest program. Wisconsin has clubs and ski trail systems with gun ranges in Madison, Green Bay, and Eagle, in the southeast of the state. For the 2020–21 season, four of the six athletes on the U.S. team's top competition squad were from Minnesota (Jake Brown and Leif Nordgren) and Wisconsin (Deedra Irwin and Paul Schommer). Interestingly, the National Guard sponsors biathlon teams, and serious biathletes often enlist to receive training and funding. The Minnesota, Wisconsin, and Michigan National Guards each have a team, but the best, the All-Guard team, trains in Camp Ethan Allen in Vermont. To avoid having to travel back and forth between the Midwest and Vermont, Midwestern biathletes often join the Vermont National Guard. Vermont is the center of the civilian biathlon world, too, and elite Midwestern biathletes often move there to practice their sport. 🎄

Kara Salmela jumps from the prone position during a biathlon event in the 2002 Winter Olympics in Salt Lake City, Utah.

than they are on actual results. Coaches brag about how many people they have rather than how fast they are." Ambitious New England youth skiers bust their butts trying to win a scholarship to a ski academy. "There's more stress to be fast in high school level there than there is here," Brochman said. "The results certainly go with that—New England is much faster than us at high school level, but at college and the U.S. team we do pretty darn well."

Brochman, in addition to coaching the St. Olaf College Nordic team, took over the Minneapolis Ski Club from Norm Oakvik and trains elite youth skiers under its banner. Two of his skiers, Molly Moening from Highland Park and Henry Snider from Mounds Park Academy, won the girls' and boys' individual state titles in 2020. Brochman's skiers, like many others, don't specialize, which is one of the more contentious issues in youth skiing. His athletes might run cross-country for their school in the fall rather than devote themselves to Nordic skiing year-around, as specialization requires. Focusing year round on a single sport requires serious commitment from a teen athlete, as well as a financial one from parents. Hiring a personal coach for ski training on top of what one's high school team offers costs a significant sum of money, and that doesn't include the rising costs of equipment. Cross-country skis have become quite expensive, running several hundred dollars for a top-notch setup, though many high school teams have assembled large collections of skis for their members.

A high-profile Twin Cities ski organization has created controversy over its specialization program for high school skiers. The Loppet Foundation was envisioned in 2002 by Minneapolis mayor R. T. Rybak. One February at the dawn of the millennium, Rybak was driving back from skiing the Birkebeiner with friends when he noted masses of skiers returning to the Twin Cities. He mused that Minneapolis should become the silent sports capital of the nation, so he called a community meeting to brainstorm ideas. One person who showed up at the meeting was John Munger. Munger had skied on the Minneapolis South High School team in the early 1990s and is the grandson of Willard Munger. Dubbed "Mr. Environment," Willard represented northeastern Minnesota in the state's House of Representatives for forty-two years. John Munger went away to college, got married, and then moved back to Minneapolis when his wife started her medical residency at Abbott Northwestern Hospital. Idolizing his grandfather, Munger would strike out on the Theodore Wirth ski trails, which

Despite being distracted by eating snow, skiers with the Minnesota Youth Ski League gather at Elm Creek Park Reserve in Maple Grove in 2019.

he'd often skied during high school; Munger often noticed the deterioration in the quality of grooming and fantasized how he might restore the trails to their former glory. So naturally he was drawn to Rybak's meeting, where the mayor suggested holding a major ski race.

Munger ran with the idea and was soon named race director for the new City of Lakes Loppet. He found a sponsor in Abbott Northwestern and used the skills he'd gained earlier in his career as a teacher to draw in youth skiers. The snow was terrible that winter. As the race date approached in early 2003, Munger beseeched volunteers from the Mora Vasaloppet to come down with a customized tiller to grind up ice on the Minneapolis lakes to make a course. A week before the race, only thirty people had registered. Luckily, a gorgeous snow fell right before the event. Eight hundred skiers showed up, and the race was a success. Munger had just graduated from law school, yet he wanted to stick with what he'd started. "I had to choose one job over the other," he said. "My wife was a doctor; financially we could do it." Munger became, and remained until 2020, the executive director of the Loppet Foundation, which in the following twenty years became a surprisingly large enterprise.

The arm of the Loppet Foundation that drew the ire of high school coaches was Loppet Nordic Racing, a yearlong training course completed in addition to, and sometimes instead of, the training offered by a skier's high school team. As one longtime Twin Cities coach said, Loppet has "created kind of a monster while they are trying really hard to develop fast Olympic level skiers. . . . Now kids are coming to high school practice and say, 'I'm going to Loppet today,' that just rubs the wrong way, and that's usually one of your better kids, but as a coach trying to make team, you want those kids there at practice, making a good team. There are a lot of high school coaches frustrated about that. It makes them better skiers, but I don't think it makes them better teammates." The feeling was echoed by another coach, who said, "Specializing is good for really fast kids at the top, but not good for the sport."

Volunteers hand out drinks to skiers during the 2019 City of Lakes Loppet in Minneapolis.

Skiers begin the classic marathon during the 2020 City of Lakes Loppet on Bde Maka Ska and Lake of the Isles in Minneapolis.

The Loppet roster of coaches is impressive, including the likes of 2010 Olympian Caitlin Gregg; second-generation fixture of the Twin Cities ski world Lynne Cecil, who grew up with her parents running the popular B.J.'s ski shop and won a Birkie; and Matt Liebsch, another Birkie winner who raced internationally with the U.S. team. To join Loppet Nordic Racing for a year will cost a skier's parents four thousand dollars, plus rides to and from practice and top-of-the-line snow and roller skis.

This more intensive coaching is an indicator that Nordic skiing has become a mainstream sport. These issues with clubs, money, and team loyalties are found in all major sports and are by no means exclusive to skiing. David Paulson, who came one warm spell away from founding the City of Lakes Loppet in 1981, has been coaching Nordic since the 1960s, currently serving at Chaska–Chanhassen. He loves it there. The affluent school district built a state-of-the-art waxing facility for the cooperative team.

"Academics is our primary emphasis," Paulson said. "The top twenty girls on the team have an average GPA of 3.9." This is an astounding accomplishment, and that mix of healthful athletics and academic success is what most parents hope for with their kids. Skiing is a salubrious, lifelong sport, and in peer groups such as this, the benefits transcend physical health. It's like the *idraet* in that sense, yet it's all too common that these benefits are often within easier reach for aspiring skiers in more prosperous communities.

🌲

The international stage of skiing was days away from rising up in the middle of Minneapolis for the 2020 World Cup sprint races on March 17 when the event became another casualty of the Covid-19 pandemic. The United States hadn't seen a cross-country World Cup since 2001 and the Midwest since 1985 at Giants Ridge, when Jessie Diggins's high school coach Kris Hansen competed. Diggins was instrumental in landing the World Cup in Minnesota when, after winning her Olympic gold medal, she started talking publicly about the merits of holding such an event in the state.

The fate of winter events at Theodore Wirth Park is increasingly dependent on faux snow. Jessie Diggins points out in her book that it is a regular skiing substrate during World Cup races in Europe.

She'd been dreaming of having a World Cup in the United States since 2017, after skiing one in Canada. With her celebrity status the following year, everyone was listening to Diggins. She had, after all, done the impossible and won gold for the Nordicly challenged United States.

Despite wanting a World Cup on home turf, the U.S. Ski Association wasn't willing to take point on landing the race. The USSA, not known for being heavily funded, was unable to make the financial and organizational commitment to an event where success wasn't guaranteed. So, partnering with Diggins, the Loppet Foundation started the process of hosting a World Cup. They needed to raise a couple of million dollars for a single-day event. Over multiple meetings, Diggins pitched local business owners, and, with Diggins being Diggins, Loppet found sponsors. They secured the money but still needed a slot on the FIS calendar. In May 2019, John Munger traveled to Greece, where that year's FIS congress was being held. The FIS didn't have much space left in its schedule for Munger and Minneapolis, but he had the money and backing, so they squeezed in a race on a Tuesday, between events in Quebec and Canmore.

Although the much-anticipated 2020 World Cup had to be canceled because of the Covid-19 pandemic, Jessie Diggins met members of the Fastenal Parallel 45 World Cup planning committee for a day of racing at Theodore Wirth Park.

The Theodore Wirth snow machines began working overtime in late 2019 to ensure coverage for the March race. "We're building a mini glacier," said Loppet coach Greg Klave in January. The edge of the trail at one point ended cleanly in a several-foot-high cliff of faux snow. The snow was so deep that near the bottom it was compacted to the plastic-like texture of a glacier and took on a dreamy blue hue. Late winter would have to unleash an extremely warm spell to jeopardize the race. But just one week before the event, with eleven thousand tickets sold and the country terrified of the exploding pandemic, Munger canceled the event. There would be no makeup date.

"It's just gone," Munger said over the phone two months later, as he worked from home. A male cardinal sang lustily in the background while Munger sat in his yard sounding crushed. Loppet was able to recoup some money from canceled transportation and hotel fees but still had lost a bundle, and Munger had to lay off much of his staff. He expressed faint hope at rebuilding and organizing another World Cup, but for now he was just trying to keep Loppet afloat. A few months later, he resigned from the foundation he had helped create.

♠

When Norm Oakvik died in 2015 at the age of ninety-four, he left money to Loppet that was used in the construction of the Trailhead, an airy timber and glass building in Theodore Wirth Park that opened in 2019. The building features a ski shop and serves as a meeting place for area skiers. The entryway, equipped with chairs and a gas fireplace, is lined with a distinctive wainscoting made from vintage wooden skis. Up until the pandemic, Theodore Wirth was bustling with activity every day. "Norm Oakvik would be in tears [of joy] to see what happened at Theodore Wirth," said David Paulson.

To skiers who came up on cross-country in the anonymity of an obscure sport, the daily winter scene outside the Trailhead is more evocative of a downhill resort. Fit city skiers stride about in Patagonia jackets and form-fitting pants. Instructors give lessons on proper kick and freestyle pole placement on the flats in front of the building. Ski instruction is far more pedagogical than in years past. Coach Greg Klave teaches six days a week. He uses phrases like "forward movement progression model" and

After opening in 2019, the Trailhead building in Theodore Wirth Park quickly became a community hub for area skiers.

cites his "PSIA 200 certification." It wasn't that long ago when Norm Oakvik summed up the whole shebang pithily with "You simply kick with the rear foot and glide with the front." These technical advancements, and perhaps even bureaucratic complications, have little bearing on the average skier, yet the increasingly specialized atmosphere of elite skiing is to credit for America's higher standing on the world stage, which translates into more casual skiers getting interested, strapping on their long boards, and hitting the trails. Like John Burton wrote back in the 1950s, the success of the Norwegian elite skiers was based on a foundation of many casual tourers.

In addition to running Loppet Nordic Racing for the city's wealthier kids, the Loppet Foundation works to diversify the Twin Cities' population of skiers. Racially, Nordic skiing is about as white a sport as one can find, yet, on a weekday in February 2020, two buses pulled up to the Trailhead and dropped off 140 kids from Park Brook Elementary in Brooklyn Park. Many of the kids were white, but more were Black, Latinx, and Asian. Loppet's goal is to introduce kids of color to skiing early so that they keep it up or feel comfortable picking up the sport later in life. For interested kids,

"Kick with the rear foot and glide with the front," quipped Norm Oakvik in the late 1960s. Oakvik's influence on Nordic skiing is felt strongly at Theodore Wirth Park today.

Loppet offers an after-school silent sports league for middle schoolers at three area schools, where youth practice canoeing, orienteering, biking, and skiing two or three days a week.

Greeting the kids was Ray Aponte, the adventure director for Loppet. Everyone seemed to know Aponte; he had served thirty years as a principal at various Minneapolis schools, most recently at South High, until retiring in June 2019. He spent his early childhood in Puerto Rico before moving to a farming town in Wisconsin when he was eight. Prompted by a friend, he started skiing twenty years ago in Minneapolis because he wanted a winter sport.

The kids exiting the bus were third graders. Their school elders, the fifth graders, had been out earlier in the day. This was the fifth graders' third year of skiing, and they were pretty solid on their boards. Usually a coach from Loppet visited the school and the kids skied on a small loop outside, but this field trip was in preparation for the Minne-Loppet, a race for kids held during the weekend of the City of Lakes Loppet.

Aponte had the veteran teacher's knack of getting boisterous kids to

Loppet Foundation adventure director Ray Aponte skis at Theodore Wirth Park in 2020. His work has been integral to the organization's mission of furthering outdoor opportunities for kids in Minneapolis.

listen without shouting at them. He kept his pep talk brief before jumping up on the wooden bench that lined the Trailhead's long wall, where he mimed classic technique in his stocking feet. "Kick, kick, glide!" he said, and the students stormed outside. They started on a one-kilometer loop on the open flats outside the Trailhead and then headed into a series of knolls wooded in bur oaks. "Are we going into those mountains?" one boy asked, referring to twenty-foot mounds while simultaneously revealing himself a Minnesotan. "We hope if we expose one or two thousand kids a year to winter sports," Aponte explained, "eventually they'll want to do that later in life. Research shows if you spend time outdoors it's healthier—it's a richer life."

Another day, Aponte brought in 175 eighth graders from Justice Page Middle School in Minneapolis. Coordinated with a former colleague and skiing buddy, art teacher Elissa Cedar Leaf, the ski experience was new

One of the Loppet Foundation's central objectives is to expand recreational opportunities for skiers of color through activities like the Minne-Loppet, seen here in 2015.

to almost all the kids. A few were refugees from Guatemala and Mexico who had never even seen snow until this winter. These kids couldn't speak English and stayed in a group with their school aide.

Thirteen-year-old Yoni Velasquez had crossed the U.S. border alone and was promptly imprisoned by U.S. authorities in what he called *la perrera*, or "the dog kennel." Whether Velasquez would get to stay in the United States and continue to practice skiing was questionable, but on this day he and his pals were living in the moment, laughing and egging each other on, their sweatpants caked in snow from frequent wipeouts as they lapped a steep hill.

Aponte's dream is to get a brown or Black kid in the Olympics. Day to day, his focus is on "getting kids outside and have them experience something really fun. . . . It's a better deal for everyone." Only time will tell whether these efforts will create a new, more equitable generation of diverse skiers. If history is any indicator, places that promote skiing to kids become homes to lots of ski enthusiasts. Students in the 1970s at Marine on St. Croix Elementary School eventually formed much of the state's first huge high school team in Stillwater. Large high school ski programs are indicators of engaged skiing communities. Parents who ski naturally get their kids into it, and, to a lesser extent, kids who ski sometimes tempt their nonskiing parents and siblings to give the long boards a try.

♠

The surge in interest among young kids and their parents isn't limited to the Twin Cities metropolitan area. Students at Mora Elementary School ski during gym class. In 2000, the Vasaloppet built the Nordic Ski Center, which includes a chalet, waxing room, and sauna, right next to the elementary and middle schools. The design for the building was donated by Duluth architect David Salmela, whose son Chad Salmela would broadcast Jessie Diggins's gold medal win for NBC, indelibly shouting the refrain "Here comes Diggins!"

Mora Elementary has a set of cross-country skis and a two-week Nordic unit in gym class in which the kids go skiing five days a week. To build from the crop of budding langlaufers, there's a popular extracurricular club for kindergarteners through sixth graders called Fast Track. No bus trip required: the kids just go out after school and ski. Once they reach seventh grade, they can join the Mora High School team, which for a small town whose annual graduating class is barely over one hundred is relatively massive, having had seventy-nine skiers in a recent season.

It will fall on the young skiers the school churns out to keep the town's landmark race alive, which is of particular interest as a major race yet run by volunteers without corporate sponsorship. Climate change and an aging volunteer base have changed the Mora Vasaloppet. The race doesn't get as many entrants as it once did, its numbers chipped away by the upstart City of Lakes Loppet and several years of poor snow. In 2019, around eight hundred skiers participated in four contests of varying lengths. Many of the baroque scenes that Glen Johnstone worked tirelessly to produce in hopes of inspiring a sense of wonder have been lost, like the costumed boys and girls ringing bells. Johnstone died in early 2019 at the age of ninety. The biggest change came when the race traded its point-to-point

The Vasaloppet Nordic Ski Center in Mora, Minnesota.

course for a series of laps, a shift necessitated by increasingly unreliable snow and new landowners. "You'd go out to check the trail in the fall and there'd be a new house where it used to go," said John Hollister, the early North Star skier who later moved to Mora.

"Those old guys worked on that trail until they were so old," said Angie Nistler, Johnstone's daughter and a ski coach in Bemidji. "Cell phones were coming out and people made them carry them." These volunteers were frequently out in the woods alone at an age advanced enough that even a minor mishap could leave them in need of help. In 2007, a volunteer in his seventies named Leroy Youngblom died of an aneurysm while doing trail maintenance.

The Vasaloppet had to be canceled in 2012 because of a lack of snow, so when conditions were terrible again the following year, volunteers were desperate to pull off a race. The Vasaloppet had always used an improvised array of grooming equipment, including a landscape tiller (made for

Mora Ski Club member Peter Larson crosses the finish line during the Dala thirty-two-kilometer freestyle race, one of four contests in the 2019 Mora Vasaloppet.

A tractor hauls snow to the trail of the Mora Vasaloppet. The organization, like many others, has begun using snow-making equipment to keep up with a changing climate.

breaking up soil, but the Vasaloppet used it on crusty snow) pulled behind a one-ton Dodge pickup equipped with snowmobile-like tracks. One of the volunteers, a machinist, sharpened the metal teeth on the tiller. Another man drove the rig onto Mora Lake, which the race always crossed, and began grinding ice. The Vasaloppet's most iconic scene comes at the far shore of the lake, where, nearing the run to the finish line in downtown Mora, the trail climbs a heartbreakingly steep little hill and passes under a wooden bell tower that chimes encouragingly at the exhausted skiers. In 2013, volunteers used the tiller to painstakingly grind a twelve-foot-wide swath of bare ice into a semblance of snow, and the entire race was held on the small lake. Jon Larson, current president of the Vasaloppet, remembered a comment a skier made about the loop trail, which was surrounded by glare ice and brown dirt: "Oh, look, they made winter!" The fifty-eight-kilometer race that year involved eleven laps. Racers joked about getting dizzy.

To avoid a repeat, the race spent sixty thousand dollars on a snow-making setup. In preparation, they had to dig a well and make a pond for cooling the pumped water. This process was difficult, but things were about to get more complicated as race organizers waited for the arrival of the snow gun they had ordered from Europe. As the race day drew nearer, they kept waiting, until eventually U.S. Customs notified them that the snowmaker was being held. Labeled a "snow gun," customs would not permit the device to ship without further documentation; specifically, the government needed ballistics information. Explaining that the gun fired water and not ammunition required filling out layers of paperwork and navigating a bureaucratic labyrinth. Finally, the snow gun was released and arrived in Mora, where snowmaking began in earnest.

At the budget-minded Vasaloppet, volunteers produce one huge pile of artificial snow and haul it to the course. This is different from, say, Theodore Wirth Park snowmaking, where a mess of hoses snake for kilometers to numerous mobile snowmakers. When the Vasaloppet crew began working with manufactured snow, they reemployed a piece of equipment they had used in the race's early days. Effective but decidedly unglamorous, and assuredly not manufactured as a specialized piece of grooming equipment, agricultural manure spreaders work wonders for transporting huge quantities of snow. Several Vasaloppet volunteers are farmers, and they loan out their manure spreaders in the weeks leading up to the race.

In front of a Nordic-looking house, a Swedish *tomte* watches over the route of the Mora Vasaloppet.

During a recent poor snow year, volunteers filled and delivered fifteen hundred spreader loads along fifteen kilometers of trail over three weeks. "It's a monumental effort," said Jon Larson, who is confident that snow-making saved the Vasaloppet. "You can get by having a flat race on a lake once, but when you have to do that every year for three years, people aren't going to come back."

Although traditionalists were saddened to lose the point-to-point course, the trails are better now than ever before. No longer do volunteers have to worry about ruts created by landowners hauling cords of stove wood or deer shot during the hunting season. The Vasaloppet trails exist today on seventy acres owned by the race, with the rest on two pieces of private property held by supportive neighbors. In the first years of working the new trails, volunteers brought their machinery and tackled trail construction with what Larson calculated to be twenty-five hundred horsepower of heavy equipment. One guy brought his bulldozer and cleared the trails, while another came through with a ripper to loosen the ground. A volunteer named Don Olson came in with his big rock picker and removed all the stones, and someone else tilled the trail to even it out further.

"We have ski trails that are as smooth as people's driveways," Larson

Medals awarded to participants of the Mora Vasaloppet.

said. Volunteers tend to the trail with a standard riding lawnmower in the summer to keep it smooth and to prevent woody growth from taking root. Such efforts on the old trail, which might get chewed up by vehicle traffic or grazing cattle, wouldn't have made sense. Aside from improving the skiing, the new trails require less snow. In the old days, to smooth over pits and mounds of the rough ground, the race needed a whopping twenty inches of snow. Today, the trails are skiable with a paltry two inches, and the race requires just four.

🌲

You can still ski Charlie Banks's trail north of Duluth. It's an old-school trail, wide enough for a single classic track and more like a hiking path, a charm that takes on special meaning when you're screaming down the trail's big hill, called Iso Mäki (meaning "big hill" in Finnish), inches away from the skeletal arms of surrounding trees. A bypass is available for those who don't want to contend with the hill, but that would mean missing the vista on top where a big white pine clings to the edge of the bluff before the ground falls away and exposes a view to the northwest of miles of lesser

It's difficult to overstate the influence that Charlie Banks has had on cross-country skiing in Minnesota. George Hovland had this sign made for Banks more than forty years ago. It stands at the Korkki trailhead.

hills and unbroken forest. After crossing over the hilltop and starting down a sidehill, Lake Superior and the Bayfield Peninsula in Wisconsin are visible, blue and dreamy in the distance, but you can't look for long because the hill demands attention. There's a wide spot in the trail at the start of the second, bigger drop where, if you're lucky and a mere mortal, you can stop to collect yourself before the howling descent ahead. From the trees at the base of the hill, Charlie Banks used to hang casualties of wipeouts—broken pieces of wooden skis and bamboo poles—as a sort of memento mori. Following that theme, various places along the trail are named with colorfully painted wooden signs tacked to trees that commemorate epic wipeouts, spots such as Cook's Fall, where Sam Cook careened off-trail, and Salmela's Curve, where four skiers, including Chad Salmela and Mark Helmer, were involved in a pileup.

Helmer has been maintaining the ten-kilometer trail system for more than twenty years since Banks's death. These days, at age sixty-six, he considers his own mortality. "I'm a northern man," he said. "I want to die in the cold." Not so long ago, a friend of his moved to Florida, gained weight, and started looking like an "older white man," Helmer said, shaking his head. Since taking a nasty tumble on Iso Mäki a few years ago, Helmer has quit running the big hill at full speed. To be sure, most skiers in their twenties would not run Iso Mäki at full speed.

One evening in late summer, Helmer sat back in a wooden rocking chair in the Korkki Nordic warming house that he and Banks built, stretched his arms over his head, and locked his hands there. He is short and muscular. Biceps like hams stick out from his shirtsleeves. His back was bothering him; after retiring from the railroad years ago, he soon started working with his former brother-in-law building houses. Influenced by the asceticism he admired in Banks, he was dressed plainly in blue jeans, a white T-shirt, navy socks, and rubberized moccasins. Helmer started rocking in his chair and didn't much stop for four hours. He recalled noting the clothes that were hanging on the line the first time he pulled into Banks's yard, decades back: three pairs of blue jeans, two denim shirts, and three denim ball caps. Banks also wore cheap white T-shirts. Banks and Helmer used to sauna and then drink beer. Banks would have two—he'd chug the first and then nurse the second for over an hour. By the end of that second beer, he'd have turned so red from the alcohol and heat that Helmer could see the blush glowing through the thin weave of Charlie's T-shirt. "This is the best thing we've ever done," Banks said to Helmer one night as they sipped beers, referring to the new sauna they'd built in 1996.

As they put the finishing touches on the sauna, Banks drove down to Lake Superior to collect stones for its firebox. He selected the stones carefully, making sure they were the right size and density so they wouldn't crack from the water that would be dumped on them. He left the newly gathered stones in buckets outside the sauna one cold fall night. Rainwater fell into the buckets and froze. The next day, as Helmer worked on the sauna's exterior, Banks sat inside, chipping the stones free from the ice with a pick. Banks hummed and talked to himself as he removed the stones. He'd extract one and hold it in his hand to admire its color and texture. "Oh, that's a beauty," Banks couldn't help but exclaim.

"He found beauty in a sauna stone!" Helmer remarked more than two

Mark Helmer at Korkki in 2017.

decades later. "He looked at life so simply and with so much joy." Helmer wanted to express something big. He glanced at the ceiling and rocked harder in his chair. "Skiing is just the vehicle for a life outside," he said. "This is all tied to ideals of skiing, sauna, and living in the woods. I don't want to say it because it sounds too corny."

On a different night, once the sauna was complete, they'd been sitting there with another guy when Banks told his younger friends that he wanted them to keep Korkki going. "Of course we'll keep it going," Helmer had said. "It's not even a thought."

Helmer remarried, built himself a house near the Korkki trailhead, and had two daughters, who both went on to ski for Bonnie Fuller-Kask's Duluth East team. Charlie Banks's old Central High School closed in 2011.

In early 2017, after another poor snow season, Helmer decided to dissolve the Korkki nonprofit and let the trail return to its original status from decades past, an intermittently maintained private trail for use by friends and family. Storms during the summer months always left a host of wind-felled trees that needed clearing. Swampy spots sometimes sucked his mower in like quicksand. As a nonprofit, Korkki had a board of trustees, yet it was always a one-man show. Banks had set a tough example by breaking the trail himself in his snowshoes and then skiing in a track.

"I don't ask for help," Helmer said, "because I'm Finnish and stubborn." He brooded over how much of his life he'd spent on the trail. The labor was worse on wimpy snow years, when he'd supplement the thin pack by shoveling snow onto the trail from the surrounding woods. One year they didn't even open, for lack of snow. "You go through all this work in the fall to get the trail going and then you don't get snow," Helmer said. "It's discouraging." It wasn't just the work, which he generally liked. A deeper frustration came from no longer knowing the skiers who used the trail. Prior to a weekend, he might get up at 3:00 a.m. to groom. On Saturday morning, the parking lot would fill. In the old days, the crowd milling about the warming cabin would be a reunion of friends, but these days he didn't know anyone. The skiers of his generation were older and no longer coming. He asked Banks's daughters how they would feel if he dissolved the Korkki nonprofit. They told him that Banks would be proud, that they understood if he let it go.

Then Helmer received a phone call from Chad Salmela, the former U.S. Biathlon Team member and Olympic sportscaster. Salmela had often trained on Banks's trail as a young biathlete. Salmela told Helmer that the Duluth Cross-Country Ski Club was giving Helmer a lifetime achievement award. The timing was not a coincidence and would secure Korkki for a while longer. "I sat there with the phone and thought, 'no, no, no,'" Helmer said. "I hung up the phone, and my wife already knew about it, and I said, 'How do I get out of this?' and she said, 'You can't get out of this.'" When he received the award at the club gathering, Helmer stood in front of the crowd and told them he was going to read a poem. "I could see the people going, 'oh, no, he's going to make a fool of himself,'" Helmer recalled. He'd written the poem on a napkin. He didn't talk long.

> For the love of the smell of pine tar on the base of a wood ski
> For the love of friends and family
> But for one friendship that comes along only once in a lifetime
> So there is a place called Korkki.

At least that's how Helmer recalled it. After his speech, he crumpled the napkin and threw it in the garbage. When Duluth outdoors writer Sam Cook called a few days later asking for it, Helmer suggested he go dig through the trash.

Things have been better at Korkki. Helmer told the board he was no longer going to plan events, write the newsletter, or take on other administrative tasks. He would keep the trail open, for Charlie, but he was done with the other stuff. The board picked up the slack. One day in late August 2019, as Helmer rocked in his chair, a volunteer had been out, a

Nordic decorations adorn the exterior wall of the Korkki warming cabin.

middle-aged man with a daughter on the Duluth East ski team. The man had walked the trail and cleared windfall. He was muddy and flecked with sawdust spat from a chainsaw. He updated Helmer on how much progress he'd made and headed off in his Subaru. Helmer looked pleased.

"A lot of people ask me what will happen to Korkki when I'm gone, and I think it will go for a couple of years, then interest will fizz out and the place will die. Maybe one of my girls will take it over, though that's a lot to ask of a young person. I keep waiting for a young Mark Helmer to walk in here like I walked up to Charlie's," Helmer said. For the time being, the Korkki trail awaits skiers, babied by Helmer on his snow machine and still hosting the Erik Judeen Memorial Race, which is approaching its sixtieth year.

When Charlie Banks put on the first Judeen Memorial, ski equipment and clothing consisted of wood, leather, and wool and all the racers were men. The ski sport has changed a great deal since then, with natural fibers replaced by space-age plastics and with women in full command in all zones of the sport, from girls toddling on skis in their backyards to the cutting edge of international competition. At the heart of it, much remains the same in the era of Jessie Diggins as it had been in that of Sondre Norheim. The elemental draw of Nordic skiing is timeless: that fusion of people's natural desire to glide quickly and quietly over the snow, the invigorating exposure to winter's spare beauty, and the pleasure found in the kinesiology of form, whether a classic stride, a Telemark turn, or the V2 skate.

When an American child of the twenty-first century masters balance on skis and can glide across the snow with confidence, that young person experiences the same glee that arose in the Hemmestveit kids as they chased after Norheim on the slopes of Morgedal. The season's joys, of course, are not limited to winter's children and may become more important with age. One thing is certain: as long as there's snow on the ground, it's a good time to grab the long boards and head out for a ski.

A cross-country skier speeds over the
forested trail at Holmenkollen, Oslo, 1969.

Epilogue

As I began writing this book at the end of 2019 and into the innocuous beginning of 2020, I skied, pursuing the modest goal of matching Torjus Hemmestveit's time from the first cross-country marathon of 1888. I'd always been a skier, ever since learning as a young boy in the eighties with the Bill Koch Junior Ski League at Coon Rapids Dam Regional Park. My dad was an instructor of the small group. He had grown up on a farm where his half-Norwegian mother skied in the cow pastures, though he never skied until he and my mother, a pair of baby boomers drawn to the era's fitness craze, bought Skilom package skis at a hardware store in Anoka County in the 1970s. I regretted not asking my grandmother about her skiing history (she was full of beguiling tales, like riding to school on a horse that walked back to the farm on its own after delivering her); her unspoken ski memories were lost with her passing.

I skied for the Anoka High School team in the late 1990s. In the early 2000s, to celebrate youth's resilience to unpreparedness, I skated the Birkebeiner three times. Then I got a pair of short, metal-edge bushwhacker skis that I adorned with a pair of universal bindings, into which I could secure my regular winter boots, allowing me to glide through untracked woods and over frozen waterways. I didn't set foot on a groomed ski trail for a decade.

In 2018, after writing an article for the *Minnesota Conservation Volunteer* about the ski culture in Marine on St. Croix, Minnesota, I dug out my twentieth-century Peltonens, melted on a layer of wax, and headed to William O'Brien State Park. After a couple of kilometers, my heart was flapping like a wren stuck in a stovepipe. I planted my poles into the snow and leaned heavily into them, wondering if my heart might literally explode. Working my heart and lungs this hard was like taking a commuter car for a fast drive on the open highway. The car might not have been a Ferrari, but the engine still revved when I pressed the pedal down.

Impressed by the depth of people's skiing stories I'd encountered while working on the magazine article, I began expanding the idea into a book by interviewing avid skiers whose enthusiasm was infectious. My fortieth birthday was nearing. Use it or lose it, I figured, and I registered for the fifty-five-kilometer classic 2020 Birkebeiner.

The 2019–20 ski season started auspiciously with snow in December. Every winter now dawned with a sense of foreboding, with doubts of whether the season would be cold enough to produce a significant window of skiing. As the year wound down, I often checked the forecast, fearing the sort of unseasonable warmup that had practically become expected. When precipitation neared, I watched nervously to see what form it would take. Late 2019, though, aside from one rainy stretch around Christmas, was the start of three solid months of skiing, the air remaining just cool enough to result in snow that lasted.

I was rusty on my skis, but the motions felt good, and after a few sessions I didn't have to stop as frequently. I racked up laps around Marine on St. Croix and on a lit trail near my home in Wisconsin. I usually skied at night, with Venus holding bright and bleary low, Orion guarding overhead, and the moon traversing through its cycles. One evening as I was skiing by the light of the full moon, cresting and bombing oak-covered knolls, eavesdropping on the serenade of a great horned owl, I felt dialed into an arc that extended back millennia and progressed directly to the present. Apropos of the bleak winter landscape in the bleached light of the moon, I pondered that arc and the dead Norwegians who inhabited much of it, Sondre Norheim and the like. More than one of the veteran skiers I'd interviewed said they wanted to die with their skis on while practicing the sport they loved. Thoughts of death and winter went hand in hand in a pleasurably gloomy way, and skiing seemed as good a method as any for staying on the surface of it all, striding quickly across the brittle crust of the melancholic before it could give way and send one plunging into the depths of the season's desolation. I thought of a Sami poem I'd come across:

> Our life
> is like a ski track
> on the white open plains.
> The wind erases it
> before morning dawns.

I put in enough kilometers that by the time the Birkie came along I was feeling confident I could match Torjus's dusty record of four and a half hours. By contemporary standards, this was a mediocre time, but for a relapsed skier who'd never done much tracked classic skiing, I thought it was reasonable, and intriguingly historical.

The night before the Birkie, I stayed at my friend Rob Dybvig's cabin an hour away from Hayward. Rob had skied the twenty-nine-kilometer Korteloppet race that day, during which he'd fallen and broken his hand. Rob was a big guy to begin with, but when I entered the cabin and he held up his fractured right hand in greeting, I was shocked to see it had swollen to the size of a rotisserie chicken. He stoically avoided treatment (other than some cans of beer) to stick to the plan of providing support for me and the other two skiers he was hosting, a pair of brothers, who like Rob were in their fifties. Natives of the Iron Range who had relocated to the Twin Cities, John and Will Johnston were smaller and leaner than Rob and serious skiers. This was John's thirty-first Birkie, gaining him the distinction of becoming, in the American Birkebeiner zeitgeist, an *Uberlegger* (someone who has skied thirty or more American Birkebeiners). We ate a big dinner of salad, bread, and spaghetti with meatballs and turned in early.

Driving to the race's start through a cold and clear dawn, John tuned the car radio to the station from the La Courte Oreilles Ojibwa reservation just outside Hayward. Usually it was a quirky independent station with spacey DJs who paused while talking in low, breathy tones like they were waiting for the words to appear out of the ether. On Birkie weekend, though, the station played on repeat a suite of singular and campy race-inspired music, the Birkie's own oeuvre of songs, like "Korteloppet Dreaming" and another tune rooted in the alliterative qualities of the word "Birkebeiner."

On doubtless the busiest day of traffic per annum on this remote stretch of Highway 77, vehicles slowed to a crawl for miles before entering a parking lot where Rob unloaded the Johnstons and me to catch a bus to the starting line. The brothers hurried to the starting line through a throng of hundreds of skiers and fans. I wouldn't start until the last classic wave. Clay Diggins, Jessie's dad, stood on scaffolding and emceed over a loudspeaker. Whenever he invoked his daughter's name, the boisterous crowd quieted in reverence to hear what he was going to say next.

Finally, my wave was off. I knew I could ski fifty-five kilometers, though I was apprehensive about my condition upon finishing. The day was sunny and gorgeous, one of those late winter days when you can feel the sun gathering strength. Several kilometers in, I calculated the distance left and shivered. I sure had a long way left to ski! I told myself to go slower, to save some energy. I was catching up to skiers from earlier waves. The hills along the course were large and frequent. People were wiping out on every descent, causing painful-looking pileups—tumbling balls of skiers with poles and legs sticking out. One large man barreling down a hill ran into the back of a much smaller woman and sent her sprawling violently into a heap. "Sorry!" he yelled as he skied on; his conscience finally got the better of him, and he stopped to make sure she was not injured.

The kilometers ground on, and my thoughts wandered in unfamiliar patterns. I recalled a conversation I'd had long ago on a hiking trail with an ultra-marathon runner. He was far gone into an endorphin-induced state of mysticism. "It takes you places," he said of his running, in what initially seemed a moronically obvious statement. I had skied thirty kilometers, and it had taken me someplace other than thirty kilometers down the trail. I better understood Jessie Diggins's "pain cave." My entire body ached. My eyes seared with sweat. I had an impulse to weep, to sob for the abuse I was inflicting on my fragile body. I was surrounded by hordes of other skiers but was in my own lonely bubble with more than twenty kilometers to go. The suffering to come weighed heavy. Confoundingly, this was funny. My endeavor was utterly unnecessary. I could stop anytime without consequence. I was putting myself through an absurd luxury. We all were. That was hilarious. I laughed and thought it would be comforting to cry, but nothing came. The kilometers kept ticking by, some like I was in fever dreams and others like my body was an engine lacking oil.

I finished after four hours and fifty minutes, twenty minutes slower than the time with which Torjus Hemmestveit had won the world's first fifty-kilometer ski marathon with a single pole. I rationalized that at fifty-five kilometers I'd skied 10 percent farther, and to deduct 10 percent of my time would put me nine minutes ahead of Hemmestveit, therefore making me world champion. Sort of.

I considered how I could have been faster—not holding back early, charging up the hills, and being in an earlier wave with the peer pressure of faster skiers. Plus, of course, I could always continue training for a year and see where that left me. I saw why people kept coming back year after year, aside from the draw of partaking in a distinctive cultural event. The Birkie was a measuring stick you could gauge yourself against. If you could beat your younger self, maybe you could keep from aging.

♠

The Birkie reminded me what I had learned in high school: that I was more of a tourer than a racer. I was fine with this—I liked skiing, and it had me in better physical shape than I had been a year before. My penchant for touring was reinforced that same month in Michigan's Upper Peninsula, after I spent some days conducting research in the USSA's Hall of Fame in Ishpeming. I spent the nights not far away at my uncle's home in the woods. Before driving home, he took me skiing on a trail system called Valley Spur, in the Hiawatha National Forest.

The air was a chilly twelve degrees that morning when we stepped out of his car at the trailhead, though a climbing sun promised warmth. Inches of lake-effect snow had fallen the day before and added to the ample layer covering the floor of the maple and hemlock forest like an excessively frosted cake. My uncle was practically drooling with excitement at the prospect of schussing the big hills he said lay along the trail. He was primarily a Telemark skier and wore a pair of old black leather boots connected by three-pin bindings to Telemark skis that were too wide to fit into the freshly groomed tracks.

The snow aside the trail was deep and pillowy, soft and soporific. It was so unlike my home trails on the outskirts of the Twin Cities, which were invariably heavily used, icy, and met on either side by frugal snowpack that sat at more or less the same level as the trail's surface. Here, the trail was a trough cut through deep white that mounded luxuriously under tall trees. The snow squeaked coldly under our skis, the only sound in the motionless air. When we stopped to look around, the resulting silence was muffled further by the snow, forming a vacuum of stillness that announced itself in a beckoning presence not unlike noise. A crystalline layer covering tree branches sparkled in the sunlight, making for a tableau so gorgeous and pure that I thought fondly of the *idraet* and how people could be divided into two groups, those who had been pulled by silence into the snowy woods and those who hadn't, and how the latter couldn't relate to the former and that was their loss.

The forest thinned as we climbed into the highlands with glimpses of Lake Superior open and blue in the distance. My uncle pointed out that the forest was airier here because the beech trees had been removed by the forest service. Beech trees in the Upper Peninsula in recent years have been massacred by a one-two punch of a tiny exotic insect and a subsequent fungus. To reduce fuel for wildfires, use the wood, and slow the spread of the bugs, the forest service logs the infected trees. Had this not been pointed out to me, I wouldn't have noticed that the beeches had ever been there. Outside the areas of cutting, occasionally I saw a healthy beech, the bole of the towering tree smooth and pale. The trunks of other beeches were covered with a whitish scuzz, an ominous sign of the tree's fate.

The story of these beech trees, I recognized, had parallels with the fate of Nordic skiing. In not so many years, a day would come when skiing on natural snow would be an uncommon event. Most people will not dwell on this. Ski touring, the type of skiing that drew baby boomers as a way to connect with nature, will disappear from much of the Upper Midwest. There will be cold weather windows resulting in snow that lasts for days, or even weeks, during which skiers will don their skis and storm forth through their favorite parks. During these times, people will think back longingly on the old cold days of winter.

More venues will farm snow, and young skiers will learn and train on loops of fake snow that stand in chromatic relief from the brown, slumbering landscape. Purists may abandon the sport. Young skiers will be fast and of good form, and when the odd natural snow lingers they will delight in skiing freely across the landscape, as their predecessors did, and they will fleetingly consider with rancor the carelessness, willful ignorance, and waste of those before.

In Valley Spur, though, the demise of the Midwest's natural snow fell far from my mind as I dropped from the highlands back into the valley. The hills along the trail had names cutely engraved on wooden signs, such as

Bigfoot, Slingshot, and Heart Attack. The hills would have been challenging had the conditions not been perfect, but on this morning, with soft and smooth snow underfoot, the rides down were pure delight. Any concerns of time and place yielded to the present, the moment elevated by the formula that had been written so many centuries ago in a place unknown, that simple and divine concoction brewed up by mingling a specimen of *homo sapiens,* a pair of long boards, and an ample coating of the sweet cold manna from above.

Sources and Acknowledgments

For an understanding of the origins of the ski, I consulted *Skis and Skiing from the Stone Age to the Birth of the Sport,* by John Weinstock (Edwin Mellen Press, 2003), and *Two Planks and a Passion: The Dramatic History of Skiing,* by Roland Huntford (Continuum Books, 2008). *Sondre Norheim: The Father of Modern Skiing,* by Anne-Gry Blikom and Eivind Molde (North American Heritage Press, 2003), told Norheim's story as well as the restoration of his legacy in later decades. Helen White's chapter "Ski-Sport Heroes from Norway" from her book *The Tale of a Comet and Other Stories* (Minnesota Historical Society Press, 1984) detailed the Hemmestveit brothers and the first boom years of the sport in the Northwest. *Sky Crashers: A History of the Aurora Ski Club,* by Frederick L. Johnson (Goodhue County Historical Society Press, 2003), was also a valuable resource regarding the first ski boom and, in subsequent chapters, the course of the Aurora club's storied history. *Pioneer Tales,* from the Pennington County Historical Society, contained an account written by Torjus Hemmestveit's granddaughter describing his final years in western Minnesota. Walter "Speedy" Spidahl's autobiography, written with Nancy A. Carter, contained the opening section on young Spidahl getting his first pair of skis. Walter O'Meara's *We Made It through Winter* (Minnesota Historical Society Press, 1987) detailed skiing in Cloquet in the early twentieth century; thanks to my mother, Linda Rodgers, for finding this book. For the first three chapters, I frequently referenced *From Skisport to Skiing: One Hundred Years of an American Sport, 1840–1940,* by E. John B. Allen (University of Massachusetts Press, 1993). *The Ishpeming Ski Club: Over a Century of Skiing,* by Burt Boyum and Jamie LaFreniere

(U.S. National Ski Hall of Fame and Museum, 2003), added more content to the NSA's early days; thanks to Dick Ziegler for giving me a copy at Suicide Hill. *Midwest Skiing, a Glance Back,* by John Pontti and Kenneth Luostari (Arcadia Publishing, 2000), features a great collection of photographs and nuggets of information in its captions. Erling Strom's delightful *Pioneers on Skis* (Smith Clove Press, 1977) contains the accounts of Strom's trips with Lars Haugen and Al Lindley. Tom Kelly's *Birkie Fever: A Ten-Year History of the American Birkebeiner* (Specialty Press, 1982) recounted the first decade of that seminal American race. *Stories of the Stillwater Nordic Team,* by Kelli Billstein and Tara Tierney (2018), contains stories about Bill Simpson, Kris Hansen, Ralph Malmberg, and Bob Hagstrom. *Endless Winter: An Olympian's Journal,* by Luke Bodensteiner (Alta Press, 1994), chronicles a year of training by an elite American skier in the early 1990s. Jessie Diggins's recent autobiography, *Brave Enough,* written with Todd Smith (University of Minnesota Press, 2020), is another account of an athlete at the top of her game.

Periodicals from the National Ski Association and, later, the U.S. Ski Association were primary sources. For years, the NSA published an annual, initially the *Ski Sport* and later *American Ski Annual.* The 1911 and 1924 editions of the *Ski Sport* were particularly helpful. In the early 1930s, the NSA published *The History of the National Ski Association and the Ski Sport, 1840–1931,* a real treasure. In chapter 5, I relied on a number of *American Ski Annual* editions to better understand the rise of alpine skiing. The American Ski Jumping Hall of Fame, in Red Wing, Minnesota, and the Roland Palmedo Ski Library at the U.S. Ski and Snowboard Hall of Fame in Ishpeming, Michigan, both have collections of these volumes. Individuals loaned me their copies. The NSA's *Central Ski Sport* newspaper helped retell the growing cross-country movement in the late 1930s. The Minnesota History Center's newspaper collection on microfiche was essential for following Mikkel Hemmestveit's time in St. Croix Falls, the Arrowhead Derby, and the national meets in Red Wing. After World War II, the periodicals *Minnesota–Wisconsin Ski News* and the *National Ski Bulletin* provided a clear picture of the ski world. I had access to these periodicals at the Norwegian-American Historical Association, at the Ski Hall of Fame, and from two private collections. The Ski Hall of Fame's Palmedo Library has a wealth of magazines through the years, particularly *Cross-Country Skier,* and newsletters from the U.S. Ski Association. A valuable source for women's jumping through the years was *Pioneers of Flight: The Story of Women's Ski Jumping,* by Ingrid Wicken, from Norco, California. Wicken maintains the California Ski Library in a building on her property and possesses a large collection of images of ski jumpers and jumps; some are included in this book. The International Skiing History Association publishes *Skiing History* magazine, from which an article by Seth Masia titled "Hart Skis: A Family Business Rebounds" informed the section on the region's last big ski maker. Greg Fangel's treatise *Minnesota's Premier Ski Makers* offered a detailed look into the Strand and Northland companies.

Prior to the pandemic, I enjoyed visiting archives and historical societies. I had planned on additional and repeat visits, but those plans had to be adjusted. The first place I visited was the Norwegian-American Historical Association at St. Olaf College in Northfield, Minnesota, which has a large collection relating to the early NSA, in addition to newspaper clippings, articles, letters, and books pertaining to Norwegian American skiers. Aside from its incredible collection of newspapers on microfiche, the Gale Library at the Minnesota Historical Society has Pastor Olaus Frederik Duus's letters detailing his ambivalent (and ultimately tragic) experience in Wisconsin territory, as well as a few early catalogs from Twin Cities ski manufacturers. Paul Rose at the New Richmond Heritage Center dug up many documents on Martin Strand and his ski company, including Strand's unfinished autobiography titled "Up to Now" ("with an apology to Al Smith," Strand quipped, referring to the 1929 autobiography by the New York governor that he had lifted the title from. Strand wrote just three pages before he apparently became bored, set the pages down, and, by all appearances, never picked them up again). Red Wing, Minnesota, is a great place for ski research, with the Goodhue County Historical Society and the American Ski Jumping Hall of Fame. Both sites contain a wealth of images, documents, books, and scrapbooks from aspiring jumpers of decades past. Goodhue County Historical Society has a pair of skis made by Torjus Hemmestveit (thanks to Afton Esson for removing the skis from the display case so I could study them), and the Hall of Fame owns an old uniform from the Aurora club. The Hall of Fame, free to visit, is in the historic St. James Hotel. The Minnesota State High School League office in Brooklyn Center has a collection of yearbooks going back to 1932 with information and statistics about the early days of high school racing. Thanks to Bob O'Hara for alerting me to its presence and Ellen Rajokowski for facilitating my visit. The Kathryn A. Martin Library at the University of Minnesota Duluth has a wealth of documents relating to the Duluth Ski Club along with a great photography collection. My thanks to archivist Aimee Brown for arranging my visit and scanning a number of the collection's wonderful photographs. Ishpeming's U.S. Ski and Snowboard Hall of Fame has a fantastic library, and the museum's collection is rich as well. Tony Wise Museum of the American Birkebeiner in Hayward, Wisconsin, documents Tony Wise, Telemark Resort, and the Birkie.

♠

I acknowledge the following individuals for providing me information and perspective while I wrote this book.

Ray Aponte talked with and let me ski with school groups at and around the Trailhead.

Brad Board recalled, over the phone, the skiing life of his uncle of the same name.

Sheri Brenden spoke of the proceedings of her sister and Toni St. Pierre against the Minnesota State High School League and emailed me excerpts of transcripts from the proceedings in Judge Miles Lord's U.S. Federal Court.

Kevin Brochman provided a valuable look into the rise of a young skier to the highest levels of international competition, as well as a glimpse into the world of coaching talented young skiers and the racing landscape today.

Barb Cartford pieced together memories from learning how to skate from the Swedish marathon team. Remarkably, Cartford saves her annual calendars and was able to tell me the exact hour when she and Bill Simpson met the Swedes at Lake Phalen.

Linda Christianson lives in a refurbished Finnish cabin that she and her husband deconstructed, moved to her property in a scenic wooded hollow northeast of the Twin Cities, and renovated into one of the cooler homes I've been in. Linda skis frequently and all over the place and told me about her girlhood on skis in Barron, Wisconsin.

Amy Cichanowski, president of the Minnesota Youth Ski League, provided league photographs and stats.

Rob Dybvig put me up the night before the 2020 Birkie and provided race support.

Greg Fangel bought his first pair of skis in Ralph Malmberg's shop. He since has been the president of the North Star Ski Touring Club and is now on the Minnesota Nordic Ski Association board, which is the citizens' advisory group for the Minnesota DNR's administration of the Great Minnesota Ski Pass. After retiring, Fangel moved to Tofte, Minnesota, where he maintains a large collection of vintage wooden skis, selling some of them through his website woodenskis.com, which I consulted dozens of times for information on ski manufacturers. From Greg I first learned about the Arrowhead Derby. Aside from hosting me at his home and supplying numerous photographs for this book, Fangel put me in touch with other skiers and generously shared the research he conducted on Minnesota's ski industry, on which he is a leading expert. He read a near final draft of this manuscript and provided valuable feedback.

John Filander lives a mile from Giants Ridge and skis 120 days a year. He was my source of information on the Ridge and the World Cup, having worked with the resort for years and continuing to serve as a Technical Delegate during races.

Bonnie Fuller-Kask talked to me on the phone about her personal history as a skier.

Christine Gessner described current challenges of pursuing jumping beyond the local level.

Peter Graves recalled details about the Edsbyn ski company's operations in the United States.

Sandy Gross and her brother Kelly Sobczak are great-grandchildren of Torjus Hemmestveit and met with me at Sandy's home in St. Paul. Thanks also to their respective partners, Mike Gross and Alisa Allen.

Bob Hagstrom initially hosted me in his wax shed to discuss the Stillwater team and then welcomed me again into his house, where he told me about his early skiing in East St. Paul.

Kris Hansen provided photographs and exchanged emails about her competitive skiing days and Jessie Diggins.

Rudi Hargesheimer helped track down an old photograph, as well as recounting details from skiing in the 1970s.

Tim Heisel talked to me about Norm Oakvik and Toni St. Pierre, early

VJC races (which he won), and high school skiing in the late sixties and early seventies.

Mark Helmer met me at the Korkki warming cabin when I was just starting this project. Helmer tells stories with a distinctive style, starting with an anecdote before veering off on long essayistic tangents before circling back and hitting the nail right on the head. I typed eight thousand words of notes during our meeting, detailing scenes that had been indelibly etched into his memory. I left Korkki that evening confident that the topic of Nordic skiing would indeed yield a book.

John Hollister told me over the phone about Norm Oakvik and the early days of the North Stars and the VJC race; later, shortly after his ninetieth birthday, he insisted on driving to my house to drop off some photographs, as he was tired of quarantining in his senior living complex. On a cold and windy October day in 2020, he gamely sat and talked in my garage because I was afraid to have him in the house inhabited by my germy family.

Patra Holter is Aksel Holter's granddaughter and an artist in Washburn, Wisconsin. As a girl, she lived next to Holter in Ashland and recalled details about Ak. Patra donated the silver teacup Martin Strand had presented Holter to the Ski Hall of Fame in Ishpeming.

George Hovland invited me to his house near Chester Park and incredibly recalled his presence at the start of the Arrowhead Derby, along with other details from his long and important life immersed in the ski world. Hovland has Peter Fosseide's worn-out skis from the Arrowhead Derby and shared firsthand memories of Fosseide and Judeen, both of whom were heroes to him. When I met with George in 2019, he expressed concern that a book about Midwestern Nordic skiing would be boring, but then he told me to hurry writing it, as he wanted to read it and would not be around forever. George passed away in May 2021 at the age of ninety-four.

Cody Inglis was my source on high school racing in Michigan, and he referred me to an informative historical article on that topic written by Ron Pesch. Before taking a post with the Michigan High School Athletic Association, Inglis was an athletic director in Traverse City.

Cavour Johnson was one of the first people I contacted during this project, after I found the video documentary he made about the Itasca Ski and Outing Club at the Minnesota Historical Society. Cavour sent me a transcript of the documentary, which contained information on the club's early stars, and newspapers clippings from his own archives. He patiently answered my many emails and put me in touch with Doug Maki. He contacted descendants of Barney Riley and Ole Mangseth on my behalf. Cavour was instrumental in establishing the grant-in-aid cross-country trails at Mount Itasca.

Dave Johnson, a longtime ski coach at both Duluth East and Marshall, spoke with me over the phone about the Duluth ski scene and the evolution of high school skiing.

Julie Judeen, the last surviving daughter of Erik Judeen, met with me in Duluth and candidly discussed the character of her father, who played such a major role in developing that region's ski world.

Pat Lanin spoke with me on the phone about watching his Finnish grandparents ski and coaching a powerhouse team for many years.

Jon Larson schooled me on the rigors of keeping the trails of Vasaloppet open and snow covered.

Joyce Macintire spoke of her mother, Natalie Bailey Gammey.

Doug Maki loaned me his ninety-five-year-old NSA annual, which had belonged to Ole Mangseth's son, Rolf, and told me about his history as a jumper and about the sport today.

Alana Maki-Foust talked over the phone about her competitive jumping days and efforts to revive the Cameron jumping club.

Kurt Mangseth provided information about his grandfather Ole.

Kristine Matlack hosted me in her deep woods home, told stories, and shared her large collection of periodicals, books, photographs, and letters detailing the dramatic lives of her parents, Grace Carter and Al Lindley. Thanks to her husband, Howard, for the smoked trout, pumpkin pie, and tour of his woodshop.

Jim McWethy spoke, over the phone and through emails, about his mother, Jinny McWethy (Mother North Star), and Norm Oakvik and provided a number of photographs.

William Meyer got me up to speed on the biathlon scene.

Larry Millett helped me understand the historical aspects of St. Paul's geography, as described in accounts of early ski contests.

Amy Moe-Hoffman, granddaughter of Harold Moe, shared family stories about her grandfather.

John Munger told me, over a couple of phone calls, about the development of Loppet and the collapse of the World Cup event in March 2020 due to the Covid-19 pandemic.

Darby and Geri Nelson spoke with me over the phone about Darby's legislation creating the Minnesota ski pass and his ongoing quest to ski fifty Vasaloppets.

Rick Nelson, who won the state jumping championship for Cloquet in 1966 and 1967, loaned me his excellent collection of jumping photographs and ephemera. Nelson talked about his life in the ski world, his friendship with coach Joe Nowak, and taught me the term "ground grippers," which the jumpers used to teasingly refer to cross-country skiers.

Angie Nistler told me about her father, Glen Johnstone, and the Mora Vasaloppet through the years.

Bob O'Hara answered many emails and invited me to his house. He told stories from his days with the North Star club, talked about his experience of coaching high school skiing, and shared details about his current role running the state meet for the MSHSL.

Solveig Olson talked about the early days of the North Star Ski Touring Club.

David Paulson shed light on the 1970s and 1980s at Telemark Resort and other episodes from the Midwestern ski world.

Kathy Pierson spoke to me about her father, Charlie Banks.

Ken Ripp exchanged emails about the Cloquet jumping club and his son Aiden's ongoing experiences in jumping at an international level.

Duane Rodgers and Patti Greethurst put me up while I was doing research in Ishpeming.

Anne Rykken allowed me to interview her in her home. She recalled the experience of starting a Koch league club, shared details about the founding of the Minnesota Youth Ski League, and showed me how to make a wooden ski.

Dave Schaeffer, who runs activities at Chester Bowl, let me dig through boxes of old photographs and borrow a stack to scan. Despite the loss of jumping, Chester is open to downhill and cross-country skiing and rents downhill skis for the season to make the costly sport more affordable to families. In the summer, and in the tradition of the place, Chester summer camps promise that kids will return home "tired, dirty, and happy."

Ken Schoville was instrumental in founding the Wisconsin Nordic Ski League and recalled details of its formation.

Rick Scott, a distant cousin of Aksel Holter and retired dentist in Superior, Wisconsin, hosted me at his idyllic home, showed me his ski collection (including a rare Holter ski), and told stories of skiing over the decades. He shared numerous articles, as well as his copies of Holter-related materials from the Ashland Historical Society (closed because of the pandemic), and provided moral support and an interesting dialogue through the strange early days of the Covid-19 pandemic.

Bill Simpson was my primary source for a magazine article that led to this book. After I offhandedly commented to him that the project could be greatly expanded, he put me in touch with an editor at the University of Minnesota Press, a gesture without which I'm not sure the project would have gotten off the ground.

David Siskind provided several great photographs of the North Star Ski Touring Club.

Bruce Slinkman caught me up on details of the grant-in-aid ski pass system in Minnesota and kindly sent me a large collection of wonderful photographs of skiing in Bemidji.

Bradford Smith, grandson of Erik Judeen, hosted me at his home and showed me relics from Judeen's racing days, along with facilitating and hosting a meeting with his aunt.

Brent Smith told me about skiing in Cloquet through the years.

Ruth Smith, my aunt and longtime Mora resident, put me in touch with members of the Vasaloppet community.

Sam St. Pierre talked with me over the phone about his sister, Toni St. Pierre.

Arne Stefferud filled me in on the history of the Great Minnesota Ski Pass.

Tory Stroshane, president of the Ashland Historical Society Museum, dug up a great photograph of Aksel Holter at the last minute, despite the museum being closed.

Ahvo Taipale sold me a pair of properly fitted skin skis and answered a variety of questions on the arc of skiing in the Twin Cities and beyond from the 1970s onward.

Aaron Troye-White, a native Minnesotan living happily in Norway, translated a couple of antiquated lines of Norwegian, written by Aksel Holter, that Google Translate wouldn't touch.

Larry Wanberg, whose father helped locate Sondre Norheim's grave, recalled that interesting series of events and his own personal history from his home in California.

Adrian Watt showed me his incredible ski collection, including a comically long "bog ski" and a beautifully engraved Finnish church ski. Along with telling me about his days as a Chester Bowl boy and a career that included participation in the Olympics and a national jumping distance record, Watt loaned me his large collection of ski periodicals, programs, and images, many of which have been used here.

I'm grateful to editors Keith Goetzman and Chris Clayton at the *Minnesota Conservation Volunteer* for assigning me the story that inspired this book. The staff at the University of Minnesota Press was great to work with, starting with Erik Anderson, who met with me in Osceola to hear my notion of a book idea. Erik put me in touch with editor Kristian Tvedten, with whom I worked extensively on completing these chapters. Kristian read through multiple drafts and dug up a marvelous array of images from the internet's dusty corners as we struggled to obtain art while much of the world was shut down during the pandemic. Thanks to Laura Westlund and the production team at the Press for pushing the book through to get it out in time for the ski season and to copy editor Anne Taylor, whose careful attention to these pages resulted in their betterment; Anne learned to ski in Norway, though she lives near Spidahl Ski Gaard, the trail system started by Walter "Speedy" Spidahl. On the home front, thanks to my girls, Grace and Ella, for occasionally letting me do some writing, and to my wife, Lily Rodgers, for putting up with my many hours sealed off from the rest of the family in my room upstairs.

Illustration Credits

Photographs and illustrations have been reprinted in this book courtesy of the individuals and organizations listed here. Every effort was made to obtain permission to reprint the illustrations published in this book. If any proper acknowledgment has not been included, we encourage copyright holders to notify the publisher.

Prologue

Title page photograph on page ii by Kenneth Melvin Wright, Minnesota Historical Society. Photographs on page vi by Anders Beer Wilse, Norsk Folkemuseum; on page 5 from the National Library of Norway; on page 6 from the Visual Arts Collections, National Museum of Art, Architecture, and Design, Norway; on page 8 from the Center for Manuscripts and Book History, Royal Danish Library, Copenhagen; and on page 9 from The Ski Museum, Holmenkollen, Oslo.

1. Just Add Norwegians

Photographs on pages 10, 15, and 16 by Hermann Christian Neupert; on pages 22 and 30 by Ludwik Szacinski; on page 37 by Christian Gihbsson, from the National Library of Norway; on page 12 from Ingrid P. Wicken, California Ski Library; on page 13 by Anders Beer Wilse, Norwegian Forest Museum; on page 14 from the *Illustrated London News,* January 12, 1856; on page 17 from the Norwegian National Archives; on page 18 by Anders

Beer Wilse; artwork on page 20 by Christian Krohg; on page 39 by Ludwik Szacinski, from Oslo Museum; on page 19 from Norsk Folkemuseum; on pages 23, 42, and 46 from Goodhue County Historical Society, Red Wing, Minnesota; on page 24 from Vest-Telemark Museum; on page 26 by Olaf Martin Peder Væring, Norwegian Museum of Science and Technology; on page 27 from Norwegian Geographical Survey; on page 28 by Otto Kjellström, Center for History of Science, The Royal Swedish Academy of Science; illustration on page 31 by *Pioneer Press,* 1887; on page 32 by Sumner W. Matteson, 1908, Milwaukee Public Museum collection, 41020; illustration on page 33 by Harry S. Watson, *The Outing Magazine,* 1893; on page 34 by T. W. Ingersoll, Minnesota Historical Society; on pages 36 (bottom), 40, and 43 from the Minnesota Historical Society; on page 36 (top) from DePauw University Archives, Greencastle, Indiana; illustration on page 38 by Thulstrip and Graham, *Harper's Weekly,* 1892; illustration on page 39 by Vincent Stoltenberg Lerche, *Die Gartenlaube,* 1872; on page 44 from Marquette Regional History Center, Marquette, Michigan.

2. Yump, Ole, Yump!

Photographs on pages 48 and 61 from Superior View Photography; artwork on page 52 by Andreas Bloch; page 55 from National Library of Norway; page 50 from U.S. Forest Service Records, National Archives; photographs on pages 51, 58, and 69 by Al Heitman; photographs on pages 82 and 84 by C. J. Hibbard, Minnesota Historical Society; pages 53 and 73 from Archives of the U.S. Ski and Snowboard Hall of Fame; photographs on pages 54, 71, and 77 by the author; page 57 from *The Winter Sport of Skeeing,* 1905; pages 59, 64, 74, 75, and 86 from Adrian Watt collection; advertisement on page 60 from *Iron Ore,* 1906; pages 63 and 76 from Goodhue County Historical Society, Red Wing, Minnesota; photograph on page 65 by Sumner W. Matteson, 1908, Milwaukee Public Museum collection, 41035; page 66 from Hennepin County Library; pages 67 and 80 from Itasca Ski and Outing Club; photograph on page 68 by Johan Bekker Larsen Lauritz, from The Picture Collection at the University Library in Bergen, Special Collections, University of Bergen; page 70 from Ingrid P. Wicken, California Ski Library; page 72 from Marquette Regional History Center; photograph on page 74 by Sumner W. Matteson, 1908, Milwaukee Public Museum collection, 41049;

page 78 from Norwegian-American Historical Association Archives; photograph on page 79 by Mathias O. Bue, Fillmore County Historical Society; page 81 from U.S. Patent and Trademark Office; page 83 from Library of Congress.

3. Ski Capital of America

Photographs on pages 88, 97, and 100 by Norton & Peel; pages 109, 114, 133, and 135 from the Minnesota Historical Society; pages 90, 119, 121, 123, and 134 from the Goodhue County Historical Society, Red Wing, Minnesota; page 91 from the Adrian Watt Collection; page 93 from Superior View Photography; photograph on page 94 by Pekka Kyytinen, Finnish Board of Antiquities–Museovirasto; page 95 from Carl Orjala family; page 96 from Itasca Ski and Outing Club; page 98 from Hennepin County Library; page 99 from Chicago Daily News Collection, SDN-060560, Chicago History Museum; pages 102, 104, and 110 from Archives and Special Collections, University of Minnesota Duluth, on permanent loan from the St. Louis County Historical Society; page 101 from Jim McWethy collection; page 103 from Ashland Historical Society Museum; pages 105, 126, and 128 from Jasper Yellowhead Museum and Archives (PA 7/26), Joseph Weiss photographs; page 108 from Admiral Richard E. Byrd Papers, SPEC.PA.56.0001, Byrd Polar and Climate Research Center Archival Program, The Ohio State University; page 107 from Large Broadsides Collection, Rare Books and Manuscripts, Indiana State Library; page 111 from Coolidge Family Papers, Vermont Historical Society; page 112 from Vesterheim Norwegian-American Museum, Decorah, Iowa; page 113, early ski party to Assiniboine, 1928, Whyte Museum of the Canadian Rockies, Erling Strom fonds, v612/lc/accn3045/na6-1373; page 115 from Library of Congress; page 116 from Tread of Pioneers Museum, Steamboat Springs, Colorado; page 117 from Tibbals Circus Collection, Ringling Museum; page 122 from Chicago Daily News Collection, SDN-064232, Chicago History Museum; page 124 from Alan K. Engen Photograph Collection P0413, Special Collections, J. Willard Marriott Library, The University of Utah; page 129 from Kristine Matlack collection; page 130 from Harry and Norma Hoyt Family Papers, Archives and Special Collections, Consortium Library, University of Alaska Anchorage; page 132 from Francis P. Farquhar Papers, 1896–1960, UAF-1981-208-51, Archives, University of Alaska Fairbanks.

4. High Times for the Ski Sport

Photographs on pages 136 and 162 by Leland J. Prater, U.S. Forest Service Records, National Archives; page 138 from Cook County Historical Society, Grand Marais, Minnesota; page 139 from Goodhue County Historical Society, Red Wing, Minnesota; page 140 from Archives and Special Collections, University of Minnesota Duluth, on permanent loan from the St. Louis County Historical Society; pages 140, 157, 161, and 165 from Minnesota Historical Society; pages 142 and 177 (bottom) from Durrance Collection, Aspen Historical Society; pages 143, 145, and 154 from Kristine Matlack collection; photograph on page 144 by Walter E. Frost, City of Vancouver Archives; page 146 from Minnesota State High School League Archives; page 147 from David Johnson; page 148 from University of Wisconsin–Madison Archives; pages 149, 155, 163, and 167 from Hennepin County Library; pages 150 and 164 from Korkki Nordic Ski Center; pages 151, 170, and 180 from Adrian Watt collection; pages 151 and 153 from Chester Bowl Improvement Club; press photo on page 158 (1938); page 160 from National Library of Norway; page 166 from Superior View Photography; page 168 from Ingrid P. Wicken, California Ski Library; page 169 from U.S. Patent and Trademark Office; photograph on page 171 by Wallace Kirkland, The LIFE Picture Collection/Getty Images; image on page 172 supplied courtesy of originalskiposters.com; page 174 from Julie Judeen collection; postcard on page 175 from Curt Teich and Company, 1946; page 177 (top) from The Community Library Center for Regional History, Ketchum, Idaho, F 05076; page 179 from Popperfoto Collection/Getty Images); page 181 courtesy of Murphy Library Special Collections, University of Wisconsin–La Crosse.

5. Nordic Decline

Page 182 from Wisconsin Historical Society, WHS-113730; page 184 from Minnesota Streetcar Museum; page 185 from St. Paul Ski Club Archives; photograph on page 186 by Finn Bergan, Norwegian Museum of Science and Technology; pages 187 and 188 from Adrian Watt collection; photograph on 189 by Christian Brun, courtesy of Erik Brun, Ninety-Ninth Battalion Educational Foundation; pages 190, 194, 195 (bottom), and 213 from Rick Nelson collection; postcard photograph on page 191 from Gallagher's Studio;

artwork on page 192 by Joseph Binder, Library of Congress collection; advertisement on page 193 from *Sports Illustrated*, December 3, 1962; pages 195 (top) and 196 from Chester Bowl Improvement Club; page 197 from the archives of George Hovland (photographer unknown); artwork on page 198 by Knut Yran, Pedersens and Company; pages 199, 200, and 205 from John Burton family; page 201 from The Community Library Center for Regional History, Ketchum, Idaho, F 09262; pages 202 and 222 from Julie Judeen collection; pages 203 and 204 from National Library of Norway; pages 207 and 217 from Hennepin County Library; page 208 from *American Ski Annual,* 1949; pages 209 and 211 from Linda Christianson collection; artwork on page 210 by Walter Harnisch; photograph on page 214 by Arthur M. Vinje, Wisconsin Historical Society, WHS-110277; artwork on page 215 by Sascha Maurer; page 218 from Laconia Historical and Museum Society; photograph on page 219 by Norton & Peel, Minnesota Historical Society; page 220 from *Sports Illustrated*, December 12, 1960; page 224 from State Historical Society of North Dakota, 0032-PI-15–09; photograph on page 225 by the author.

6. Cross-Country Revolution

Pages 226 and 259 from Archives and Special Collections, University of Minnesota Duluth; pages 228, 229, 230, and 268 from Rick Nelson collection; pages 231, 238, and 244 from David Siskind collection; page 232 from National Archives of Norway; page 234 from Korkki Nordic Ski Center; photograph on page 235 by Gunnar Bergbom, Luleå Municipality City Archives; photograph on page 237 by Charles Bjorgen, copyright 1967 *Star Tribune*; page 239 from Jim McWethy collection; page 240 (top) from St. Louis Park Historical Society; page 240 (bottom) from Bonnie Fuller-Kask; page 242 from John Hollister; advertisement on page 243 from *Minneapolis Tribune*, November 17, 1968; pages 245, 246, and 255 from Hennepin County Library; advertisement from page 247 from *Birch Scroll* 1988 Official Results of the American Birkebeiner; photograph on page 248 by Steve Schluter, copyright 1982 *Star Tribune*; photograph on page 250 by John M. Kuhn; pages 251 and 257 from Minnesota Historical Society; page 252 from Washington County Historical Society; photograph on page 253 by David Simpkins, courtesy *Minnesota Trails* magazine; page 254 from Ralph

Malmberg; page 261 from National Library of Norway; pages 262 and 263 from Tony Wise Museum of the American Birkebeiner; page 264 from the archives of George Hovland (photographer unknown); photograph on page 265 by Ralph Thornton, copyright 1985 *Star Tribune*; page 266 from Vasaloppet USA; page 267 from Kevin Brochman collection; page 269 from Chester Bowl Improvement Club; page 270 from St. Paul Ski Club Archives; press photo on page 271 (1979).

7. Modern Nordic

Photograph on page 272 by Bruce Bisping, copyright 1979 *Star Tribune*; page 275 from Buck Hill Ski and Snowboard Area; pages 276 and 309 from Korkki Nordic Ski Center; page 277 from Hennepin County Library; page 278 from Maplelag Resort; page 279 from Denver Public Library, Special Collections; page 280 from David Siskind collection; photograph on page 281 by Clint Austin, *Duluth News Tribune*; page 283 from Vasaloppet USA; page 284 from Bruce Slinkman; pages 285, 295, and 297 from Angie Nistler; page 286 from *Sports Illustrated,* 1966; photograph on page 287 by Richard Tsong-Taatarii, copyright 2014 *Star Tribune*; pages 288 and 291 from Tony Wise Museum of the American Birkebeiner; page 289 from Archives of the U.S. Ski and Snowboard Hall of Fame, licensed under Creative Commons BY-SA 4.0; page 290 from *Sports Illustrated,* February 17, 1958; page 293 from Giants Ridge Ski Patrol; page 294 copyright *Duluth News Tribune*; page 298 from Ramsey County Historical Society; photograph on page 299 by Tom Sweeney, copyright 1986 *Star Tribune*; page 300 from Itasca County Historical Society; page 302 from Kevin Brochman collection; photograph on page 304 copyright Dr. James Gaffney; page 305 from Eric Iverson; page 306 from Adrian Watt collection; (top) photograph on page 307 Dan Kraker/Minnesota Public Radio News, copyright 2014 Minnesota Public Radio®, reprinted with permission, all rights reserved; page 307 (bottom) from Kris Edlund; page 308 from St. Paul Ski Club Archives; page 310 from David Arvold.

8. A Thriving Ski Scene

Pages 312, 335, 336, 338, and 343 copyright Steve Kotvis, f/go, www.f-go
.us; page 314 from Three Rivers Park District; page 315 from Anne Rykken;
page 317 from Ishpeming Ski Club; pages 318 and 319 from Sue Kavanagh;
page 321 from Sue Denney; pages 322 and 326 from Kris Edlund; page 323
from Archives and Special Collections, University of Minnesota Duluth, on
permanent loan from the St. Louis County Historical Society; photograph
on page 324 by Harley C. Petersen, Wisconsin DNR Collection, University
of Wisconsin–Madison Libraries, licensed under Creative Commons BY-ND
4.0; page 325 from Alana Maki-Faust; page 327 copyright Ailura, licensed
under Creative Commons BY-SA 3.0 AT; page 329 from Bruce Slinkman;
pages 330 and 331 from Kris Hansen; photograph on page 332 by Preston
Keres, Department of Defense Records, U.S. National Archives; page 334
from Charlie Plain; photograph on page 337 by Jeff Wheeler, copyright 2011
Star Tribune; page 340 from Minneapolis Park and Recreation Board; photograph on page 341 by Charles Bjorgen, copyright 1967 *Star Tribune*; page
342 copyright Lucy Hawthorne, produced by *Minnesota Monthly*; page 345
from Jan Lasar, *Minnesota Trails* magazine; pages 346 (top), 348, and 349
copyright Lorie Shaull, licensed under Creative Commons BY-SA 2.0; page
346 (bottom) from Vasaloppet USA; page 350 from Korkki Nordic Ski Center; page 352 from David Johnson; photograph on page 354 by the author.

Epilogue

Photograph on page 356 by Jac Brun, National Library of Norway.

Index

Ryan Rodgers learned to ski with the Bill Koch Junior Ski League. He is a freelance writer and avid skier. His work has been published in *Minnesota Conservation Volunteer,* the *Boundary Waters Journal, Backpacker, The Sun,* and *Northern Wilds.* He lives with his family in northern Minnesota.